TRUE
HALLUCINATIONS

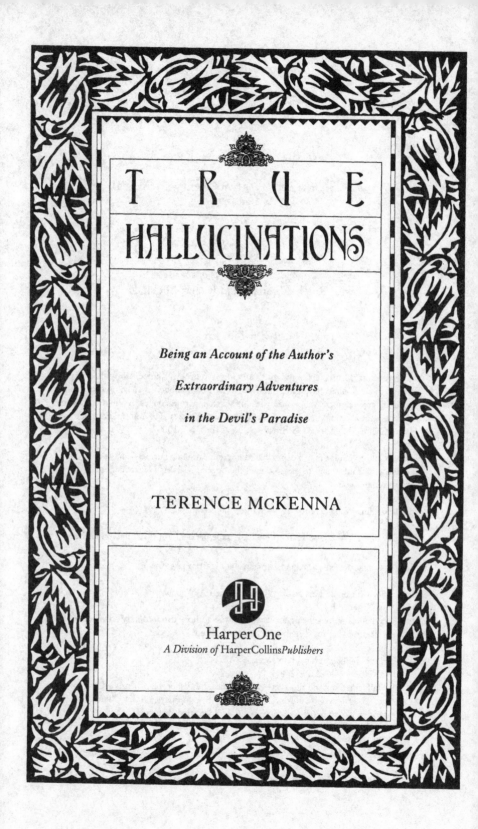

TRUE HALLUCINATIONS

Being an Account of the Author's

Extraordinary Adventures

in the Devil's Paradise

TERENCE McKENNA

HarperOne
A Division of HarperCollinsPublishers

HarperOne

Also by Terence McKenna

The Invisible Landscape (with Dennis McKenna)

Food of the Gods

The Archaic Revival

Trialogues at the Edge of the West
with Ralph Abraham and Rupert Sheldrake)

Synesthesia
(with Tim Ely)

HarperCollins books may be purchased for educational, business, or sales promotional use. For information, please e-mail the Special Markets Department at SPsales-@harpercollins.com.

HarperCollins Web site: http://www.harpercollins.com

HarperCollins®, 📖®, and HarperOne™ are trademarks of HarperCollins Publishers.

FIRST HARPERCOLLINS PAPERBACK EDITION PUBLISHED IN 1994

An Earlier Edition of This Book Was Catalogued As Follows:
McKenna, Terence K.
    True hallucinations: being an account of the author's extraordinary adventures in the devil's paradise / Terence McKenna.—1st ed.
        p. cm.
    Includes bibliographical references.
    ISBN: 978-0-06-250652-8
    1. Hallucinations and illusions—Miscellanea. 2. Psilocybe cubensis—Psychic aspects. 3. Psilocybin. 4. McKenna, Terence K.—Journeys. 5. La Chorrera (Amazonas, Colombia)—Description. 6. Unidentified flying objects.
7. Shamanism. I. Title.
BF1999.M453   1993
133—dc20   91-58904

22 23 24 25 26 LBC 49 48 47 46 45

To
Dennis McKenna,
who realized that
"A stitch in Time saves nine."

CONTENTS

PREFACE

SOMETIME DURING THE EARLY 1980s, while visiting the Esalen Institute, where I had been invited to participate in a conference on shamanism, I realized that my innate Irish ability to rave had been turbo-charged by years of psilocybin mushroom use. Aided by my devotion to psilocybin and the experiment at La Chorrera that is the subject of this book, I had apparently evolved into a sort of mouthpiece for the incarnate Logos. I could talk to small groups of people with what appeared to be electrifying effect about the peculiarly transcendental matters that you will read about in these pages.

These verbal performances seemed to me rather mundane while they were occurring, but relistening to them on audiotape I could see the source of other people's fascination. It was as though my ordinary, rather humdrum personality had simply been turned off and speaking through me was the voice of another, a voice that was steady, unhesitating, and articulate—a voice seeking to inform others about the power and the promise of psychedelic dimensions.

Dozens, now perhaps nearly a hundred, of my talks and lectures were recorded, distributed, sometimes pirated, passed among friends, and played on small underground radio stations. I began to make my living as a lecturer and teacher at various spas and growth centers. I was discovered by the notorious Roy of Hollywood, whose late-night radio show made me an underground mini-star, at least among the insomniacs of Los Angeles. Merely by talking about the events at La Chorrera I had become a minor celebrity.

Eventually rumor of my status as a raver and a West Coast underground figure reached even into the great glass boxes along Fifth Avenue in Gotham itself. Publishers that I had imagined would not give me the time of day were suddenly interested in my work. Let us hope that as you read this, my books—this one and others that have preceded it—are spreading these strange ideas and making my life comfortable and others rich.

There is a strange paradox surrounding all of this: my ideas are now in the public arena and an informal plebiscite is being held on them. If they spread, become popular, and function as catalysts of social change then the hope that they may have a special destiny will be sustained. If, on the other hand, they have their moment in the sun and then fade from public notice, my work and my vision will have been judged to be no more than another fleeting facet of our surreal and paranoia-infected culture. I have no idea where these ideas may lead. Certainly with several books now in print I cannot claim that I was not given a fair hearing. It is apparently the public who will decide if this phenomenon has run its course or if it is only beginning to make itself felt.

I mention all of this not to inform my reader of the less-than-interesting details of my personal effort to feed a family, but because this career of mine is now the only and best evidence that something extraordinary, perhaps something of historical importance, may have happened at La Chorrera. For the loquacious mushrooms encountered there have spun a myth and issued a prophecy, in quite specific detail, of a planet-saving global shift of consciousness. They have promised all that has happened in my life over the last twenty years, and they have promised much more for the future. If you read onward you become a part of this tale. *Caveat lector.*

CHAPTER ONE

THE CALL OF THE SECRET

In which our cast of characters, including a mushroom, are introduced, and their peculiar interests sketched. The Amazon jungle is invoked and the descent of one of its rivers undertaken.

FOR THOUSANDS OF YEARS the visions imparted by hallucinogenic mushrooms have been sought and revered as a true religious mystery. Much of my thought over the past twenty or more years has been caught up in describing and contemplating this mystery. Closely guarded by the chaotically jeweled Angels—"Every angel is terrible," wrote Rilke, and at once sacred and profane—the mushroom has risen in my life much as it may rise at some future point in human history. I have chosen a literary approach to the telling of this tale. A living mystery could take any shape—it is master of place and space, time and spirit—yet my search for a simple form to convey this mystery brought me to follow tradition: to write a chronological narrative of a story that is both true and extraordinarily bizarre.

In early February of 1971, I was passing through southern Colombia with my brother and some friends on our way to an expedition into the Colombian Amazonas. Our route led us through

Florencia, the provincial capital of the Departmento of Caquetá. There we paused a few days awaiting an airplane to carry us to our embarkation point on the Rio Putumayo, a river whose vast expanse is the border between Colombia and her two southern neighbors, Ecuador and Peru.

The day we were to depart was especially hot, and we left the oppressive confines of our hotel near the noisy central market and bus station. We walked southwest, out of town, perhaps a mile. Here were the warm waters of the Rio Hacha, visible across rolling pastures of tall grass. After swimming in the river, exploring deep pools carved by the warm torrent in the black basaltic stream bed, we returned through the same meadows. Someone more familiar than I with the appearance of the mushroom *Stropharia cubensis* pointed out a single large specimen standing tall and alone in an old bit of cow manure. Impulsively and at my companions' suggestion, I ate the whole mushroom. It occupied but a moment, and then on we trudged, tired from our swim, a tropical thunderstorm moving toward us along the eastern edge of the Andean cordillera where Florencia is located.

For perhaps a quarter hour we walked on, mostly in silence. Wearily I hung my head, almost hypnotized by the sight of the regular motion of my boots cutting through the grass. To align my back, to throw off my lethargy, I paused and stretched, scanning the horizon. The feeling of the bigness of the sky, which I have come to associate with psilocybin, rushed down on me there for the first time. I asked my friends to pause and then I sat down heavily on the ground. A silent thunder seemed to shake the air before me. Things stood out with a new presence and significance. This feeling came and passed over me like a wave just as the first fury of the tropical storm burst overhead, leaving us soaked. The eerie sense that some other dimension or scale of being had intersected with the bright tropical day lasted only a few minutes. Elusive but strong, it was unlike any feeling I could recall.

In our sodden retreat, the extended, oddly shimmering moment preceding our frantic withdrawal went unmentioned by me. I recognized that my experience had been induced by the mushroom, but I did not want to let thoughts of it distract me, for we were after bigger game. We were involved, I imagined, in a deep jungle search for hallucinogens of a different sort: plants containing the orally active drug di-methyltryptamine (or DMT) and the psychedelic brew *ayahuasca*. These plants were long associated with telepathic abilities and feats of the paranormal. Yet the patterns of their use, which were unique to the Amazon jungles, had not been fully studied.

Once I had come down, I dismissed the mushroom experience as something to look into another time. Longtime residents of Colombia assured me that the golden-hued *Stropharia* occurred exclusively on the dung of Zebu cattle, and I assumed that in the jungles of the interior—where I was shortly to be—I could expect no cattle or pasture. Putting the thought of mushrooms from my mind, I prepared for the rigors of our descent down the Rio Putumayo toward our target destination, a remote mission called La Chorrera.

Why had a gypsy band such as ours come to the steaming jungles of Amazonian Colombia? We were a party of five, bound by friendship, extravagant imagination, naiveté, and a dedication to travel and exotic experience. Ev, our translator and newly my lover, was the only member of the group not a long acquaintance of the others. She was an American, like the rest of us, and she had lived several years in South America and had traveled in the East (where I had passed her once in the Kathmandu airport at a moment of great duress for us both—another story). She was recently free of a long relationship.

On her own and having nothing better to do, she had fallen in with our group. By the time we reached La Chorrera, she and I would have been together less than three weeks. The other three members of the group were my brother, Dennis, the youngest and least traveled of us, a student of botany and a colleague of long standing; Vanessa, an old school friend of mine from the experimental college in Berkeley, trained in anthropology and photography and traveling on her own; and Dave, another old friend, a gay meditator, a maker of pottery, an embroiderer of blue jeans, and like Vanessa, a New Yorker.

Four months before our descent into the watery underworld of the lower Putumayo, my brother and I had endured the grief of our mother's death. Before that I had been traveling for three years in India and Indonesia. Then I had worked as a teacher in the English

mills of Tokyo and, when I couldn't put up with that any more, fled
to Canada. In Vancouver our crew held a reunion and planned this
Amazon expedition to investigate the depths of the psychedelic
experience.

I deliberately do not say much about any of us. We were mis-
educated perhaps, but well-educated certainly. None of us was yet
twenty-five years old. We had been drawn together through the political turmoil that had characterized our years shared in Berkeley.
We were refugees from a society that we thought was poisoned by
its own self-hatred and inner contradictions. We had sorted through
the ideological options, and we had decided to put all of our chips
on the psychedelic experience as the shortest path to the millennium, which our politics had inflamed us to hope for. We had no
idea what to expect from the Amazon, but we had collected as
much ethno-botanical information as was available. This data told
us where the various hallucinogens were to be sought, but not what
to expect when we found them.

I have given some thought to how predisposed we might have
been to the experiences that would eventually befall us. Often our
interpretations of events did not agree, as is common among strong
personalities or witnesses to an unusual event. We were complex
people or we would not have been doing what we were doing.

Even at age twenty-four, I could look back on nearly ten years
of involvement with matters most people might consider fringe in
the extreme. My interest in drugs, magic, and the more obscure
backwaters of natural history and theology gave me the interest
profile of an eccentric Florentine prince rather than a kid growing
up in the heartland of the United States in the late fifties. Dennis
had shared all of these concerns, to the despair of our conventional
and hardworking parents. For some reason we were odd from the
start, chosen by fate for a destiny too strange to imagine.

In a letter written eleven months before our expedition I find
that Dennis even then had the clearest conception of what might
happen. He wrote to me while I was on Taiwan in 1970 to say:

As to the central shamanic quest and the idea that its
resolution may entail physical death—indeed a sobering
thought—I would be interested in hearing just how likely

you consider this possibility and why. I had not thought of it in terms of death, though I have considered that it may well give us, as living men, willful access to the doorway that the dead pass daily. This I consider as a kind of hyperspatial astral projection that allows the hyper-organ, consciousness, to instantly manifest itself at any point in the space-time matrix, or at all points simultaneously.

His letters to me made it clear that his imagination had suffered no atrophy during the years of finishing high school in our small Colorado hometown. A steady diet of science fiction had made his imagination a joy to watch at play, but I wondered, was he serious?

A UFO is essentially this hyperspatially mobile psychic vortex, and the trip may well involve contact with some race of hyperspatial dwellers. Probably it will be an encounter similar to a "flying lesson": instruction in the use of the transdimensional stone, how to navigate in hyperspace, and perhaps an introductory course in Cosmic Ecology tending.

He was struggling, as was I, to come to terms with the elf-haunted psychic landscapes revealed by di-methyltryptamine, or DMT. Once we had encountered DMT, in the heady and surreal atmosphere of Berkeley at the apex of the Summer of Love, it had become the primary mystery, and the most effective tool for the continuance of the quest.

Retention of the physical form under such circumstances would be, it seems, a matter of choice rather than necessity; though it could be a matter of indifference, since in the hyperspatial web all existing physical manifestations would be open. I would say that time is not of the essence for the venture except insofar as the culture-deaths of the tribes we are seeking are proceeding at an appalling rate.

It was not our colorful fantasies alone that were centered on DMT-type hallucinogens. Our operational approach to discovering the secrets of the hallucinogenic dimension was centered on them as well. This was because, of the psychoactive compounds we knew, the action of DMT-containing hallucinogens, though very brief, seemed the most intense. DMT is not an object of common experience, even among psychonauts of inner space, and so a word must be said about it. In its pure synthetic form, it is a crystalline paste or powder that is smoked in a glass pipe with nothing else. After a few inhalations the onset of the experience is rapid, fifteen seconds to a minute. The hallucinogenic experience that it triggers lasts three to seven minutes and is unambiguously peculiar. It is so bizarre and intense that even the most devoted *aficionados* of hallucinogens usually pass it by. Yet it is the most common and the most widely distributed of the naturally occurring hallucinogens, and it is the basis, when not the entire component, of most of the hallucinogens used by aboriginal tribes in tropical South America. In nature, as a product of plant metabolism, it never occurs in anything like the concentrations at which it comes from the laboratory. Yet South American shamans, by chemically predisposing themselves to its effects in various ways, do find the same levels of reality-obliterating intensity achievable with pure DMT. Its strangeness and power so exceeded that of other hallucinogens that di-methyltryptamine and its chemical relatives seemed finally to define, for our little circle at any rate, maximum exfoliation—the most radical and flowery unfolding—of the hallucinogenic dimension that can occur without serious risk to psychic and bodily integrity.

We thought, therefore, that our phenomenological description of the hallucinogenic dimension should begin by locating a strong DMT-containing aboriginal hallucinogen and then exploring with an open mind the shamanic states that it made accessible. To this end we had sifted the literature on tryptamine drugs in the Upper Amazon Basin and learned that *ayahuasca* or *yagé*—the brew of *Banisteriopsis caapi* with the DMT admixtures—is known over a wide area,[*] just as are several kinds of DMT-containing snuffs, but there

---

[*] *Ayahuasca* is a term in general use throughout the upper Amazon Basin. It refers not only to the prepared hallucinogenic beverage but also to its main ingredient, the woody liana *Banisteriopsis caapi*. This often gigantic jungle vine is pulverized and boiled with a DMT-containing plant, usually *Psychotria viridis*, occasionally *Diploterus cabrerena*. The watery extraction is then concentrated through further boiling. *Ayahuasca*, also called *natema*, *yagé*, or *pildé*, is the most widely distributed and used of the equatorial New World shamanic hallucinogens.

was one DMT-containing hallucinogen that was severely restricted in its usage.

Oo-koo-hé is made from the resin of certain trees of the Myristicaceous genus *Virola* mixed with the ashes of other plants and rolled into pellets and swallowed. What was eye-catching about the description of this visionary plant preparation was that the Witoto tribe of the Upper Amazon, who alone knew the secret of making it, used it to talk to "little men" and to gain knowledge from them.

These little people are one bridge between the motifs of alien contact and the more traditional strange doings of woodland elves and fairies. The worldwide tradition of little people is well studied in *The Fairy Faith in Celtic Countries* by W. E. Evans-Wentz, a pioneering study of Celtic folkways that was influential on UFO researcher Jacques Vallee's quest as well as our own. The mention of little men rang a bell, since during my own experiences smoking synthesized DMT in Berkeley, I had had the impression of bursting into a space inhabited by merry elfin, self-transforming, machine creatures. Dozens of these friendly fractal entities, looking like self-dribbling Fabergé eggs on the rebound, had surrounded me and tried to teach me the lost language of true poetry. They seemed to be babbling in a visible and five-dimensional form of Ecstatic Nostratic, to judge from the emotional impact of this gnomish prattle. Mirror-surfaced tumbling rivers of melted meaning flowed gurgling around me. This happened on several occasions.

It was the transformation of language that made these experiences so memorable and peculiar. Under the influence of DMT, language was transmuted from a thing heard to a thing seen. Syntax became unambiguously visible. In searching for parallels to this notion I am forced to recall the wonderful scene in the Disney version of *Alice in Wonderland*, in which Alice encounters the hooka-smoking caterpillar seated on a mushroom. "Who R U?" the caterpillar inquires, spelling out his question in smoke above his head. There has always been a suspicion of psychedelic sophistication associated with Lewis Carroll and his nineteenth-century story of a self-transforming wonderland. In the hands of Disney's animators, the synesthesia-like blending of sense perception is exaggerated and made explicit and literal. What the caterpillar intends to communicate is not heard but seen, floating in nearby space; a visible language whose medium is the convenient smoke that the caterpillar possesses in abundant supply.*

Which is not to say that DMT is to be thought of as a stimulus for mere inner cartoons. It is not. The feeling that radiates from the DMT encounter is hair-raisingly bizarre. It is as much as one can stand without the categories of consciousness becoming permanently rewritten. I am occasionally asked if DMT is dangerous. The proper answer is that it is only dangerous if you feel threatened by the possibility of death by astonishment. So great is the wave of amazement that accompanies the dissolving of the boundary between our world and this other unsuspected continuum that it approaches being a kind of ecstasy in and of itself.

The sense of being literally in some other dimension, which these bizarre DMT experiences had provoked, had been the focus of our decision to concentrate on tryptamine hallucinogens. After reading all that there was on psychoactive tryptamines, we came eventually to the work of the pioneering ethnobotanist Richard Evans Schultes. Schultes's tenured position as a professor of botany at Harvard had allowed him to dedicate his life to collecting and cataloging the world's psychoactive plants. His paper on "Virola as an Orally Administered Hallucinogen" was a turning point in our quest. We were fascinated by his description of the use of the resin of *Virola theiodora* trees as an orally active DMT drug, as well as by the fact that the use of this hallucinogen seemed to be limited to a very small geographical area. Schultes was an inspiring voice when he wrote of the hallucinogen *oo-koo-hé*:

> Further field work in the original home region of these Indians will be necessary for a full understanding of this interesting hallucinogen. . . . Interest in this newly discovered

---

*That a Disney film should be a showcase for this notion is not as surprising as it might first appear. One has only to recall the carefully choreographed dances of Oriental mushrooms in *Fantasia* to wonder whether some portions of the Disney production group might have been shamanically inspired. After all, *Fantasia* was a very serious and ambitious effort to make synesthesia a motif for popular entertainment. Rumors persist that many of the European animators whom Disney hired for his extravagant projects were aware of the psychedelic experience. Among the Czech animators who joined the Disney group during this period were some who probably knew of the vision-producing power of peyote and its chemical constituent, mescaline.

hallucinogen does not lie wholly within the bounds of anthropology and ethnobotany. It bears very directly on certain pharmacological matters and, when considered with the other plants with psychotomimetic properties due to tryptamines, this new oral drug poses problems which must now be faced and, if possible, toxicologically explained.[*]

Based on Schultes's paper, we decided to abandon our studies and careers and to pay our own way to the Amazon and the vicinity of La Chorrera in search of *oo-koo-hé*. We wanted to see if the titanically strange dimensions that we had encountered in the DMT trance were even more accessible via the DMT plant combinations that the shamans of the Amazon had developed.

It was of these shamanic sacraments that I had been thinking when I had dismissed the *Stropharia* mushroom encountered in the pasture near Florencia. I was eager to press on with the quest for the exotic, barely reported, Witoto *oo-koo-hé*. Little did I imagine that soon after our arrival at La Chorrera the search for *oo-koo-hé* would be all but forgotten. The Witoto hallucinogen became totally eclipsed by the discovery of psilocybin mushrooms growing abundantly there and by the strange power that seemed to swirl around the fog-bound emerald pastures in which they were found.

My first intimation that La Chorrera was a place different from other places came when we arrived at Puerto Leguizamo, our proposed point of embarkation on the Rio Putumayo. It can be reached only by airplane, since no roads make their way through the jungle to it. It is as tired and oppressive a South American river town as you could ever hope to see. William Burroughs, who passed this way in his search for *ayahuasca* in the fifties, described it then as "looking like some place after a flood." By 1971 it had changed little.

We were scarcely installed in our hotel, having just returned from the ritual registration of foreigners that goes on in the frontier areas of Colombia, when the matron of the hotel informed us that

* R. E. Schultes, "Virola as an Orally Administered Hallucinogen," in the *Botanical Leaflets of Harvard University*, vol. 22, no. 6, pp. 229–40.

a countryman of ours was living nearby. It seemed incredible that an American could be living in such an out-of-the-way and thoroughly rural river town in Colombia. When *la señora* remarked that this man, *El Señor Brown*, was very old and also a black man, it became all the more puzzling. My curiosity piqued, I left immediately in the company of one of the loutish sons of the hotel woman. As we walked along, my guide could hardly wait for us to get out the door of the hotel before informing me that the man we were to see was *"mal y bizarro."*

"*El Señor Brown es un sanguinero,*" he said.

A killer? Was I on my way to visit a murderer, then? It seemed unlikely. I did not believe it for a moment. "*¿Un sanguinero, dice?*"

The horror that the rubber boom brought to the Amazon Indians in the early years of this century has lived on, a memory for the oldest people and a terrifying legend for younger Indians. In the area surrounding La Chorrera, the Witoto population had been systematically reduced from forty thousand in 1905 to about five thousand in 1970. I could not imagine that the man I was to meet had any real connection to those distant events. I supposed that this story I was hearing meant that I was about to meet a local bogey man around whom extravagant stories had grown up.

We soon reached a ramshackle and undistinguished house with a small yard hidden behind a tall board fence. My companion knocked and yelled and soon a young man, similar to my guide, came and opened the gate. My escort melted away and the gate closed behind me. A large pig lay in the lowest, wettest part of the yard; three steps up was a veranda. Upon the veranda, smiling and motioning me forward, sat a very thin, very old, much wrinkled black man: John Brown. It is not often that one meets a living legend and, had I known more about the person I confronted, I would have been more respectful and more amazed.

"Yes," he said, "I am an American." And, "Yes, hell yes, I am old, ninety-three years. Me hee-story, baby, is so long." He laughed dryly, like the rustle of roof thatch when tarantulas stir.

The son of a slave, John Brown had left America in 1885, never to return. He had gone to Barbados and then to France, had been a merchant seaman, and had seen Aden and Bombay. Around 1910, he had come to Peru, to Iquitos. There he had been made a work-crew foreman in the notorious House of Arana, which was the main force behind the ruthless exploitation and mass murder of the Indians of Amazonas during the rubber boom.

I spent several hours that day with *El Señor Brown*. He was an extraordinary person, at once near and yet ghostly and far away, a living bit of history. He had been the personal servant of Captain Thomas Whiffen of the Fourteenth Hussars, a British adventurer who explored the La Chorrera area around 1912. Brown, who is described in Whiffin's now rare work, *Explorations of the Upper Amazon*, was the last person to see the French explorer Eugène Robuchon, who disappeared on the Rio Caquetá in 1913. "Yes, he had a Witoto wife and a big black dog that never left him," mused Brown.

John Brown spoke Witoto and once had lived with a Witoto woman for many years. He knew the area into which we were going intimately. He had never heard of *oo-koo-hé*, but in 1915 he had taken *ayahuasca* for the first time—and at La Chorrera. His description of his experiences was an added inspiration to continue toward our goal.

It was only after I returned from the Amazon that I learned that this was the same John Brown who had exposed the atrocities of the rubber barons along the Putumayo to British authorities. He first spoke to Roger Casement, then the British Consul in Rio de Janiero, who had gone to Peru in July 1910 to investigate the atrocity stories.[*] Few remember, so strewn with horror is the history of the twentieth century, that before Guernica and Auschwitz the Upper Amazon was used as a rehearsal stage for one of the episodes of mechanized dehumanization so typical of our age. British banks, in collusion with the Arana clan and other laissez-faire operators, financed wholesale use of terror, intimidation, and murder to force the Indians of the deep forest to harvest wild rubber. It was John Brown who returned to London with Casement to give evidence to the Royal High Commission investigation.[†]

---

[*] For details, see W. E. Hardenburg, *The Putumayo: The Devil's Paradise* (London, 1912). Extracts from Casement's report are reprinted there as well. Also see Michael Taussig's *Shamanism, Colonialism and the Wildman* (Chicago: University of Chicago Press, 1987).

[†] John Estacion Riverá, a Colombian historian, has told the story differently and implicates Brown in the murders, thus providing the basis for the *sanguinero* story.

I returned to talk with him the next two days while preparations were made for our trip downriver. I was impressed by Brown's sincerity, by the depth of his understanding of me, by the way that Roger Casement and a world nearly forgotten—a world known to me only from its brief mention in the pages of James Joyce's *Ulysses*—lived and moved before me in those long, rambling conversations on his veranda.

He spoke long and eloquently of La Chorrera. He had not been there since 1935, but I was to find it much as he described it. The fever-haunted old town on the lowland across the lake no longer stood, but the dungeons for the Indian slaves could still be seen, crumbling iron rings set deep in sweating basaltic stone. The notorious House of Arana was no more, and Peru long ago abandoned her claims to that area to Colombia. But the old town of La Chorrera was ghostly indeed, and so was the old rubber trail, or *trocha*, that we would shortly use to walk the hundred and ten kilometers that separate La Chorrera from the Rio Putumayo. In 1911, up to twenty thousand Indians gave their lives to push that trail through the jungle. Indians who refused to work had the bottoms of their feet and their buttocks removed by machete. And for what? So that, in a surreal act of hubris typical of techno-colonialism, a motorcar could be driven the entire length of the trail in 1915. It was a ride from nowhere to nowhere.

Walking those gloomy, empty trails, I seemed often to hear a grumble of voices or the rustle of chained feet. John Brown's rambling monologues barely prepared me for its strangeness. On the morning that our boat was leaving to carry us downriver, we stopped at his house on our way to the landing. His eyes and skin shone. He was the gatekeeper of the Plutonic world downriver from Puerto Leguizamo, and he knew it. I felt like a child before him, and he knew that too.

"Bye, bye, babies. Bye bye," was his dry farewell.

CHAPTER TWO

INTO THE DEVIL'S PARADISE

*In which Solo Dark and Ev are introduced and
the past history of each of our party is outlined.
Philosophical musings during a languid descent
of the Putumayo River.*

DID I SAY WE WERE a party of five? We would be
five when we arrived at La Chorrera, but we were six departing
from Puerto Leguizamo. Ev and I were living together as much as
a couple can live together when they pile off a boat every night
with four other people to hang their hammocks in the trees. But *he*
was with us too. Solo Dark.

I must explain Solo. He was part of a fringe religion happening
in South America, which I had not found in India, called the New
Jerusalem. Devotees, who seemed to be primarily fruitarian, were a
tribe of mostly Americans who since 1962 or 1963 had been drifting
down through Latin America, chiseling on each other, living with
each other, hating each other, and weaving intrigues. They communicated through Ouija boards with entities they called "Beings
of Light." An entire mythology had been constructed around reincarnation. According to them, everyone was a reincarnation.

One person assumed himself to be the reincarnation of Rasputin; another, who was a refugee from the inner circles of the Hari Krishna cult and wore white robes and white rubber rain boots, was the reincarnation of Erwin Rommel. The burning-eyed leader of this whole group was Solo. He had been Ev's companion for four years.

Need I mention that Solo was strange? With his depthless baby blues and his wreath of wild long hair, he presented an imposing sight. He believed that he had been incarnated as several prominent historical personages: Christ, Hitler, Lucifer. It was a gamut both depressing and predictable.

I was in a peculiar dilemma, as my categories were themselves not very rigid. I had spent most of the previous three years living either as a hermit scholar studying dead Asian languages or as a lone lepidopterist in the Indonesian outback. I was unfamiliar with the protocols that had developed among the more exotic of my peers in the post–Charles Manson era. I thought, "Can't we work this out? Aren't we all happy hippies?" Perhaps I had been in Asia too long. In any case, I was soon to learn that among the enthusiasts of the New Jerusalem there were a lot of weird personae difficult to tolerate.

If Solo did not approve of something you were doing, he would look blank for a moment and then announce that it had been revealed to him that instant, by the Beings of Light, that you shouldn't, for example, peel fruit with metal knives. The tiny minutia of existence were controlled by these hidden forces. Solo traveled with animals: dogs, kittens, monkeys (he had a monkey that he supposed to be Christ incarnate). He insisted that all the animals be vegetarian, so the animals became twisted and unhealthy. As their eyes were going around in circles he would tell me, "This is Buddha; this is Christ; this is Hitler." It was not quite this demented— I exaggerate to give the flavor—but it was clear that in Solo's head it *was* this loose.

As we put off from Puerto Leguizamo, we were, therefore, six: Vanessa, Dave, Ev, Dennis, and myself. And Solo. Six freaks.

Our group had first come together on New Year's Eve, a little over two months before, when we met with Solo and Ev, who were still a couple then and not intending to join us. Our encounter had occurred in the fog-girt town of San Augustine in Colombia. Now that night seemed long in the past. Only a day or two after that evening, Vanessa, Dave, and I had left for Bogotá. In the days following our departure, Ev and Solo raged at each other. At the pinnacle of the final row, Solo deliberately unhorsed her into a deep mud puddle in front of a number of guests. Ev left him then and came to Bogotá to live in an apartment that she and Solo had said we could all use. In the two weeks while we gathered together the equipment for the expedition, Ev and I made our way to each other, and she joined our original group of four. The harsh Andean light streaming through the skylight of the pension was transformed into a lush intensity by rites of parting and defiling that drew Ev and me together. But this was no idyll for everyone. For Vanessa, who had once been my lover, it was surely a source of resentment. Doorways within the mirrored labyrinth of feelings opened and beckoned.

I said to her, "Look, I like this woman, *and* she speaks Spanish." This was my best argument, appealing as it did to reason. "Are you seriously suggesting that we trek many days into the Amazon Basin with our specious grip on the local language? It makes very good sense that Ev come."

Eventually Vanessa agreed. In the meantime the situation grew more complicated: Dave, unaware of Ev's attachment to me or of her abandonment of earlier plans to travel to Peru, had invited Solo along. Dave had been much impressed with Solo's knowledge of the Colombian outback during our first meeting in San Augustine, and so he cabled Solo, inviting him to meet us in Florencia and travel into the Amazon! When we piled off a vintage Colombian Air Force plane at Florencia, we were Dave, Vanessa, Ev, Dennis and I, Ev's puppy Lhasa, and a half-ton of equipment to be transported down the Putumayo. Waiting for us at the airport was Solo, thinking that the woman he had lived with for four years had gone to Peru with the incarnation of Rommel in white robes and matching rubber boots. When he discovered the truth, there was an emotion-fraught sorting out scene at the airport fence.

Later, in town, Ev and I took one room at the hotel, leaving Solo to figure it out for himself. With no possibility of grace on anyone's part, I was hoping that Solo, seeing that Ev's life had taken a new direction, would hit the road. I was disconcerted to encounter Solo, and as I am a bit of a wimp, hating tension, I chose not to address the situation directly.

Solo came to our room. He talked about the need to see all points of view, then he cut to the chase:

"Well, it looks like there is nothing here for me. I'm planning to fly back to Bogotá."

"Thank God," thought I.

Then he went to his room and went into communication with the Beings of Light. He came back two hours later to say, "You can't find it without me."

By this he meant the *oo-koo-hé*. "You don't know anything about the jungle. I'm a man of the forest."

With great reluctance I went along with this idea. When next we flew, it was on to Puerto Leguizamo. And we now had Solo, his dog, his cat, and his monkey. He wore robes and had a staff adorned with bright flowing *fajas*, locally woven strips of fabric. He looked both menacing and ridiculous.

I knew that the boats left Puerto Leguizamo very irregularly, and I thought we would have to wait, perhaps even up to two weeks. The hotel was tiny; the food terrible. I figured we would rub up against each other and then Solo would leave. He enjoyed cornering Ev into long, intense conversations. It was becoming a strain on everyone.

But it did not happen as I had anticipated. It turned out that there was a boat, the *Fabiolita*, departing downriver in two days. And so, in what seemed like hours, the arrangements had fallen together and we had paid six hundred pesos to secure our fare. At dawn on the appointed morning, all our animals, cameras, the *I Ching*, butterfly nets, formaldehyde, notebooks, a copy of *Finnegans Wake*, insect repellent, chloroquine, mosquito nets, hammocks, binoculars, tape recorders, granola, peanut butter, and dope—and all the other things one must have to go into the Amazon Basin—were piled at the river's edge. On the tiny trading boat that was to be our vessel, Ernito, our captain, indicated that our berth would be the area on top of the cases of bottled sodas colored fluorescent chartreuse, electric lemon, and magenta. We were informed that it was six to twelve days to where we wanted to go, "depending on business." John Brown came down to wave good-bye. He actually pulled out a large, white handkerchief and waved it. Then he dwindled to a speck. Puerto Leguizamo disappeared and the river, the green bank, the shrill of insects and parrots, and the brown water became our world.

We made our way under power, but slowly, to the middle of the shining brown river beneath an immense sky and an immense sun. A delicious moment—when one has done all that one can for a journey and is at last in motion, no longer responsible, since that burden has been given to pilot or engineer, boatman or ground control. The world one is leaving has been truly broken away from and the destination is still unknown. A favorite kind of moment, more familiar, yet less considered in the sterile environs of ocean-crossing passenger planes, and so how much richer here, surrounded by the cargo of sun-dried fish and local bottled sodas toxic with brilliant dyes.

I made a small space where I could sit cross-legged and rolled a joint out of the extraordinary kilo of Santa Marta Gold that we had laid in as a part of our provisions during the month in Bogotá. The flow of the river was like the rich smoke I inhaled. The flow of smoke, the flow of water, and of time. "All flows," said a beloved Greek. Heraclitus was called the crying philosopher, as if he spoke in desperation. But, why crying? I love what he says—it does not make me cry. Rather than interpret *pante rhea* as "nothing lasts," I had always considered it a Western expression of the idea of Tao. And here we were, going with the Putumayo's flow. What a luxury to be smoking, again in the tropics, again in the light, away from the season and places of death. Away from living under Canada's State of Emergency, on the edge of war-bloated, mad America. Mother's death and coincidentally the loss of all of my books and art, which had been collected, carefully shipped back and stored, and then had burned in one of the periodic brushfires that decimate the Berkeley hills. Cancer and Fire. Fire and Cancer. Away from these terrible things, where Monopoly houses, waxy green, go tumbling into fissures in the animated psychic landscape.

And before all that, Tokyo: its outer-planet atmosphere, the pretension of fitting into the work cycle. How inhuman does one become in an inhuman situation for a little while? The nights on the trains. The airless rooms of the Akihabara English language schools. Tokyo demanded the spending of money, the saving of which was the only way out.

I thought back over ten months of deepening alienation that had begun with leaving tropical Asia and, like a comet being drawn in to nearly brush its star, I was being drawn through Hong Kong, Taipei, Tokyo, and Vancouver before being hurled over war-toiling America and on into the outer darkness of other, new, and wretchedly poor tropical countries. The flight from Vancouver to Mexico City passed over my mother sleeping in her grave for the first winter. On over Albuquerque, only a pattern of freeway interchanges in the desert's night emptiness. On and on into what was then only an idea: the Amazon.

Out on the river, the past could enter the stillness and exfoliate before the mind's eye, unfurling a dark fabric of interlocking casuistry. Forces, visible and hidden, stretching back into one's past; migrations; religious conversions—our self discoveries make us each a microcosm of the larger pattern of history. The inertia of introspection leads toward recollection, for only through memory is the past recaptured and understood. In the fact of experiencing and making the present, we are all actors. But in the lacunae—in the rare moments of sensory deprivation when experience in the present is a minimal thing, as on a long plane ride, or any indolent, self-examining trip—then memory is free to speak and call forth the landscapes of our striving in moments now past.

Now—the now that is a time beyond the confines of this story, a now in which this story is past—I do not worry the past as I did then. Now it is set for me in a way that it was not set then. Not set then because so recent, still to be relived in memory and learned from. Five days of river travel lay before us—undemanding, freeing the mind to rove and scan.

Two all-inclusive categories emerged for us on the broad river whose distant banks were no more than a dark green line separating river and sky: the familiar and the unfamiliar. The unfamiliar was everywhere forcing us to draw inane analogies in common conversation: The Putumayo is like the Holy Ganga. The jungle evokes Ambon. The sky is similar to the skies of the Serengeti Plain, and so on. The illusion of understanding was a lame way of getting one's bearings. The unfamiliar does not give up its secrets in this game—the Putumayo does not become like the Ganga. The unfamiliar must become known as itself before it is correctly recognized.

The familiar things here are the people who have come with me. They appear as known quantities because I knew them in the past. So long as the future remains like the past, they would remain known. Certainly this is not New York, Boulder, or Berkeley, and it is not easy to become extra-environmentals, to develop a sense of appropriate action that is never at a loss for *savoir faire*. The cool aesthetic of the stranger: "Me, Ma'am? I'm just passing through." It is the familiarity of these people that makes them windows in my imagination opening into the past.

Dennis, of course; his is still the time line longest on a track parallel to my own. No need to mention the matter of shared genes. Back our connection goes until lost in primal, unlanguaged feeling. We grew up in the same household, shared the same constraints and freedoms until I left home at sixteen. But I had held close to Dennis.

Two and a half years earlier, in the middle of my twenty-second year, in the hold of the British Steam Navigation Company liner *Karanja*, I was weak and semi-delirious, wracked with hives, heartbreak, and dysentery. The eight days of passage from Port Victoria, Seychelles, to Bombay was then, in 1968, thirty-five dollars. In spite of being ill, I was obliged to travel the lowest class or my funds would not carry me home. My bunk was a metal plate that folded down from the wall. Public toilets and the hammer of the engines. Bilge water sloshed from one corner of the passageway to the other. Fifteen hundred displaced Indians from Uganda, victims of the Ugandan government's policy of Africanization, were traveling in the hold. All night long Indian women came and went from the toilets down my passageway, which was filled with bilge and engine throb. Without hashish and opium, I would have found it unbearable. To these middle-class Indians, my consolations and I were a stark example of depravity and moral failure, which they self-righteously pointed out to their children in long bird-like lectures on the evils of hippies and life in general.

After many days and nights of this, I awoke feverish in the middle of the night, the air redolent with curried food, excrement, and machine oil. I made my way to the exposed deck on the stern. The night was warm, the smell of curry not altogether lost even there. I sat down with my back against a heavily painted metal box of fire-fighting equipment. I felt my fever lift and a great sense of relief come through me. The recent past, my romantic disappointment in the Seychelles and in Jerusalem, seemed to release its hold on me. I had a clear space in which to turn toward the future and discern it. Unbidden came the thought that I would go with Dennis to South America. Even then, I knew it for a certainty.

And, in time, it happened. Not immediately, not before much more wandering in the East, but eventually, by February 1971, the prophecy was all round us. River, jungle, and sky enclosed us now and bore us toward La Chorrera. This boat was very little like the *Karanja*, but its small diesel engine was an echo of the larger engines further away in time. Yes, Dennis came first, came in with the sepia-toned memories of our growing up in a small Colorado town. There he was, always there beside me; we were two flies frozen in the backlit world of amber memories of summer outings and afternoons.

These others, different histories.

Vanessa and I had been student radicals together at Berkeley from 1965 to 1967. She was from New York—the Upper East Side. Father a prominent surgeon; older sister a practicing psychoanalyst; a mother who gave teas for the wives of U.N. delegates. Vanessa first attended private schools, then in a gesture of liberal chic, her parents supported her in her choice of Berkeley, a state university. She is intelligent, with a slightly feral twist to her gawkish sexuality. Her large brown eyes cannot hide a kitten cruelty and a mean love of puns. We were part of the Experimental College at Berkeley, but in the fall of 1968, I went to New York to try to sell the tortured manuscript that had been generated by my self-enforced seclusion in the Seychelles Islands, from where I had returned only a few months earlier. This was a rambling, sophomoric, McLuhanesque diatribe that was to die a bornin', fortunately. But in the complex autumn of that year, I took that work and flew to New York, in which place I knew no one but Vanessa.

She dug me out of a flophouse on West 43rd Street where I had crash-landed and persuaded me to move up to the Hotel Alden on

Central Park West, a place her mother had chosen for me. Our current riverine departure for the heart of Comisaria Amazonas followed by three years the languid moment when Vanessa and I sat together at the outdoor restaurant near the fountain in Central Park, she with her Dubonnet and I with my Lowenbrau. In the eyes of the poor scholar and revolutionary that I then imagined myself to be, the scene seemed staged in its casual elegance, the production values definitely higher than I could usually afford. The conversation had arrived at the subject of my brother, then only eighteen, whom Vanessa had never met:

"Dennis really is some sort of genius, I guess. Anyway, I'm his brother and am quite in awe of him, having seen it all from close up, as it were."

"And he had an idea that you think has great potential?" she asked.

"Actually, that's putting it mildly. I think that he may have seized the angel of Gnosis by the throat and forced the beast to the mat. This idea he has that some hallucinogens work by fitting into the DNA is startling. It has a ring of truth that I just can't ignore. The political revolution has become too murky a thing to put one's hope in. So far, the most interesting unlikelihood in our lives is DMT, right?"

"Reluctant agreement."

"Reluctant only because the conclusion that it leads to is so extreme. Mainly that we should stop fucking around and go off and grapple with the DMT mystery. Because, you know, anybody who has studied Western Civ. for ten minutes can readily see that the places this stuff puts you in touch with. . . . It's some kind of outrage that, properly understood, might—you know that I think it would—have tremendous importance for the historical crisis everybody is in."

"Okay. So say that I suspend my judgment. Then what's up?"

"I'm not sure. How about a trip to the Amazon? That's where these psychedelic plants are endemic. And that's where there is, God knows, enough solitude for anyone."

"Maybe. I'm trying to get on a dig that will happen in the Gibson Desert in Australia next year."

"I understand. And I am committed to this hash thing in Asia in a few months, for who knows how long? No, this Amazon trip, if it happens at all, is off in the future. But you should think about it, and something else. . . ."

"He lowered his voice mysteriously . . ." Vanessa provided in a radio drama aside.

"Right. The something else is flying saucers. I know it sounds nuts but they're mixed up in this somehow. It's pretty murky now. Fortunately it doesn't matter yet, but DMT is somehow linked to the whole psychic, you know Jungian, side of the notion of saucers. Deep water, I know. It's a hunch, but strong."

🍄   🍄   🍄

Dave was something else. We called him "the flower child." He was a delight-provoking, paradoxical amalgam of naiveté and strong-willed insight. If they sold harlequin suits off the rack he would have worn one. A Polish count, Ambassador to the Court of Great Elizabeth and friend of my personal idol, Dr. John Dee, brightened his genealogy. I had met Dave during the summer of 1967 in Berkeley. We had both been hitchhiking from the corner of Ashby and Telegraph, and when one kind soul picked both of us up, we became acquainted on the ride over the bridge to San Francisco. In Berkeley, Dave supported himself selling the *Berkeley Barb* and whatever else you sell when you loiter a lot. Since those days, Dave had graduated, both from the upstate New York commune he idealized and from Syracuse University with a degree in ethnobotany. In letters that passed between us when I was in Benares he became determined to be part of the venture to the Amazon Basin. He was to find in the jungles and mountains of South America a world even more spellbinding than he expected. To this day he has not returned from our initial voyage.

It was nearly two years before we could begin to put our plans into effect. Late in August of 1969 fate turned me from hash smuggler to fugitive when one of my Bombay-to-Aspen shipments fell into the hands of U. S. Customs. I went undergroud and wandered throughout Southeast Asia and Indonesia, viewing ruins in the former and collecting butterflies in the latter. Then came my time in Japan. Whether this gave me an edge on the others in experience seemed unlikely. Yet even my new status as desperado did not deter my passion for the Amazon. I still dreamed of visiting the green places of the vine people.

Eventually, Vanessa, Dave, and I gathered in Victoria, British Columbia. We lived there three months in a clapboard house, which we rented from a family of Sikhs—we ransacked articles, wrote letters, and maintained a constant correspondence with Dennis, who was in Colorado. Building momentum, we amassed information on a near-mythical world that none of us had ever seen.

While I lived in Canada, my mother died after a long bout with cancer. She was laid to rest, and then eventually Vancouver Island, lost in swirling snow, had fallen behind us as if by a series of telescoping leaps. At last our journey loomed: One by one the barriers to our entry into the anticipated magical world fell away, until we came to this indolent moment, our first day on the river. From my journal:

February 6, 1971

We are at last freed of our umbilical connection to civilization. This morning, under the uncertain skies which mark the Amazon during the dry season, we have at last gotten underway. Part of a flotilla of gasoline and fruit soda suppliers who are on their way to La Chorrera and will certainly carry us as far as El Encanto on the Rio Cara-Parana. Moving toward the absolute center of the geography of the secret, I am moved to ponder, as ever, the meaning of this truly strange search. I am having difficulty processing the intense content of my expectations. There can now be little doubt that, given that we continue to press forward as we have, we shall reach a state of satisfaction. We have been so long seeking this thing and it is so difficult to understand. Projections concerning who we will be or what we will do when this excursion is over are unconsciously based on the assumption that our experience will leave us unaffected, an assumption which is doubtless false, but its alternative can hardly be imagined.

Later: Two hours out of Puerto Leguizamo, upriver winds have caused us to tie up on the Peru side to await calmer weather. We are at Puerto Naranja. It is not shown on the Atlas Codazzi. The pattern of river travel immediately asserts itself. Following the channel means moving from side to side of the river, usually near one of the banks. The land is thickly covered by a dense canopy of jungle reminiscent of Central Seram or the coast of Ambon—a Venusian forest. The dull drum of the engine, the cooing of pigeons (part of our cargo), like the sacred Ganga, the brown, smooth water of the Putumayo soon flows through all our dreams and daydreams.

Solo watches me fixedly.

The familiar falls behind. The river is broad. The mystery for the present is in the strangeness of this place. The watery flatness. Five days descent of the Rio Putumayo will put us at the mouth of the Rio Cara-Parana. There is a mission there called San Raphael. We are looking for Dr. Alfredo Guzman, mentioned in one of our papers as the source of an authentic sample of the *oo-koo-hé* we are looking for. Guzman is an anthropologist working with the Witoto upriver from San Raphael at a tiny village charmingly called San Jose del Encanto. This village is situated at the beginning of the old rubber-gatherers' trail that leads through the jungle to La Chorrera. Not only can Guzman aid us in our search, but he can help us hire bearers for the trek overland. Many days to anticipate this personage.

In the meantime, the cramped world of this trading vessel, the *Fabiolita*, is ours, its mission, to sell plastic shoes, tinned food, and fishing line at the small clusters of houses on stilts that appear several times during each day of travel. We arrive, tie up, and while the *jefe* of our vessel makes *negocios* with the *colonistas*, I take my butterfly net and walk to the jungle, hoping to escape the stinging flies that swarm near the boat landings.

Sometimes there are long, opinionated conversations, with everyone animated and taking part. Sometimes a silence falls among us that lasts for several hours once each of us is comfortable, watching the riverbank slide by or nodding on the edge of siesta.

February 7, 1971

A Sunday. Last night we arrived at an unnamed place and spread our mosquito nets and hammocks for the first time in the Amazon. Eight A.M. found us back out on a rainy river under leaden skies. The moods of the approach to the secret are many. The air is delicious with oxygen, and the odors which reach us from the passing liana-hung forest change with the frequency and subtlety of a sonata. Brief stops at police inspections and ever more isolated riverside dwellings mark this day as well. Today, after forty minutes early morning travel, we passed a shallow depression in a clay bank on the Peruvian side of the river. There, thousands of parrots gathered around a salt source. The sonic shrill of their many-throated voice and their iridescent green bodies cleaving the air heightened the impression of moving in an aqueous Venusian world. We tied up opposite the lick and some of our crew went across the river to capture some parrots to add to the trader's already large menagerie. With our own small monkey, the nonhuman population of this ark of fools numbers two dogs, three monkeys, a kitten, a danta, a cock, a pig, and a crate of pigeons. Today is the day of the full moon and tomorrow we will arrive at El Encanto. There, if present plans hold, we will meet Dr. Guzman. The tensions that divide us have also surfaced. Vanessa and Solo, who have very little in common, seem warm friends. Is this because I have miffed Vanessa? It is not going well at all. Dennis is very quiet. Dave is worrying about the food supply; he is a chronic worrier. And naive. He seems to have thought that one just takes off one's shoes and goes to an Indian brother and says that one wants to learn the secrets of the forest and they say, "Come, my son, come with us and you will learn the secrets of the forest." Now that he is actually confronted with the Amazon jungle, he seems a bit taken aback. Solo's animals are falling off the boat into the river once an hour. The captain of the boat hates us because we have to stop to drag these soaking monkeys out of the drink.

That night we camped on the Peruvian side of the river. After dark, around the fire, the conversation anticipated a total eclipse of the moon said to be due. We wondered after the fate of the Apollo

14 crew which was returning that night from that same moon. These were the last bits of news we had received before our departure from Puerto Leguizamo.

Sometime in the dead of the night I awoke in my hammock, and after listening to the seething insect-filled night, pulled on my boots and silently made my way to the bluff of a little hill overlooking our portage. There I had a view of the river and the way along which we had traveled in the fading light of the late afternoon. Now all was transformed, the jungle eerily silent very suddenly, the moon washed an orange-red, the eclipse in progress and near totality.

The scene and the feeling were profoundly "Other." Alone in an immensity of jungle and rivers more vast than any I had ever known, we seemed witnesses to the emergence of strange dimensions, the clash of unearthly geometries, lords of places unseen and undreamed of by humanity. A few miles away, rain was falling from a cloud standing still in the sky; nearby foliage glistened black with orange highlights.

Unknown to me in that moment was that the eclipse that had drawn me as a lone observer from my hammock to this eerie scene would in a few short hours trigger a groaning shift of billions of tons of impacted rock along the San Andreas Fault in Southern California. Chaos was about to break out in the hell-city of Los Angeles. In a pitiless cartoon, I could imagine the pop-eyed denizens in beehive hairdos pouring out under incandescent lights into choking pollution to wail their hysteria to mobile news teams. Knowing nothing of the world beyond the forest and the river I returned to my hammock oddly cheered and exalted—the bizarre moment seemed a portent of great things.

CHAPTER THREE

ALONG A GHOSTLY TRAIL

In which we meet a peculiar anthropologist and his wife, and we depart from Solo Dark and make our way to our destination at Mission La Chorrera.

SHORTLY AFTER DAWN the next day, our vessel left the broad course of the Putumayo and turned into the Rio Cara-Parana for the last few miles of the journey to San Raphael, where the boat would leave us. The Cara-Parana more correctly fitted my conception of a jungle river, it being only several hundred feet across at its widest point, with lush vegetation overgrowing the banks and trailing in the water. Its flow was so sinuous and unpredictable that we could seldom see more than a half mile or so ahead. By mid-morning we arrived at a low bluff surmounted by a white flagpole and a few corrugated buildings appearing lavish in a land of thatched huts on stilts.

This was Mission San Raphael. We were properly, if unenthusiastically, received by Padre Miguel. He was thin, Castilian, with deep-set eyes and a barely noticeable palsy that was the result of malaria contracted years before. He had been in the Amazon over thirty years. It was not possible to read from his face what he thought of us. He had seen many anthropologists, botanists, and adventurers pass through, but I sensed that our longer hair and loose manner made him uneasy. His uneasiness increased when I asked about Dr. Guzman. In fact it was clear then, by the stiffening of the old priest's face, that my question hit a sore point. Nevertheless we were offered a ride upriver to where there was an inland trail to San Jose del Encanto.

"Yes, Dr. Guzman is doubtless there. He passed through on his way to return to his language studies only three weeks before. And his wife was with him." The priest's gaze hardened. "You may be assured of finding him."

We were given lunch by the nun in charge, *La Madré* being the form of address to the number-one nun at these missions. While we ate, Ev questioned the priest more carefully concerning La Chorrera. Yes, he confirmed, the trail took five days for a fully loaded expedition to traverse. We anticipated the need for porters to help carry our equipment. Padre Miguel said that we could get some help in El Encanto, but now was the time of hunting and men would be reluctant to leave the hunt to travel to La Chorrera. Since we were determined not to be over-burdened with equipment on the last leg of the push to reach La Chorrera, after lunch we sorted all of our equipment once again. Many books were reluctantly left behind; our plant and drug file was thinned down to only the essential articles; excess camera and insect-collecting equipment was stored: all went into a trunk to be left in the priest's keeping until we should return. Ev's pup Lhasa ended up with *La Madré*, whose admiration for the beast had seemed an opportunity too good to pass up.

The chore finished, we stowed our lightened supplies in the priest's powerful speedboat—an immense luxury in a world where the paddle canoe is the standard mode of transportation. In a few minutes we were tearing over the surface of the brown river, the moving center of a cresting wave of tremendous mechanical noise. The priest looked considerably more human and at ease here, with his brown cassock beating furiously in the wind and his long beard trembling in the spray and the sunlight. After forty minutes of this furious travel, we had gone a day's distance by canoe. Suddenly the priest turned the small boat at a right angle to the flow of the river, making directly for a long, low spit of white sand. The engine cut off at what seemed the last instant, and in the shattering silence, we slid lightly aground on the sand bar. It was a spot that seemed no less desolate than any other place we had passed in our wild ride, but the priest clambered up the bank and pointed out a broad trail much overgrown with vines. It was half a mile to the village, Padre Miguel explained, as we moved our supplies into a jumbled heap on the sand.

"I'm sure you will be well received," called the priest from the river as he wheeled the little speedboat around. Then he was gone. Long after he had turned a bend in the river and the sound of his departure had faded, the glassy surface of the river still moved and sucked against the banks as a last echo of the unusual commotion.

Silence. Then a shrill wave of insect sound swept like a drawn curtain through the area. Silence again. There was jungle, river, and sky—nothing else. We were on our own now, without a seasoned expert in control, and we all became aware of it in that moment on that spit of sand on the shore of a jungle river identical to hundreds of other such rivers.

The sense of time suspended could not last. We had to find the village and make whatever arrangements we could to move our supplies from the river. We had to act before dark; there would be time later to contemplate our situation. No one wanted to stay with the mound of supplies, so we hid them in the bushes away from the shore and started down the trail. Vanessa brought her box of cameras; I carried my telescoping fiberglass butterfly net.

The trail was broad and easy to follow, obviously cared for. As we moved away from the riverbank, the vegetation became less lush, and we were walking through an eroded, scrubby, brush land. The soil was red, lateritic clay, and where it was exposed to the sun, it baked and shattered into sharp-edged, cubical fragments. After half an hour of walking the trail we topped a long, slow rise and looked down on an assemblage of huts on sandy soil under a scattering of palms. Striking us immediately was a single unusual house near the center of the village, which was not of the thatched and stilted variety. As we surveyed the scene below, we were ourselves observed, and people began running and shouting. Some ran one way and some another. To the first person who reached us, we asked for Dr. Guzman. Surrounded by people giggling and whispering, we reached the anomalous house.

The structure was made of palm leaves expertly woven between long arched sticks. It was windowless and rested on the ground, looking vaguely like a loaf of brown bread. We all recognized it as a *malloca*, the traditional type of house peculiar to the Witoto people.

Inside, resting in a hammock that hung between two smoke-darkened supporting posts, was Dr. Alfredo Guzman. His face was unnaturally gaunt, his eyes were dark and deep-set, and his hands were skeletal, nervous. He did not get up, but gestured for us to sit on the ground. Only when I sat did I see beyond the hammock to the shadowed rear of the *malloca*, where a plump white woman in khaki pants sat cleaning pebbles from beans in a stone-polished Witoto pot. After we were all seated she looked up. She had blue eyes and even teeth.

Seeming to address us all equally, Guzman spoke: "My wife shares my professional interests."

"How fortunate. It must make it much easier," Vanessa offered.

"Yes." The flat reply became an unnerving pause. I decided to address the issue directly.

"Doctor, our apologies for disturbing your solitude and the local social environment here. We can appreciate your wish to be undisturbed in your work. We are anxious to push on to La Chorrera, and we hope that you will help us arrange bearers here to go with us. Also, we are here with a special purpose. I refer to the Virola hallucinogens that you reported to Schultes."

I am telescoping my account, of course; it all took longer and moved less directly. We talked for perhaps twenty minutes. At the end of that time, we learned that Guzman would help us find bearers and depart, but that this would take some days. We also learned that Guzman was an ardent Structuralist, Marxist, and male chauvinist, that his involvement with the Witoto approached the maniacal, and that he was regarded by his colleagues back in Bogotá as bonkers. He gave us no encouragement that we would find the *oo-koo-hé*, which he said was a secret of the men that was slowly dying out. At the end of this discussion, our small party and a dozen of the village people walked back to the river and carried our gear to a rundown, unused hut on the edge of the village.

As we set up camp, Annalisé Guzman approached us with several cups of steaming coffee and chatted with us. Unlike her husband, she seemed more relieved than dismayed by our presence. As she talked, a picture emerged. She had gone to the London School of Economics, studied anthropology, and did graduate work in Colombia, meeting the impassioned older man in a similar profession. She was now living a pendulum life, going between the striving, contentious world of the university in Bogotá and the tiny village of San Jose del Encanto. Her husband's addiction to chewing coca was much on her mind.

Like the males of the Witoto group, Guzman was a coca enthusiast, and he had become quite paranoid from constantly chewing it. When we saw him in the morning, he always had coca staining his lower chin. Because the tribe is very hard on women, Annalisé had been told by Alfredo that, in order to become integrated into this society, she had to take on the women's role. This required pounding yucca root with stones and also making the coca, which the women are not allowed to chew at all. The men lie around in hammocks and listen to transistor radios. The women live with the dogs and the children *under* the houses, while the men lived *in* the houses. At five o'clock in the afternoon, the women are all sent to the sleeping place with the children and the dogs. The men retire into the long house for storytelling and coca chewing until four-thirty in the morning. The fart is their most highly appreciated form of humor. There are ten thousand variations on the fart and all are thought riotously funny.

We lived with these people elbow-to-elbow, staying in that uncomfortable setting until the morning of the eighteenth of February. It took that long—nearly a week—to arrange for two young boys to leave the hunting to help us carry our supplies over the trail to La Chorrera.

We were grateful for the pause in travel, since the voyage on the *Fabiolita* had left us rather worn. I spent part of each day collecting insects, or writing, or thinking in my hammock. That week we saw Dr. Guzman very rarely. He treated us with the same remote disdain that the other male leaders of the community affected. Not everyone was so shy; there were always several Witoto of all ages intently watching whichever one of us was most active at any given moment. In one of his oddest moves, Dr. Guzman asked us to answer any questions about the relationships prevailing within our group by saying that we were all brothers and sisters. This assertion brought the expression of amazement expected of any reasoning being. And so I think we were especially interesting to the people of the village because they were asked by their expert informant concerning all things in the outside world to believe that such a disparate group as we were all siblings. It was only one of the good doctor's peculiarities.

Once in the heat of the afternoon when I was alone, collecting insects in the forest, I came around a large tree to surprise Guzman, who was standing absolutely still, poised above a small stream with a fish spear in his hand. We walked back to the village together, and as we walked, he told me his view of life.

"Danger lurks everywhere. Never swim alone in the river. Huge forms move beneath its surface. There is the anaconda. The rivers abound with them. Snakes are everywhere. Be aware of this as you make your way to La Chorrera. The forest is unforgiving of error."

I had spent months in the jungles of Indonesia, and I had been collecting insects every day in these Amazonian forests since the journey to San Jose del Encanto had begun. I had my own idea of the risks of the forests, not nearly so dark as the thoughts of the wildly gesticulating figure who strode raving at my side. Clearly, it had been our misfortune to stumble onto what was a very peculiar scene. Guzman had been ruling his wife with an iron hand. He lived in a nightmare world of delusions brought on by coca addiction. His wife had not had any *Anglos* to talk with since arriving in the jungle. Naturally she was wondering what was going on. She wasn't allowed to chew coca and he was behaving more and more like a male Witoto of the tribe.

There were strange incidents that set everyone on edge. A bushmaster, most deadly of vipers, was killed near the village and brought back and shown around. Incidents? Say rather omens or ominous events. One morning an enormous tarantula, the largest I had ever seen, made a dash through the village, or so it seemed, since it was suddenly discovered very much in the middle of things. Had someone released it?

Two nights before we were to leave the village, a tree burst into flames near our hut. This seemed unambiguously unfriendly and we accelerated our plans for departure. But we could not continue on without bearers, and only when the men came back from the hunting party could we expect to hire them.

From Guzman we would learn almost nothing. About the *oo-koo-hé* he said, "Ridiculous, my friend. You're not going to get it. These people don't even speak Spanish. They speak only Witoto. There were forty thousand of them killed here fifty years ago. They have no reason to like you and the drug is supersecret. What are you doing here? I urge you to leave the jungle while that is still possible." But in his way he was informative; we learned that the *oo-koo-hé* was always made with the ash of other trees mixed into the DMT-containing resin. We felt that these additional ingredients must be the key to its oral activity, since normally DMT would be destroyed by enzymes in the large intestine. Dennis was determined that we make a firm botanical identification of the "secret activators." Ideally we hoped to be the first to get good collections of these plants. It would be our small contribution to Amazonian ethnobotany.

Finally, on the eighteenth, we departed, the six of us in the company of two Witoto adolescents. The *capitan* of the village turned out to wish us a good journey. Even Dr. Guzman was smiling, delighted no doubt at the prospect of the village returning to normal after a long week playing host to a delegation from the global electronic tribe.

There was no one more pleased to leave the village than I. As we strode along the wide path, or *trocha*, I felt my spirits rise. At last we had put all the encumbering obstacles behind us. Only Solo remained to plague me. I decided, Walter Mitty or not, I was going to have to burst his bubble. Relations inside our group were becoming too odd. Solo was doing things. He insisted on going first on the *trocha*. He would get far ahead, then sharpen sticks and put them on the ground in odd patterns, fetishes.

During our journey downriver, before we got to El Encanto, we had been smoking weed all the time. Solo would just sit staring for hours and hours. I finally came to understand that he was probably going to kill me and was most likely completely deranged. That, strange as it may seem, would be my fate—I was going to be bumped off by somebody's psychotic old boyfriend who had somehow managed to sneak onto this Amazon expedition.

I contemplated the irony of the situation. I recalled that mushroom maven Gordon Wasson and his wife had been accompanied by an undercover CIA agent during their second journey to the mushroom village of Huatla de Jimenez in the remote uplands of Mazatecan, Mexico. Psychedelic history would have been different if Wasson had detected that clumsy effort at co-option. Then the CIA's absurd notion that psilocybin might forever remain what it termed an "in-house prerogative" could never have been entertained. It was only the speedy publication of the molecular structure of psilocybin by Swiss pharmacologist and LSD-inventor Albert Hofmann that had short-circuited that dark and grandiose fantasy. I thought about turning points generally. I recalled John Wayne's observation that, "A man's gotta do what a man's gotta do."

At this thought, I seized the moment and stopped on the trail and observed out loud that Solo was the world's most outrageous jackass. In other words, I just pitched the shit straight into the fan. For a moment it looked like we were going to punch each other out right there. Vanessa began yelling and shoving. Witoto bearers were standing around open-mouthed. The incident ended as a standoff, but as the day wore on Solo decided to turn back. He had no money, and he was in terrific pain because of an abscessed tooth. There was no reason for him to be there. The stress of isolation and bad food can push even a healthy person to the edge, and I had become convinced that he was deeply disturbed and capable of anything. He chewed coca to cut the pain of his tooth, but it didn't help. He needed medical attention. That night he came to me and explained that he did not have enough money to get back upriver. He offered me a kilo of his own crop, and I jumped at the chance to pay him a hundred dollars. When we broke camp the next morning he was already gone.

Around us, the jungle; ahead of us, the Secret. After Solo's departure, I buttoned up my stash, hefted my butterfly net, and felt like Van Veen, the priapic hero of Nabokov's surreal love story *Ada*. After all, how often does one have the satisfaction of overcoming a rival? Especially a rival who claims to believe sincerely that he is Jesus Christ and Hitler?

It was as lovely as a Bierstadt as we wended our way toward La Chorrera under the liana-tangled canopy of the climaxed Amazonian forest. Iridescent, blue *morphos*, butterflies the size of dinner plates, would occasionally be surprised while lounging languidly on broad leaves overhanging the trail. They would start upwards suddenly with an amazing show of watery, splendiferous sapphire quickly lost in the gloomy heights. We set a brisk pace and as we moved along my thoughts returned to Nabokov and the seemingly prophetic lines written in *Pale Fire* by his character, the apocryphal American poet John Shade:

> . . . that rare phenomenon
> The iridule—when, beautiful and strange
> In a bright sky above a mountain range
> One opal cloudlet in an oval form
> Reflects the rainbow of a thunderstorm
> Which in a distant valley has been staged—
> For we are most artistically caged.

That night we made our camp at a thatch-roofed shelter with a marker indicating we had come twenty-five kilometers during the day. We ate well that night on tinned cheese with reconstituted minestrone, and in the morning we were back on the trail as the ground fogs of dawn departed. It was a day of hard work, carrying the heaviest loads by a method that allowed each person two hours on and then an hour off. Quite a physical feat. I think that we were already feeling the effects of "the phenomenon," a backwash from our experimental tampering with the laws of physics that still lay days in the future. But it is impossible to say. We stopped eating.

The women announced that we would eliminate breakfast and lunch to make better time. It was their decision since they were doing the cooking; it was too much of a chore to make a fire in the damp Amazonian forest.

We would get up at four-thirty in the morning, have coffee, and walk twenty-five kilometers until about three-thirty in the afternoon. It was an ass buster, absolutely. The *trocha* went up and down, up and down. We would arrive at a river to find no bridge and have to figure out how to cross. We had to be aware of the possibility that the bearers might steal something or desert us. In spite of the exertion, the days were an exquisite immersion in the truly immense and vibrant forest through which we were passing. All day long on the second day we pushed forward against our flagging energies. At last we reached a shelter similar to the one we had used the night before. It was set on the top of a small hill just beyond a crude bridge arching a small river. After dark, around the fire, we smoked and talked long into the night, anticipating the adventure soon to come that we could sense but not yet imagine. The Witoto bearers unfolded their leaf-wrapped packets of food and ate apart from us, friendly but distant.

Toward the afternoon of the fourth day, the bearers were visibly excited in anticipation of our arrival at La Chorrera. During one of our breaks, Vanessa pointed out a rainbow that lay directly over the path we were traveling. The appropriate jokes were made and we hoisted our loads and hurried onward. In a few minutes we were walking through secondary forest and shortly thereafter emerged on the edge of a huge clearing of rough pasture. Mission buildings could be seen across this expanse. As we walked into the clearing, an Indian came to meet us. We spoke with him haltingly in Spanish, and then he spoke to our bearers rapidly in Witoto and started off with us in the direction from which he had come.

We passed through a space fenced by a wood enclosure and across a semi-enclosed courtyard, perhaps a ballcourt. On the walls of this enclosure were paintings in tempera of cartoon elves with pointed ears. We were led finally to the back porch of a more substantial wooden building that was obviously the priest's house. A huge man, bearded and bearish, emerged in his shirt sleeves. Peter Ustinov could have played him to perfection. A basically merry person, he nevertheless did not seem happy to see us. Why were these people always so withdrawn? Something about not liking anthropologists—but we were basically botanists: how could we put that across? Our reception was hospitable and correct. We asked no more, and as we hung our hammocks in the empty guest house to which we were shown, there was a sense of relief among us all at having reached our destination.

CHAPTER FOUR

CAMPED BY A DOORWAY

In which we become acquainted with the
mushrooms and shamans of La Chorrera.

MOST OF THE AMAZON BASIN is made up of alluvial deposits from the Andes. La Chorrera is different. A river, the Rio Igara-Parana, narrows and flows into a crack. It becomes very rapid then drops over an edge—a lip—creating not exactly a waterfall but a narrow channel of water (*chorro* means "chute"), a flume whose violent outpouring has made a sizable lake.

La Chorrera is a paradisiacal place. You push very hard and suddenly you are there. There are no stinging or biting insects. In the evening, mist drifts across a large pasture creating a beautiful pastoral scene. There is the mission, the foam-flecked lake below, the jungle surrounding, and much to my surprise, white cattle.

The afternoon following our arrival, at the edge of the pasture, which had been cleared by the Spanish priests who had managed Mission La Chorrera since its establishment in the 1920s, I held and turned over in my hand perfect specimens of the same species of mushroom that I had eaten near Florencia. In the pasture before me were dozens of these mushrooms. After examining several, my brother concurred, pronounced them the same *Stropharia cubensis* we had found before, one of the largest, strongest, and certainly the most widely distributed of any of the known psilocybin-containing mushrooms.

What to do? We had no data on the proper dosage of psilocybin. Our expedition's thinned-down drug and plant file was concerned with flowering plants, not with fungi. Collectively we seemed to remember that in the Oaxacan mushroom rituals described by Gordon Wasson, in *Life* magazine of all places, mushrooms were always eaten in pairs, with several pairs consumed. We determined to eat six mushrooms each that same evening. My journal entry for the next day spoke clearly:

February 23, 1971

Are we indeed now in some way camped on the edge of another dimension? Yesterday afternoon Dave discovered Stropharia cubensis *in the damp pastures behind the house where we had hung our hammocks. He and I gathered thirty delicious psilocybin-saturated specimens in about a half an hour. We each ate about six and spent last night on an enormously rich and alive, yet gentle and elusive, trip. In between strange lights in the pasture and discussion of our project, I am left with the sense that by penetrating the local psychedelic flora this way we have taken a giant step toward deeper understanding. Multifaceted and benevolent, as complex as mescaline, as intense as LSD—the mushroom, as is said of peyote, teaches the right way to live. This particular mushroom species is unclaimed, so far as I know, by any aboriginal people anywhere and thus is neutral ground in the tryptamine dimension we are exploring. Through this unclaimed vegetable teacher one can gain entry into the world of the elf chemists. The experience of the mushroom is subtle but can reach out to the depth and breadth of a truly intense psychedelic experience. It is, however, extremely mercurial and difficult to catch at work. Dennis and I, through a staggered description of our visions, noticed a similarity of content that seemed to suggest a telepathic phenomenon or some sort of simultaneous perception of the same invisible landscape. A tight headache accompanied the experience in its final stages, but this was quick to fade, and the body strain and*

*exhaustion often met with in unextracted vegetable drugs such as
peyote and Datura was not present.*

*This mushroom is a transdimensional doorway which sly
fairies have left slightly ajar for anyone to enter into who can find
the key and who wishes to use this power—the power of vision—
to explore this peculiar and naturally occurring psychoactive
complex.*

*We are closing distance with the most profound event
a planetary ecology can encounter.
The emergence of life
from the dark chrysalis of matter.*

Such were my impressions after only one exposure to the realm
of vision over which the mushroom holds sway.

The reference to "strange lights in the pasture" should be explained, since perhaps it has some bearing on some of what followed.
An hour after we had eaten the mushrooms, and everyone was comfortable with the pleasant plateau of colorful, drifting, behind-the-
eyelids imagery, someone initiated a discussion.

It was Dave or my brother, Dennis; Dennis, I believe. He said
that we were now stoned in the home territory of the Secret and so
should not remain in the confined space of our thatched hut, but
we should move out into the night and the warm, enfolding fog
over the pasture. Not all should go, but a delegation. Who should
it be? Dennis nominated Dave and myself, calling Dave the least
skeptical and me the most. Vanessa objected to me as "most skeptical," suggesting instead that Dave and Dennis should go. I
heartily agreed, not actually wishing to visit the dark and dewy pasture myself, and having no faith, so skeptical was I, in the transcendental potential of the errand.

So off they went, first loudly proclaiming the total enveloping
power of the ground fog, and then in a theatrically absurd short
time and from offstage, they hollered out that they saw a hovering,
diffuse light in the pasture nearby. Investigation pursued. Hollering
continued but faded. Light persisted. Diffuseness persisted. I decided it was time for cooler heads to intervene. Off into the enfolding, wet night I went. I crossed carefully through the barbed wire

that surrounded the pastures; it was wet to my fingers but warm-seeming even at night, so steamy is the Amazon. Once united with Dave and Dennis I found the situation closer to their description than I had expected. There *was* a dim light on the ground a few yards away. It seemed to retreat as one walked toward it.

We moved about thirty meters in its direction in a series of short advances. Enveloped in dense and drifting fog, we felt far from our companions back at the house.

"We can follow this light but we had better not go too far or we'll get lost since we don't know the area at all."

Dave was pleading for a retreat, but we continued to press on. Sometimes the light seemed to be hovering above the ground just twenty feet ahead and then, leaping and falling again, it would recede as we approached. We would run forward to catch up with it, yet it continued to remain ahead of us. For ten minutes, we chased this hovering, receding light, but then decided to go no farther. As we turned to depart I seemed to see a flickering of the diffuse light that, to my mind, suggested someone dancing before a fire.

I momentary abandoned thoughts of UFOs and recalled instead the series of ominous incidents preceding our departure from Dr. Guzman and his scene at San Jose del Encanto. Was this a shaman dancing around a small fire? Did it have something to do with us? No illumination was ever shed on this incident, but the general eeriness of it anticipated all that was to follow.

The words of my journal are revealing. I wrote matter of factly of "gaining entry into the world of elf chemists"; I called the mushroom a transdimensional doorway and linked it to a transformation of life on the planet. A younger, more naive, more poetic self is revealed—a more intuitive self, at ease with proclaiming wild unlikelihoods as hallucinogenically derived Gnostic Truth.

And yet these ideas have changed very little in twenty years; then I was eager to be convinced by demonstration, and demonstration was given. I was changed and was obviously eager to be changed. It was true of me then and is still true now, for since the coming of the mushroom all has been continuous transformation. Now, years later and with two decades of reflection on these things, I can still discern in that earliest experience many of the motifs that have persisted through the years and remained mysterious. At one point during that evening, Dennis and I both seemed able to see and describe the same inner visions. Off and on over the years this has happened several times with psilocybin. The wonder of it remains.

In those early mushroom experiences at La Chorrera there was an aura of the animate and the strange, the idea that the mushroom was somehow more than a plant hallucinogen or even a shamanic ally of the classic sort. It had begun to dawn on me that the mushroom was in fact a kind of intelligent entity—not of earth—alien and able during the trance to communicate its personality as a presence in the inward-turned perceptions of its beholder.

In the days following that first mushroom experience, the lives of my brother and I underwent a tremendous and bizarre transformation. Not until Jacques Vallee had written *The Invisible College* (1975), noting that an absurd element is invariably a part of the situation in which contact with an alien occurs, did I find the courage to examine the events at La Chorrera and try to fit them into some general pattern. I have told various parts of our story over the years, never revealing the entire incredible structure to any one listener, knowing full well what it seems to imply about our mental condition during the time of the experiences.

Any story of alien contact is going to be incredible enough by itself, but central to our story as well are the hallucinogenic mushrooms with which we were experimenting. The very fact that we were involved with such plants would make any story of alien contact seem highly dubious to anyone not sympathetic to the use of hallucinogens. Who would fail to attribute our "UFO experience" to the fact that we were tripping? But that is not the only difficulty with telling this story. The events at La Chorrera generated a great deal of controversy and subsequent bitterness among the participants. Several ideas of what was taking place were represented, each basing itself on data unavailable to or deemed irrelevant by the competing interpretations. What some of us took to be a metamorphosis toward the transcendental, others took for an outbreak of obsessional fantasy.

We were poorly prepared for the events that overwhelmed us. We began as naive observers of something—we knew not what— and because our involvement with this phenomenon went on for many days, we were able to observe *some* aspects of it. I feel satisfied that the method of approach described here is generally effective for triggering whatever it is that I am calling the alien contact experience. (It may also be dangerous, so don't try this at home, folks.)

Our first *Stropharia* trip at La Chorrera occurred on the twenty-second of February, 1971, only a little more than twenty-four hours after our arrival at La Chorrera and following the four-day walk through the jungle from San Jose del Encanto on the Rio Cara-Parana. My journal entry on the following day makes it clear that I was spellbound. It was the last thing I could bring myself to write for several weeks. All day I was suffused with contentment. I knew only that the mushroom was the best hallucinogen I had ever had and that it had a quality of aliveness I had never known before. It seemed to open doorways into places I had assumed would always be closed to me because of my insistence on analysis and realism.

I had never had psilocybin before and was amazed at the contrast with LSD, which seemed more abrasively psychoanalytic and personal. In contrast, the mushrooms seemed so full of merry elfin energy that casting off into a visionary trance was all the more enticing. I sensed nothing of the magnitude of the forces that were gathering around our small expedition. I was thinking only that it was great these mushrooms were here. Even if we didn't find *oo-koo-hé* or *ayahuasca*, we would always have them to fall back on, and certainly they *were* interesting.

Our plan was to spend about three months slowly getting to know the botanical and social environment of the Witoto, who were living traditionally in a village about fourteen kilometers down a trail from the mission at La Chorrera on the Rio Igara-Parana. We knew *oo-koo-hé* was taboo, so we were in no hurry. The day after our first mushroom experience was spent checking our equipment, after the rigors of the overland walk, and generally relaxing in the *casita* to which Father José Maria, the Capuchin in charge, had kindly shown us. We gathered more mushrooms that afternoon and dried them near the cooking fire.

We decided we would take mushrooms again that night. I pulverized them into a snuff, which we all took. It was delicious, like some chocolate-related essence, and it was generally thought a success. I felt elated and very pleased with everything and impressed with what an extraordinarily beautiful place we had come to be in.

But it was a different sort of experience. We were exhausted from the trip the night before, and as we all sat around waiting to get stoned, there was a lot of bickering between Vanessa and Dennis. Apparently he had had enough of her and said, "You know, you're pretty weird, and I'm going to tell you why," at which point he launched into a long monologue of accumulated gripes.

The next day was spent relaxing, catching up on insect and plant collecting, washing clothes, and chatting with the priest and brother in residence, who were both part of an austere Franciscan order that did missionary work. Through them we put out the word that we were interested in people who knew things about medicinal plants.

That afternoon a young Witoto named Basilio came to the *casita* and, having heard of our interest from the priest, offered to take us to see his father, a shaman with a local reputation. Basilio assumed we were interested in *ayahuasca*, the better-known hallucinogen in the area, which is generally available for the asking.

The *oo-koo-hé* was a much more sensitive subject. There had been a murder at La Chorrera a month or two before we arrived—actually several murders—and Guzman claimed they all had to do with *oo-koo-hé*. Supposedly a shaman had murdered one of two shaman brothers by painting the top rung of a ladder with a DMT-containing resin. When the victim grabbed the rung, the resin had absorbed through his fingers and he had gotten vertigo and fallen, breaking his neck. The shaman whose brother had been killed struck back by causing an accident. The alleged murderer's wife, daughter, and grandchild had been in a canoe above the *chorro* and, unaccountably unable to reach the shore, they had been swept over it. It was generally assumed that they were victims of magic. Only the wife had lived through it. It was not the time to be poking around asking about *oo-koo-hé*.

Basilio insisted that the *ayahuasca* was a day upriver at his father's *malloca*, or house. He had a small canoe, so only two of us could go with him. After consultation, it was decided that Ev and I should go. We left at once for the river and I took my film canister of snuff with us.

The day was calm and the sky blue. An extraordinary peace and depthless serenity seemed to touch everything. It was as if the whole earth was softly exhaling its exhilaration. Had such a mood developed no further it would have passed into being but a pleasant memory; in light of later events, I now look back to that afternoon of deepening contentment and almost bucolic relaxation as the first faint stirring of a current that was shortly to sweep me toward unimaginably titanic emotions.

When we arrived at Basilio's village late in the day, we found our new Witoto acquaintances very kind, a different sort from the Witoto of San Jose del Encanto. We were shown a matted tangle of cultivated *ayahuasca* plants and given cuttings and a bundle of the vine so that we could make our own brew. Basilio described to us his own single experience with *ayahuasca* when, several years before, after days of fever from an unknown cause, he had taken it with his father. He described the *ayahuasca* as a cold water infusion, rare for that area, where vigorous boiling usually plays a part in the preparation. After soaking the shredded *ayahuasca* for a day and a night, the unboiled water becomes hallucinogenically potent. There had been many "fences" to cross in Basilio's visions. He had a sense of flying. The father had seen the "bad air" that had weakened his son as coming from the mission, which was recognized as a place of ill omen. After this experience, Basilio recovered his health and was less often at the mission, he told us. It was all very interesting, our first exposure to "field conditions," and it accorded well with our data on *ayahuasca* usage and beliefs in the area.

We hung our hammocks in a small hut near the main *malloca* that night. I dreamed of fences and the pasture back at the mission. Early the next morning we were rowed back to the mission by Basilio. Our collections of *Banisteriopsis caapi* were reason enough for pride, but again I felt the elation whose depth could not be found.

"Peculiar," I muttered to myself as we swung into sight of the mission overlooking its placid lake, with a row of date palms sweeping up from the boat landing.

"Peculiar."

CHAPTER FIVE

A BRUSH WITH THE OTHER

*In which we move to a new home, and Dennis
has a bizarre experience that divides our group.*

RETURNING TO OUR FRIENDS, we learned that
during the day that we were gone some teachers, *professores* who
had been expected to arrive to teach in the mission school, had finally appeared. They had been ferried in by a bush pilot, the notorious George Tsalikas, who served as La Chorrera's emergency link
to the outside world and who brought the mail once a month. This
meant that we needed new lodging, since we had been staying in
the *professores'* quarters. The priest offered us the temporary use of
a run-down hut that stood on stilts on a small rise below the mission, though it was well above the broad lake created by the *chorro.*
It was in this small hut, instantly christened "the knoll house," that
we proposed to live while we made arrangements to move farther
into the nearby jungle and away from the somewhat confining atmosphere of the mission. That morning we rested, passed a joint
around, and planned our next move.

Dave and Vanessa had learned in conversations with Brother
Luis, a white-bearded ancient who was the only other resident rep-
resentative of the Church aside from Father José Maria, that there

47

was a quite sturdy Witoto house which was unused and lying down the trail toward the village where our hopes for *oo-koo-hé* centered. It normally stood empty but was now occupied by the people who had brought their children to the mission for the beginning of the school year. It is the practice of the Witoto to leave their children in the keeping of the padres for six or more months out of the year; the times of gathering at the mission at the beginning and end of the school year are high points of the Witoto social swirl and an excuse for soccer games and evening *bailes,* for the Witoto are inveterate dancers. We were in the midst of such a gathering time, but in a few days all the families would leave and there would be ample empty housing in the jungle. Dave, Dennis, and Vanessa had already inspected one place and determined it to be ideal, close to good insect- and plant-collecting and definitely in the jungle itself.

We transferred our equipment to the knoll house and reslung our hammocks. It was cramped, but it would do until we could move into the forest. Then, almost in a collective motion, we set out in the early afternoon to the pastures behind the mission. *Find the mushrooms.* That was the thought on everyone's mind. We returned that evening to the house, each with six or eight carefully chosen specimens. These we ate and then, as the evening's trip deepened, we smoked joints rolled out of shavings of the freshly gathered *Banisteriopsis caapi.* The *caapi* smoke was delicious; it smelled like a light incense, and each toke synergized beautiful slow-motion volleys of delicate hallucinations, which we immediately dubbed "vegetable television."

Each burst of imagery would last about fifteen minutes and subside; then we would take another hit of the *caapi* smoke. The cumulative effect persisted for a couple of hours. We triggered it repeatedly, and excitedly discussed it as an example of the sort of thing that sophisticated shamanic technicians must have been whipping up for each other's amazement since the late paleolithic.

As the evening wore on, our conversation drifted toward and around the possibility of violating normal physics, discussing it in terms of a psychological versus a naive/realist view of shamanic phenomena. We were especially interested in the obsidian liquids that *ayahuasqueros* are said to produce on the surface of their skins and use to look into time.* The idea of a kind of hologramatic alchemical fluid, a self-generated liquid crystal ball, seemed to me very strange and somehow compelling. The question of whether or not such things are possible is actually a more gut issue in disguise: Is what we moderns have remaining to learn about the nature of reality slight and will it require only light fine-tuning of our current way of looking at things; or do we understand very little, missing the point entirely about the nature of our situation in being? I found myself arguing that reality is made of language and that we somehow had to step outside the cultural prison of language to confront a reality behind appearances. "If you would strike, strike through the mask!" That sort of thing.

Rhetoric waxed hot and heavy. Ev, Dennis, and I became passionate defenders of this view. Vanessa and Dave insisted on a psychological-reductionist approach to unusual events. They argued that everything could be seen in a context of fantasy, delusion, and wish-fulfillment. For them nothing that occurred during hallucinations happened in the real world; only mental events were taking place. Then, ideology forgotten, they denounced the passion of our commitment as naive and obsessive. We retorted that they repressed the real power of the unconscious and that if they had come along to try to vindicate some behaviorist/materialist view of man, then they would be in for a surprise. And so on.

The life of an expedition is full of stress and aggravated differences, and tension had simmered under the surface for weeks. But I believe that the real cause of tension even then was a sense that something in the mushroom experience was pulling everyone toward it, or at least precipitating a crisis during which we had to decide whether or not to go deeper into a dimension whose precise nature could not yet be seen.

Each exposure to the mushroom was a learning experience with an unexpected conclusion. Three of us were ready to become alchemical children, ready to strip down and climb into the sophic fountain and take the measure of the thing from the inside.

---

* See Terence McKenna and Dennis McKenna, *The Invisible Landscape* (New York: The Seabury Press, 1975), chapter six.

Call it Faustian or obsessed, that was our position. I considered it
continuing the program of investigations that brought us to La
Chorrera in the first place. For Vanessa and Dave, however, the
reality of the dimension we were exploring, or rather our growing
insistence that somehow it was a dimension with elements more
than merely psychological, was seen as a threat. So there we were,
a group of friends sharing a common set of symbols, completely
isolated in the jungle, struggling with an epistemological problem
upon whose eventual solution our sanity would seem to depend.

And so, and in short, Dave and Vanessa withdrew from us,
withdrew from the excited speculative conversations with their intimations of the possibility of being overwhelmed by the unseen.
There were no arguments or scenes, but after that night there was
a tacit and mutual understanding that a fork in the road had been
reached. Some of us were committed to going more deeply into the
idea systems of the mushroom trance, and some were disturbed by
the sudden depth of things and preferred only to witness the occasion. The cramped knoll house and the polarizing of our two approaches combined to inspire Vanessa to expand her checker-
playing contacts with the police garrison of three young Colom-
bians forlornly homesick for their Andean homes. After several
closely fought games, she had a full-fledged invitation to relieve
our crowded conditions by moving with Dave into an unused riverside house nominally in the care of the police. Later, this house,
which was at the river landing of La Chorrera, would be the site of
my own brush with the Other. Vanessa and Dave took down their
hammocks and quietly moved down the hill to the new "riverside
house." Their departure was friendly. They would spend more
time in the water now, Vanessa laughed.

It was the sixth day of our residence at La Chorrera. We had
taken the mushrooms three times. We were healthy, relaxed, and
delighted with ourselves for having come so far in such good shape.
There were insects and plants to collect and the lake beneath the
chorro to swim in. My new relationship with Ev seemed promising
and was well launched by then. We were being lulled by the warm,
tropical sun in the depthless blue sky. Such unconsciousness seems
almost the precondition for change. Events were stirring on some
deep and unseen level.

That morning, after the departure of our two friends, Dennis, Ev, and I each lay in our own hammock, lost in thought as the heat and insect shrill built toward midday. My journal entries had ceased, my careful writing now replaced by long flights of reverie, dizzying and beautiful, the faint traces of the deepening contact with the Other, though I did not then recognize it for that. Another warm night came upon us, and we slept long and well. When the morning ground fogs had burned away, this new day was revealed to be as pristine and as flawless as the days always seemed to be in this marvelously beautiful, jungle-isolated settlement. Each day seemed like an alchemical pearl born from the warm and starry night preceding.

We used that day to explore the extraordinary lake edge in the direction of the *chorro*. With its abrupt narrowing of the Igara-Parana and sudden terrible increase of power and speed, the *chorro* is impressive enough. But the lake into which it empties its waters is no mere catch-basin for the rapids; it is the site of some ancient geological catastrophe that shattered the basaltic layer deep beneath the earth's surface, peeling back a great hole and laying thousands of house-sized rock fragments near the cliff, on the northern side of the lake. The mission is perched on the top of this basaltic knoll and is the highest point in the immediate vicinity.

We followed the river and then made our way along the bluffs leading down to the *chorro*, until finally, a couple of hundred feet from the *chorro*, it was so steep that we could go no further. But at that distance the ground was shuddering with the throbbing reverberations of millions of tons of water cascading through the rock walls of the *chorro*. Unusual ground-clinging plants seemed endemic there in that turbulent atmosphere of mist-whipped sand and thundering noise. The feeling of being so small among such sharply shattered stone and so close to the energy of the rapids was eerie and somewhat disturbing. I felt considerably relieved as we climbed hand over hand up the bluffs and made our way back through the meadows and pastures that the mission had cleared over the years with the free labor of its Witoto parishioners.

Once on level ground and still well within the aura of the *chorro*, we rested. There, on the point of land overlooking the entire surrounding area, the mission had long ago established a small cemetery. Within a rudely fenced, hexagonal area, perhaps two dozen graves, many of them obviously of children, were eroding away. The shocking red of the lateritic soil was here laid bare. It was a place touched with sad loneliness even on a perfect sunny day. Our respite finished, we hurried away from the odd combination of emptiness, solitude, and the distant roar of moving water.

Our walk and the exposure to so much sun and stone sent us as if by instinct toward the unbroken green wall of the jungle across the pastures behind the mission. Broad sandy trails led to the system of Witoto, Bora, and Muinane villages that are the "indigenous component" of Comasaria Amazonas, the rest being a few missions, police, and unclassifiables—traders mostly—and ourselves.

We wandered down the trail, checked on our home-to-be, and found it still occupied. Returning through the pastures under a spectacular sunset, we gathered more mushrooms, enough for Ev, Dennis, and I to each take more than we ever had before, perhaps twenty mushrooms apiece.

It was during that walk through the pasture that I noticed for the first time, or at least mentioned for the first time, that everything was very beautiful and that I felt so good that I had a strange sense of being in a movie, or somehow larger than life. Even the sky seemed to have a slight fish-eye lens effect, as though everything were cinematically exaggerated. What was this? Was it a slight distortion of space brought on by accumulating levels of psilocybin? Psilocybin can induce such perceptual distortions. I felt ten feet high; just a touch of the superhuman, or a bit like Alice, whose mushroom eating made her alternately tall and small. It was odd, but very pleasing.

Back at the knoll house we kindled a fire and boiled rice for a light supper. Rain was falling intermittently. After dinner, we smoked and waited a long time, thinking that Vanessa and Dave might visit. Finally it began to drizzle a bit harder, and so we withdrew into the house and each of us ate a large pile of mushrooms. The onset of the *Stropharia* was rapid, and the hallucinations very vivid, but despite the larger dose, after an hour or so the experience did not seem to be particularly different from the earlier trips. We came out of our reveries and conversed softly about our reactions.

Dennis complained that he felt blocked from a deep connection by concern for our father in Colorado, about whether or not he had gotten our last messages to him before we set off down the Rio Putumayo. Dennis seemed melancholy, as if his homesickness had been amplified by the hallucinogen. At least that's what I supposed. I tried to reassure him, and we talked softly in the darkness for several minutes. He said that his trip consisted of many things, a suffusing inner heat and a strange inaudible buzzing that gave him, so he said, insight into glossolalia-like linguistic phenomena, which I had experienced on DMT and had described to him before. I asked him to imitate the sounds that he was hearing, but he seemed to think it was not possible. While we talked, the drizzle lifted somewhat, and we could faintly hear the sound of a transistor radio being carried by someone who had chosen the let-up in the storm to make his or her way up the hill on a small path that passed a few feet from our hut. Our conversation stopped while we listened to the small radio sound as it drew near and then began to fade.

What happened next was nothing less than a turn of events that would propel us into another world. For with the fading of the radio Dennis gave forth, for a few seconds, a very machine-like, loud, dry buzz, during which his body became stiff. After a moment's silence, he broke into a frightened series of excited questions. "What happened?" and, most memorably, "I don't want to become a giant insect!"

Dennis was clearly quite disturbed by what had happened, and both Ev and I attempted to calm him. It was obvious that what to us had seemed only a strange sound had far different effects on the person who made it. I understood his predicament because it was familiar to me from DMT experiences, where a kind of glossolalia of thought, which had seemed the very embodiment of meaning to me, seemed mere gibberish when verbalized and heard by other people.

Dennis said there was a tremendous energy in the sound and that he had felt it like a physical force of some kind. We discussed it for several minutes, then Dennis decided that he wished to attempt the effect again. This he did, but for a much shorter time, again reporting that he experienced a great amount of energy being unleashed. He said he felt as if he might have left the ground if he had directed his voice downward. We wondered if one could make a sound capable of having a synergistic effect on metabolizing drugs, while Dennis suggested that chanting might make some drugs metabolize more rapidly. According to Dennis, from the inside it felt as if he had acquired a shamanic power of some sort.

He began pacing around and wishing aloud that Vanessa would appear out of the gloom with her skepticism, which he felt would crumble when confronted with his testimony of the reality of something strange. I told him that she would only think of it as a peculiar sound in combination with a hallucinogen she was growing uncertain of.

At one point Dennis became so excited that we all left the hut and stood looking out into the pitch darkness. Dennis contemplated going immediately to find Vanessa and Dave to discuss with them what had happened. Finally, a bewildered Ev and I convinced him to return to the hut and leave it all for the morning.

Once back in the hut, we tried again to figure out what was going on. I felt Dennis's amazement was perfectly reasonable; it was my own encounter with the visionary and linguistic powers of DMT that had originally sent me looking into hallucinogens and their place in nature. It is incredible to see all that you believe about reality changed around by these plant metabolites. Excitement is a reasonable reaction to such an edifying, even terrifying, experience.

My brother and I had been close over the years and especially close since our mother's death, but there were experiences that I had had while traveling in Asia that we had not yet shared. To calm us all and to argue for the universality of the kind of experience that Dennis had just had, it occurred to me to tell a story.

CHAPTER SIX

KATHMANDU INTERLUDE

*In which a flashback to Tantric excesses in the
head nests of hippie Asia illuminates strange
mushroom experiences at La Chorrera.*

TWO YEARS BEFORE, during the spring and summer of 1969, I had lived in Nepal and studied the Tibetan language. The wave of interest in Buddhist studies was just beginning, so those of us in Nepal with Tibetan interests were a tightly knit group. My purpose in studying Tibetan was different from that of most Westerners involved with the language in Nepal. They were nearly all interested in some aspect of Mahayana Buddhist thought, while I was interested in a religious tradition that antedated the seventh century and the introduction of Buddhism into Tibet.

This indigenous pre-Buddhist religion of Tibet was a kind of shamanism closely related to the motifs and cosmology of the classical shamanism of Siberia. Tibetan folk shamanism, called Bön, continues to be practiced today in the mountainous area of Nepal that borders Tibet. Its practitioners are generally despised by the Buddhist community, being thought of as heretics and as generally low types.

My interest in Bön and its practitioners, the Bön-po, arose out of a passion for Tibetan painting. It is common in such painting that the most fantastic, extravagant, and ferocious images are drawn from the pre-Buddhist substratum of folk imagery. The terrifying, multi-armed, and multi-headed guardians of the Buddhist teaching, called *Dharmapalas*, with their auras of flame and light, are autochthonous Bön deities whose allegiance to the late-arriving Buddhist religion is maintained only by powerful spells and rituals that bind and secure the loyalty of these forceful demons.

It seemed to me that the shamanic tradition that spawned such outlandish and fantastic images must at some time have had the knowledge of a hallucinogenic plant. Shamanic ecstasy in Siberia was known to be attained through the use of the mushroom *Amanita muscaria*, and Gordon Wasson has made a good case for the use of the same mushroom in Vedic India. Since Tibet is situated roughly between these two areas, it did not seem impossible that, before the coming of Buddhism, hallucinogens were part of the indigenous shamanic tradition.

Amanita muscaria was only one of several candidates that might have served as a hallucinogen in ancient Tibet. *Pegamum harmala* of the *Zygophallaceae* family is another suspect. It, like *Banisteriopsis caapi*, contains the hallucinogenic beta-carboline alkaloid harmaline in considerable quantities and is probably hallucinogenic by itself. Certainly in combination with a DMT-containing plant, of which the flora of India boasts several, it should yield a strong hallucinogen whose composition would not differ chemically from the *ayahuasca* brews of the Amazon.*

My interest in Tibetan painting and hallucinogenic shamanism led me to Nepal. I had learned there were refugee camps in Nepal and near Simla in India whose populations were nearly entirely outcast Bön-po, unwelcome in the camps where Buddhist refugees were housed. I wanted to learn from the Bön-po whatever knowledge they still retained of hallucinogens they might once have known and used. I wished, in my naiveté, to prove my hypothesis

---

* The giant river reed, *Arundo donax* for example, occurs in India and its roots contain DMT. See S. Ghosal, S. K. Dutta, A. K. Sanyal, and Bhattacharya, "Arundo donex L. (Graminae), Phytochemical and Pharmacological Evaluation," in the *Journal of Medical Chemistry*, vol. 12 (1969), p. 480.

about the influence of plant hallucinogens on Tibetan painting and then write a monograph about it.

As soon as I arrived in Asia, the enormity of the task and the effort that this project would require were seen more nearly in their correct proportions. My proposed plan was actually an outline for a life of scholarly research! Naturally, I found that nothing could be done at all until I was familiar with the Tibetan language, so I put aside all my research ideas and resolved to dedicate myself to learning as much Tibetan as I could in the few months that circumstances gave me in Nepal.

I moved out of Kathmandu, away from the pleasures of the hashish dens and the social swirl of the international community of travelers, smugglers, and adventurers that has made the town its own. I moved to Boudanath, a small village of great antiquity a few miles east of Kathmandu and recently flooded with Tibetans from Lhasa—people who spoke the Lhasa dialect that is understood throughout the Himalayas. The people of the village were Buddhist and I made my arrangements to study with the monks there without mentioning my interest in the Bön-po. I sought lodging and came to terms with Den Ba-do, the local miller and a Newari, one of the main ethnic groups of Nepal. He agreed to rent me a room on the third floor of his prosperous adobe house, which fronted the muddy main street of Boudanath. I struck a bargain with a local girl who agreed to bring me fresh water each day, and I settled comfortably in. I whitewashed the adobe walls of my room, commissioned a huge mosquito net in the market in Kathmandu, and arranged my books and small Tibetan writing bench inside. Finally at ease, I set about cultivating my image as a young traveler and scholar.

Tashi Gyaltsen Lama was my teacher. He was a very kind and understanding Gelugpa. In spite of his advanced age, he would arrive every morning promptly at seven for our two-hour lesson. I was like a child; we began with penmanship and the alphabet. Each morning, after the lama departed, I would study for several more hours and then the rest of the day was my own. I explored the King of Nepal's game sanctuary farther east of Boudanath and the Hindu cremation ghatts at nearby Pashupathinath. I also made the acquaintance of a few Westerners who were living in the vicinity.

Among the latter were an English couple my own age. They were self-consciously fascinating. He was thin and blonde, with an aquiline nose and an arch manner typical of the model product of the British public school system. He was haughty and urbane, but eccentric and often hilarious. She was small and unhealthily thin— scrawny is the word I used to describe her to myself. Red-haired, wild-tempered, and cynical, she, like her companion, possessed a razor wit.

They had both been disowned by their families and were traveling hippies, as we all were then. Their relationship was bizarre— they had come together from England, but the relaxation of tension, which arrival in bucolic Nepal had brought, had been too much for their fragile liaison. Now they lived apart, he at one end of Boudanath and she, alone, at the other. They met only for the combined purpose of "paying calls" or of abrading each other's nerves.

For some reason, in that exotic setting they managed to charm me completely. Whether they were alone or together, I was always willing to pause from my studies to pass the time with them. We became fast friends. Naturally we discussed my work, since it involved hallucinogens; they were very interested, being familiar with LSD from their days in the London scene. We also discovered that we had mutual friends in India and that we all loved the novels of Thomas Hardy. It was a very pleasant idyll.

During this time the method I had evolved for probing the shamanic dimension was to smoke DMT at the peak point of an LSD experience. I would do this whenever I took LSD, which was quite occasionally. It would allow me to enter the tryptamine dimension for a slightly extended period of time. As the summer solstice of 1969 approached, I laid plans for another such experiment.

I was going to take LSD the night of the solstice and sit up all night on my roof, smoking hashish and star-gazing. I mentioned my plan to my two English friends, who expressed a desire to join me. This was fine with me, but there was a problem; there was not enough reliable LSD to go around. My own tiny supply had arrived in Kathmandu, prophetically hidden inside a small ceramic mushroom mailed from Aspen.

Almost as a joke, I suggested that they substitute the seed of the Himalayan Datura, *Datura metel*, for the LSD. Daturas are

annual bushes and the source of a number of tropane alkaloids—
scopalamine, hylosciamine, and so on—compounds that produce a
pseudo-hallucinogenic effect. They give an impression of flying or
of confronting vague and fleeting visions, but all in a realm hard to
keep control of and hard to recollect later. The seeds of *Datura metel*
are used in Nepal by *saddhus* (wandering hermits and holy men), so
their use was known in the area. Nevertheless my suggestion was
made facetiously, since the difficulty of controlling Datura is legendary. To my surprise, my friends agreed that this was something
they wanted to do, so we arranged that they would arrive at my
home at six P.M. on the appointed day to make the experiment.

When the evening finally came, I moved my blankets and
pipes up to the roof of the building. From there I could command
a fine view of the surrounding village with its enormous *Stupa*, a
conical temple with staring Buddha eyes painted on its higher portion in gold leaf. The upper golden levels of the Stupa were at that
time encased in scaffolding, where repairs necessitated by a lightning strike suffered some months previously were under way. The
white-domed bulk of the Stupa gave the whitewashed adobe mud
village of Boudanath a saucerian and unearthly quality. Farther
away, rising up many thousands of feet, I could see the great Anna-
purna Range; in the middle distance, the land was a patchwork of
emerald paddies.

Six o'clock came and went, and my friends had not arrived. At
seven they still had not been seen, and so I took my treasured tab
of Orange Sunshine and settled down to wait. Ten minutes later,
they arrived. I could already feel myself going, so I gestured to the
two piles of Datura seeds that I had prepared. They took them
downstairs to my room and ground them with a mortar and pestle
before washing them down with some tea. By the time they had returned to the roof and gotten comfortably settled, I was surging
through mental space.

Hours seemed to pass. When they seated themselves, I was too
distant to be aware of them. She was seated directly across from me,
and he farther back and to one side, in the shadows. He played his
flute. I passed the hash pipe. The moon rose full and high in the
sky. I fell into long hallucinatory reveries that each lasted many
minutes but felt like whole lifetimes. When I had emerged from

a particularly long spell of visions, I found that my friend had stopped playing and had gone away, leaving me with his lady.

I had promised them both that I would let them try some DMT during the evening. My glass pipe and tiny stash of waxy orange DMT were before me. Slowly, and with the fluid movements of a dream, I filled the pipe and gave it to her. The stars, hard and glittering, stared down from a mighty distance on all of this. She held the pipe and took two deep inhalations, sufficient for a person so frail, then the pipe was returned to me, and I followed her into it with four huge inhalations, the fourth of which I held onto until I had broken through. For me it was an enormous amount of DMT, and I immediately had a sense of entering a high vacuum. I heard a high-pitched whine and the sound of cellophane ripping as I was transformed into the ultra-high-frequency orgasmic goblin that is a human being in DMT ecstasy. I was surrounded by the chattering of elf machines and the more-than-Arabian vaulted spaces that would shame a Bibiena. Manifestations of a power both alien and bizarrely beautiful raged around me.

At the point where I would normally have expected the visions to fade, the pretreatment with LSD synergized my state to a higher level. The cavorting hoards of DMT elf machines faded to a mere howling as the elfin mob moved on. I suddenly found myself flying hundreds of miles above the earth and in the company of silvery disks. I could not tell how many. I was fixated on the spectacle of the earth below and realized that I was moving south, apparently in polar orbit, over Siberia. Ahead of me I could see the Great Plain of Shang and the mass of the Himalayas rising up in front of the red-yellow waste of India. The sun would rise in about two hours. In a series of telescoping leaps, I went from orbit to a point where I could specifically pick out the circular depression that is the Kathmandu Valley. Then, in the next leap, the valley filled my field of vision. I seemed to be approaching it at great speed. I could see the Hindu temple and the houses of Kathmandu, the Temple of Svayambhu-nath to the west of the city and the Stupa at Boudanath, gleaming white and a few miles to the east. Then Boudanath was a mandala of houses and circular streets filling my vision. Among the several hundred roof tops I found my own. In the next moment I slammed into

my body and was refocused on the roof top and the woman in front
of me.

Incongruously, she had come to the event wearing a silver
satin, full-length evening dress—an heirloom—the sort of thing
one could find in an antique clothing store in Notting Hill Gate. I
fell forward and thought that my hand was covered by some cool,
white liquid. It was the fabric of the dress. Until that moment neither of us had considered the other a potential lover. Our relationship had functioned on quite a different level. But suddenly all the
normal sets of relations were obviated. We reached out toward each
other, and I had the distinct impression of passing through her, of
physically reaching beyond her. She pulled her dress over her head
in a single gesture. I did the same with my shirt, which ripped to
pieces in my hands as I took it off over my head. I heard buttons fly,
and somewhere my glasses landed and shattered.

Then we made love. Or rather we had an experience that
vaguely related to making love but was a thing unto itself. We were
both howling and singing in the glossolalia of DMT, rolling over the
ground with everything awash in crawling, geometric hallucinations.
She was transformed; words exist to describe what she became—
pure anima, Kali, Leucothea, something erotic but not human,
something addressed to the species and not to the individual, glittering with the possibility of cannibalism, madness, space, and extinction. She seemed on the edge of devouring me.

Reality was shattered. This kind of fucking occurs at the very
limit of what is possible. Everything had been transformed into or-
gasm and visible, chattering oceans of elf language. Then I saw that
where our bodies were glued together there was flowing, out of her,
over me, over the floor of the roof, flowing everywhere, some sort of
obsidian liquid, something dark and glittering, with color and lights
within it. After the DMT flash, after the seizures of orgasms, after all
that, this new thing shocked me to the core. What was this fluid and
what was going on? I looked at it. I looked right into it, and it was the
surface of my own mind reflected in front of me. Was it translinguistic matter, the living opalescent excrescence of the alchemical
abyss of hyperspace, something generated by the sex act performed
under such crazy conditions? I looked into it again and now saw in

it the lama who taught me Tibetan, who would have been asleep a mile away. In the fluid I saw him, in the company of a monk I had never seen; they were looking into a mirrored plate. Then I realized that they were watching me! I could not understand it. I looked away from the fluid and away from my companion, so intense was her aura of strangeness.

Then I realized that we had been singing and yodeling and uttering wild orgasmic howls for what must have been several minutes on my roof! It meant everyone in Boudanath would have been awakened and was about to open their doors and windows and demand to know what was going on. And what *was* going on? My grandfather's favorite expostulation seemed appropriate: "Great God! said the woodcock when the hawk struck him." This grotesquely inappropriate recollection brought uncontrollable laughter.

Then the thought of discovery sobered me enough to realize that we must get away from this exposed place. Both of us were completely naked, and the scene around us was one of total, unexplainable chaos. She was lying down, unable to rise, so I picked her up and made my way down the narrow staircase, past the grain storage bins and into my room. The whole time I remember saying over and over to her and to myself: "I am a human being. I am a human being." I had to reassure myself, for I was not at that moment sure.

We waited in my room many minutes. Slowly we realized that by some miracle no less strange than everything else that had occurred, no one was awake demanding to know what was going on. No one seemed even to have heard! To calm us, I made tea and, as I did this, I was able to assess my companion's state of mind. She seemed quite delirious, quite unable to discuss with me what had happened only a few moments before on the roof. It is an effect typical of Datura that whatever one experiences is very difficult, indeed usually impossible, to recollect later. It seemed that while what had transpired had involved the most intimate of acts between two people, I was nevertheless the only witness who could remember anything at all of what had happened.

Pondering all of this, I crept back to the roof and collected my glasses. Incredibly, they were unbroken, although I had distinctly heard them shatter. Obsidian liquids, the ectoplasmic excrescences of tantric hanky-panky, were nowhere to be seen. With my glasses and our clothes, I returned to my room where my companion was sleeping. I smoked a little hashish and then climbed into the mosquito net and lay down beside her. In spite of all the excitement and the stimulation of my system, I immediately went to sleep.

I have no idea how long I slept. When I awoke it was with a start and from a deep slumber. It was still dark. And there was no sign of my friend. I felt a stab of alarm; if she was delirious then it would be dangerous for her to be wandering alone around the village at night. I jumped up and threw on my *jalaba* and began to search. She was not on the roof, nor near the grain storage bins.

I found her on the ground floor of my building. She was sitting on the earthen floor staring at her reflection in the gas tank of a motorcycle, which belonged to the miller's son-in-law. Still disoriented in the way that is typical of Datura, she was hallucinating persons not present and mistaking one person for another. "Are you my tailor?" she asked me several times as I led her back to my room. "Are you my tailor?"

When we were once again upstairs in my quarters, I took off my *jalaba*, and we both discovered that I was wearing what she delicately described as her "knickers." They were too small on me and neither of us knew how they had come to be there. This little crossdressing episode capped an amazing evening, and I roared with laughter. I returned her knickers and we went to bed, puzzled, reassured, exhausted, and amused.

As this experience passed behind us, the girl and I became even closer friends. We never made love again; it was not really the relationship that suited us. She remembered nothing of the events on the roof. About a week after all this was over, I told her my impression of what had happened. She was amazed but accepting. I did not know what had happened. I christened the obsidian fluid we had generated "luv," something more than love, something less than love, perhaps not love at all, but some kind of unplumbed potential human experience very little is known about.

This is the story I told Dennis and Ev that night at La Chorrera as our hammocks swung in the lamplight and the intermittent rain beat down on the thatched roof of the knoll house. It was this incident that had kindled my interest in the violet fluids that *ayahuasca* shamans are said to generate on the surface of their skins and to use to divine and cure. Whenever I tell this story, it is the phenomenon of the liquid that I stress. That was what I accentuated to reassure Dennis that foggy night. I did not tell the absurd part about waking up wearing someone else's drawers. It was damned embarrassing and contributed nothing to the story. At that time I had never told anyone that part of the incident; it was a personal memory. I mention this because that absurd incident was later to become the focus of an instance of telepathy that was the most convincing I have ever witnessed.

CHAPTER SEVEN

A VIOLET PSYCHOFLUID

*In which Dennis begins to outline his approach
to the Alchemical Opus and a psychofluid that
may or may not be translinguistic matter is
debated.*

MY STORY FINISHED, we all went to sleep for a
few fitful hours. In the dim light of dawn, Ev and I made our way to
a cluster of huts about three-quarters of a mile away on the shore of
the Igara-Parana above the *chorro*. We knew that Witoto, coming
down the river to the mission to deliver their children to school,
would be staying in those normally empty houses. Our hope was to
buy some eggs, papayas, or squash to supplement our diet of brown
rice, yucca, and plantains.

We found only a small group of people whose only item for sale
was a grapefruit-sized, green, heart-shaped fruit filled with slimy,
vaguely sweet seeds awash in a light, purple syrup. At the time this
fruit was unknown to science; a few years later Schultes would describe it and name it *Macoubea witotorum*. I have yet to encounter
this fruit again. It was very inexpensive and since we had come
with the expectation of buying *something* we spent fifteen pesos and
got nearly fifty pounds of this curious food. Even though I had
been up most of the night plying the hallucinogenic oceans of

mind, I felt fit and full of vitality. I hoisted a bulging *costal*—our entire buy—and set off back toward the mission at a brisk pace.

I enjoyed this chore. The *costal* seemed light, almost a pleasure to carry along. Without pause, even to rest for a moment, Ev and I returned to the mission and to Vanessa and Dave's riverside residence for our breakfast in common. When we had left our hut in search of food, Dennis had been deeply asleep, but he was up now and had apparently gone immediately to awaken Vanessa and describe to her his experiences of a few hours previous. The interior buzzing sound, the feeling of being possessed—it was all being excitedly told as we arrived at the house and I set down my load. Throughout the making of breakfast the events of the last evening were discussed and dissected. Vanessa and Dave were unmoved by Dennis's excited assertion that some extremely peculiar energy field had been tapped into and verified. At the end of breakfast I suggested to Dennis that, rather than arguing with people about the nature of the experience, he should go off by himself and write down all that he thought about the strange sound that he had made. He accepted this advice and made his way back up the hill to the knoll house to be alone and to write:

February 28, 1971

I approach these pages with a peculiar sense of urgency as a man might who had confronted an unexplainable phenomenon as some impossible creation of dreams or unaccountable natural principle. The task facing such a man would be a very subtle one; that is, to describe the phenomenon as accurately as possible. My task is compounded by the fact that the phenomenon I must try to describe has itself to do with the very tools of description; i.e., language. This rather peculiar statement will begin to make more sense as we explore the concept more fully.

Before going further, something tells me it is necessary to consider who I am. Twenty-four hours ago I thought I knew—now this has become the most perplexing question I have ever been confronted with. The questions leading from it will provide the answers that will allow us to understand and use the phenomenon which is so difficult to describe. These may be the last characters of a crude language that I will ever apply to the description of any-thing; since the phenomenon begins at the edge of language, where the concept-forming faculty gropes but finds no words, I must be careful to avoid not distinguishing between mere language-symbol-metaphor and the reality I am attempting to apply it to.

When I read this prologue later, it seemed to me both grandiose and alarming, but Dennis had an aura of calm certitude that seemed to command respect. I felt that the Logos was struggling with the vocabulary of its newest vessel. He seemed to be making more and more sense, to be on to something. I read on:

Since any phenomenon is, to a point, describable in empirical terms, so too with this one. It has to do with controlling one's body chemistry in such a way as to produce very specific vocal and au-dial phenomena: the state becomes possible when highly bio-dynamic vegetable alkaloids, specifically tryptamines and MAO-inhibitors,* are introduced into the body under very carefully regulated para-meters. This phenomenon is apparently possible in the presence of tryptamines alone, though MAO inhibition definitely helps to trig-ger it by facilitating tryptamine absorption. The phenomenon has now been triggered by two people within our immediate group: Terence has been experimenting with vocal phenomena under the influence of DMT for some years now.†

Until last night, when I triggered and experienced this sound wave for a few brief seconds under the influence of nine-teen Stropharia *mushrooms, Terence was the only person I knew who claimed ability to perform this sound. But last night, after*

---

* MAO-inhibitors are chemical compounds whose activity in the body slows down or interferes with Mono Amine Oxidase, an enzyme system that oxidizes many compounds in foods and drugs into harmless byproducts. In the presence of MAO-inhibitors, compounds that would normally be metabolized into inac-tive by-products instead have the duration of their physiological and psycho-logical activity extended.

†My experiments had consisted of having observed that the spontaneous glos-solalia that DMT caused in myself sometimes triggered a kind of seizure of synesthesia in which syntactical structures, spoken language, actually became visible. Some effect such as this may have been behind my rooftop experience in Nepal. Unusual linguistic and vocal displays seem to typify DMT intoxi-cation.

ingesting the mushrooms, we lay waiting in our hammocks; the heavy poisoned feeling that commonly passes briefly over the limbs at the beginning of the Stropharia visions had by this time passed completely. It had given way, in me at least, to a warm suffusion of contentment and good feeling that actually seemed to burn away somewhere inside of me. Such feelings I have had before, both on mushrooms and just after DMT flashes. Then we began to discuss people far away and how we might attempt to contact them fourth-dimensionally; since apparently magical connection at a distance is a concern of shamanism this was not such a strange rap for us. But it was definitely at some point in time near to that conversation that I first heard the sound, immeasurably distant and faint, in the region between the ears, not outside, but definitely, incredibly there, perfectly distinct on the absolute edge of audible perception. A sound almost like a signal or very, very faint transmissions of radio buzzing from somewhere, something like tingling chimes at first, but gradually becoming amplified into a snapping, popping, gurgling, cracking electrical sound. I tried to imitate these noises with my vocal chords, just experimenting with a kind of humming, buzzing vocal sound made deep in the throat. Suddenly, it was as if the sound and my voice locked onto each other and the sound was my voice—but coming out of me in such a way that no human voice could possibly distort itself the way mine was doing. The sound was suddenly much intensified in energy and was like the sound of a giant insect.

While Dennis wrote, the rest of us swam indolently in the river and washed our laundry under a clear, infinitely blue, and empty Amazonian sky. The background drone of the cicadas would occasionally rise in a coherent wave and sweep over the warm and shining surface of the gently drifting Igara-Parana, falling like electricity across the land in the heat of the equatorial day.

Late that afternoon, Dennis came back down to the edge of the river looking for me. He found me washing out my tennis shoes on a large, flat rock that the shifting height of the river had conveniently exposed just a foot or so above the water line. Doubtless whenever it was so exposed it served as the favorite local laundry spot. It was a magic spot, but its magic at that moment was still fourteen days into the future. There we sat and talked. It had been about sixteen hours since the previous evening's episode with the strange sound. Dennis said that the writing exercise had been very useful.

"Great! And so what have you come up with?"

"I'm not sure. I'm very excited, but whatever it is that's the cause of my excitement is also developing ideas in my mind nearly faster than I can write them down."

"Ideas? What sort of ideas?"

"Funny ideas. Ideas about how we can use this effect, or this stuff, or whatever it is. My intuition is that it is related to the psychofluids that Michael Harner reported in the July 1969 issue of *Natural History* and to what happened to you in Boudanath. Remember how Harner implied that *ayahuasqueros* vomited a magical substance that was the basis of their ability to divine? This is like that, some sort of translinguistic stuff made with the voice."

We talked at length there by the river's edge, ranging over the options and the possibilities. He was insistent in linking my experience in Nepal with a very strange phenomenon that occurred in Jivaro shamanism in Ecuador. The people take *ayahuasca* after which they, and anyone else who has taken *ayahuasca*, are able to see a substance that is described as violet or deep blue and that bubbles like a liquid. When you vomit from taking *ayahuasca*, this violet fluid comes out of your body; it also forms on the surface of the skin, like sweat. The Jivaro do much of their magic with this peculiar stuff. These matters are extremely secret. Informants insist that the shamans spread the stuff out on the ground in front of them, and that one can look at this material and see other times and other places. According to their reports, the nature of this fluid is completely outside of ordinary experience: it is made out of space/time or mind, or it is pure hallucination objectively expressed but always keeping itself within the confines of a liquid.

Harner's work among the Jivaro did not stand alone. Since the beginnings of ethnographic reporting out of the Amazon there have been rumors and unconfirmed reports of magical excrement and magically empowered psychophysical objects generated out of the human body using hallucinogens and song. I recalled the alchemical observation that the secret is hidden in feces.

"Matter that is hyperdimensional and therefore translinguistic? Is that what you mean?" I asked Dennis.

"Yes. Whatever that means, but something like that, I suppose. Gad! Why not? I mean it's pretty nuts, but it's also the symbol system we brought with us running into the shamanic magic that we came here looking for. 'This is what you shipped for, man, to chase the White Whale over all sides of ocean and both sides of earth till he spout black blood and roll fin out.' Isn't that your rap?"

The resort to Melvillian rhetoric was unexpected and not like him. Where did he get this stuff?

"Yes, I suppose."

"But here is the thing; if there is something weird going on, then we should observe it and see what it is and try to reduce it to some coherent framework. Granted we don't know what it is that we are dealing with, but on the other hand, we know that we came here to investigate shamanic magic generally, so now we have to go to work on this effect, or whatever it is, and just hope that we know what we are doing and have enough data to crack it. We are too isolated to do anything else, and to ignore it might be to squander a golden opportunity."

"Yes, you're right," I said. "So here we are, very much on the brink of deep water. We are having something like beginner's luck, you know, finding the 'Other' so accessible. The mushroom is doing this, or the mushroom and the *ayahuasca* smoking—it is hard to be sure. So many variables. There is a lot of synchronistic activity as well."

"Right. I feel on the brink of something tremendous. We must just observe our active fantasy closely and try to ride herd on what is developing. The good old Jungian method, that's all."

"Yes," I said, "ideally all of this could be distilled down to the point where some sort of test of the validity of the effect could somehow be set up."

I recalled that there is an instance in *The Teachings of Don Juan* where the Peyote entity, Mescalito, holds up his hand, and in its palm Carlos Castaneda sees a past incident in his life.

If this phenomenon has any empirical validity, perhaps what happens is that a very thin film of this projection-sensitive transdimensional goo is present. And when you look at it, it is like perfect feedback. It is a mirror—not of your physical reflection but of who you are. All this lays in the realm of speculation, of course. Does this stuff exist? Or is it just hallucination? Who can believe in a thing like that?

Dennis felt strongly that it was connected with sound. One could either stabilize the stuff or cause it to appear by doing something with one's voice. It was a strange, slippery idea because one could extrapolate it infinitely, since whatever it was, it was made of the very stuff of imagination itself. If one shaped this stuff in three dimensions, it could be anything, yet this violet ectoplasmic mental liquid must only exist in the fourth dimension. It seemed possible to suppose that one might pierce the other dimension and have this fluid come boiling out. Flubber for eggheads. Mental silly putty. He talked a lot about it. I was ecstatic; I thought his ideas were wonderful. I felt it was yet another idea from the tryptamine ocean that had floated up into our nets. The question was: What could we do with it?

Recalling it now, having learned so much in the intervening twenty years, it is hard to be sure just what we did believe at La Chorrera, just what level of sophistication we did achieve. Our mood was one of lightness and delight, the several mushroom experiences in that remote and beautiful place leading us to a gently swelling euphoria. It was a very happy time. We were excited with the prospect of actually grappling under near perfect conditions with "the Secret," as we called it then, meaning the spectrum of effects encountered in tryptamine-induced ecstasy. These had become the compass and the vehicle of our quest: the rose window topologies of the galacterian beehives of the di-methyltryptamine flash, that nexus of cheap talk and formal mathematics where wishes became horses and everybody got to ride. We were not unused to the idea of the Other, but we had only glimpsed it in brief flashes and in its manifestation as the *lux natura*, the spiritual radiance behind organic nature. We were in that moment the fans of the goddess, not yet her lovers.

Everyone in our small expedition felt, I think, the sense of something opening around us, of the suspension of time, of turning and turning in a widening green world that was strangely and almost erotically alive, surrounding us for thousands of miles. The jungle as mind, the world hanging in space as mind—images of order and sentient organization came crowding in on all sides. How small we were, knowing little, yet fiercely proud of what we knew, and feeling ourselves somehow the representatives of humanity meeting something strange and Other, something at the edge of human experience since the very beginning. A proud and eerie grandeur seemed mixed with our enterprise as those first days at La Chorrera went by.

The next day, the first of March, passed uneventfully. Dennis worked on his journal. I collected insects, and Vanessa photographed around the mission. At evening we were all gathered again at the edge of the knoll where our small lodging stood. In silent communion with each other and the river, Ev and I sat looking out over the lake.

It was Ev who noticed it first. The lake beneath the *chorro* was flecked with foam generated by the rush of water through the narrow channel. The foam floating on the brown water served to mark the currents of the river as it widened into the lake and continued on the other side. It was at this that Ev exclaimed. After several minutes of watching the water, a change had suddenly stolen over the moving, marbled surface at the far side of the river. The water there appeared to have stopped. Just that, just simply to have stopped moving. The surface appeared frozen, yet the near half of the river was seen to continue as before.

Dennis and Vanessa were called out of the hut, and they agreed that the effect was remarkable. I wandered away as they began to speculate on the causes—the time of day, the light conditions, optical illusions, and all the rest. I seemed to have no heart for these arguments; each time they broke out, I found myself with some deep, inner assurance that the situation was moving forward just as it should and that everyone was playing a part and doing it very well.

This mood of calm and insightful resignation was something new to me, perhaps enhanced by the taking of the mushrooms, but it had developed during the month in Colombia preceding our trek into the jungle. A few weeks earlier, I would have participated in these sorts of discussions; now I let them take their own course. As I walked, I looked for a place to sit down—Dennis had offered me his journal entry for that day to read:

March 1, 1971

Last night I again triggered the phenomenon after having eaten one mushroom and smoking grass. It was almost identical to the first experience—a lifting, pulsing wave of vocal buzzing growing loud very quickly and picking up shock energy as it did so. Though I could have prolonged the sound beyond a brief burst, I did not because of the energy. I am certain that soon it will become possible to trigger the sound completely without tryptamines or other drugs. It is becoming easier to plug-in on each time, and I feel now that it is accessible at any time. It is clearly a learned activity that tryptamines can initiate and trigger, but it can happen without tryptamines once it is understood and mastered. We have thus far been able to establish the existence of peculiar vocal phenomena in two individuals subject to similar experimental controls. We must now attempt to understand what it is that the phenomenon could be. We must perform experiments with the sound and from our results develop theories to understand the processes at work. Terence has experimented with these sounds far more than anyone else (and I am the only other that I know of), and he has discovered some interesting things.

Things such as that the normally invisible syntactical web that holds both language and the world together can condense or change its ontological status and become visible. Indeed there seems to be a parallel mental dimension in which everything is made of the stuff of visible language, a kind of universe next door inhabited by elves that sing themselves into existence and invite those who encounter them to do the same.

The DMT-initiated state, which allows prolonged bursts of this vocal energy, he describes as being one of seeing the levels of sound become more dense as they finally materialize into small, gnome-like, machine-like creatures made of material like obsidian froth, which pours from the body, mouth, and sex organs as long as the sound continues. It is effervescent, phosphorescent, and indescribable. Here is where the linguistic metaphors become useless, for what the material actually is is supra-linguistic matter; it is a language, but not made of words—a language which becomes and which is the things it describes. It is a more perfect archetypal Logos. We are convinced that through experimentation with these vocal phenomena, with and without the aid of drugs, it will be possible to understand and use translinguistic matter to accomplish any reality, for to say anything in this voice is to cause that thing to happen!

Non-chemists ourselves at that point, we had been able to turn the condensation of spirit into the idea of translinguistic matter. Word, object, and cognition had become fused in the best tradition of the higher Tantric yogas. My brother was in the grip of a revelation of the alchemical mystery in the most traditional sense.

Such a rash statement would be outlandish if it were not for our long and tedious speculations on the matter. Our studies in the chemistry of mind, the metabolism of tryptamine, the nature of thought, of consciousness, history, magic, shamanism, quantum and relativistic physics, metamorphosis in insects, alchemical processes, etc., together with the intuitive understanding of acausal and synchronistic events that we are deriving from the Stropharia, *allows us to venture a not entirely wild guess as to what this sound which takes form may be. Hallucinogens, by effecting the neural matrix, can produce changes in consciousness in the temporal dimension. Clearly, consciousness can work changes in three dimensions as well. On tryptamines it is possible, under special conditions, to hear and vocalize a sound that turns through a higher dimensional manifold and condenses as translinguistic matter, i.e., matter reduplicated upon itself through time, much as a hologram is reduplicated through space. The substance whose appearance the sounds initiate is tryptamine metabolized by mind through a higher spatial dimension. It is a hyperdimensional molecule carrying its trip on the outside of itself in "this" world. The hyperdimensional nature of this material is such that it is all material, concepts, events, words, people, and ideas homogenized into one thing via the higher dimensional alchemy of mind.*

This is the idea of the mysterious magical phlegm, the legend of which survives on the less-traveled side tributaries of the Amazon. There, persistent rumors circulate of a magical material, generated out of one's body by master shamans, that allows one to cure, work magic, and obtain information unavailable by any normal means. Like the magic mirrors familiar from fairy tales, the magical fluids of rainforest rumor are windows on distant times and places. Our task was to create a credible model of how such a phenomenon could operate without leaving the known or suspected laws of physics and chemistry far behind. It was a real challenge. Dennis speculated in his journal:

Many questions occur concerning the phenomenology of this temporal hologram as fluid matrix. We speculate it is hyperdimensionally metabolized tryptamine—an alchemical phenomenon which is a correct union of tryptamine (a compound nearly ubiquitous in organic nature), with vocally produced sound mediated by mind. It is the mind that directs this process, and that direction consists of a harmonic atunement to an interiorized audiolinguistic phenomenon which may be an electron-spin resonance "tone" of the psilocybin molecule. When this tone is locked in on— a process which consists of vocally imitating the interior tone to perfection, the hyperdimensional tryptamine is produced. Is this substance mental as an idea is mental? Is it as real as an ordinary liquid, like water? Harner insisted that Jivaro shamans under the influence of MAO-inhibiting tryptamine plus Banisteriopsis caapi *(ayahuasca) infusions produce a fluorescent liquid by means of which they accomplish all of their magic. Though invisible to ordinary perception, this fluid is said to be visible to anyone who has ingested the brew. Ayahuasca is frequently associated with violet auras and deep blue hallucinations. This may indicate a thermal plasma, perhaps only visible in the UV spectrum. If this phenomenon is found to fall into the category "mental," indicated above, functioning as described, but with the limitation of not being tangential to ordinary space/time, it will*

still represent perfected understanding of the hyperdimension Jung
named the collective unconscious.

Looking back from the vantage point of over twenty years, these notes seem both arcane and naive. The idea of a possible unitary metamorphosis of the mental and physical worlds is counterintuitive and conceptually difficult, yet the belief that something real lies behind this phenomenon, or the idea of it, was a central factor in leading us to explore the shamanism of the Amazon Basin. At the time when I first read these notes, I doubted what I read. It seemed to go against the grain of common sense; I could not really understand them. Today, after years of education pushed toward understanding the events at La Chorrera, these ideas seem as magically near and yet as far away as they did then. We had a theory and we had an experience, and we soon decided to try to link them through an experiment whose results would have been preposterous unless there were some seed of operational truth in the bizarre ideas born in that period.

Later that same evening, Ev, Dennis, and I smoked a joint of Santa Marta Gold before turning in. It was a calm, perfectly clear night when we sat down and began this ritual. Ev commented on the clarity of the night, and we all stared for a moment out into the galaxy. The night was awash with millions of stars. We smoked in awed silence. Perhaps five minutes went by, each of the three of us lost in our own ideas. The reverie ended with Dennis's exclamation.

"Look how quickly the air conditions have changed. Now there is a ground fog just springing up."

It was true. For about seventy feet in all directions there was a thick fog, only a few feet deep, hugging the ground. Even as we watched, the condition thickened and spread outward, becoming finally a general fog over the whole area. We had come from depthless, clear night sky to dense fog in a few minutes. I was frankly amazed. Dennis was the first to offer an explanation, with a certainty that seemed as puzzling as the thing itself:

"It's some kind of barometric instability that our burning joint was able to push over some critical threshold."

"You must be putting me on!" I said. "You're saying that the heat from our joint started water condensing into visible fog right near us and that that was like a chain-reaction to all of the super-saturated air nearby? You can't be serious!"

"No, no. That's it! And what's more, this is happening for a reason, or rather something, perhaps the mushroom, is using it as an example. It is a way of showing us that small instabilities in a system can trigger large general fluctuations."

"Hoo-boy."

This rap of Dennis's unsettled me. I could not imagine that his explanation was correct or exactly why he thought it made sense.* It passed through my mind for the first time that he might be spacing out mentally. I used no psychoanalytical jargon in thinking about it, but I noted a reaction in myself that included the idea that he might be unfolding into a mythopoetic reality, or as I thought of it then, "going bananas."

By this time the fog was impenetrable, and we all retired for the night, but not before Ev related that in the silence before the appearance of the fog she had a hallucination. With her eyes closed, she saw a strange, elf-like creature rolling a complicated polyhedron along the ground. Each facet of this polyhedron seemed, she said, like a window onto another place in time or another world.

"It's the stone!" I breathed. I could almost see her vision of the *lapis philosophorum*—the glittering goal of centuries of alchemical and Hermetic speculation glimpsed in the Amazonian night, now seeming a great multi-dimensional jewel, the philosopher's stone, in the keeping of a telluric gnome. The power of the image was deep and touching. I seemed to feel the spiritual dreams of the old alchemists, the puffers great and small, who had sought the *lapis* in the cloudy swirling of their alembics. I could feel the golden chain of adepts reaching back into the distant Hellenistic past, the Hermetic Opus, a project vaster than empires and centuries; nothing less than the redemption of fallen humanity through the respiritualization of matter. I had never seen or imagined the mystery of the stone thus, but in listening to Ev's description of what she had seen, an image formed in my mind that to this day remains with

---

* Of course, none of us could have known that much of the mathematical research of the decades ahead would explore just such ideas under the name of chaos theory and dynamics.

me. It is the image of the philosopher's stone as hyperdimensional jewel-become-UFO—the human soul as starship. It is the universal panacea at the end of time, all history being the shock wave of this final actualization of the potential in the human psyche. These thoughts, these reveries, seemed to me then like the stirring of something vast, something dimly sensed that was stretched out over millions of years, something about the destiny of humankind and the return of the soul to its awesome and hidden source. What *was* happening to us?

The sense of the peculiar was nearly palpable. Dark oceans of time and space seemed to swell and flow beneath our feet. The image of the earth hanging in space was everywhere emotionally superimposed on the situation around us. And what was that situation really? I lay in my hammock, thrilled and uneasy at the edge of sleep, then I fell into deep sleep and deep dreams from which nothing remained in the morning save the sense of yawning interstellar space.

CHAPTER EIGHT

THE OPUS CLARIFIED

In which Dennis reveals his strategy for
commencing the Great Work.

THE MORNING OF MARCH 2, 1971, dawned crys-
talline and hot at La Chorrera. It was the much anticipated day
when Ev, Dennis, and I would at last be able to take possession of
the house in the forest, which was finally being vacated. This particular morning there was more than the usual amount of excitement associated with our frequent moves. For three days, ever
since the glossolalia episode of the twenty-seventh, Dennis had
been saying that the energy of the phenomenon was so great that
we should not go any further unless we had the greater isolation
that the forest house provided.

Our move began shortly after dawn in order to avoid the heat of
the day. The trek to move ourselves and our equipment to the new
home involved going through pastures we had not seen since our
mushroom experience three days before. The *Stropharia* seemed to
be everywhere. There seemed not to be a cow-pie without its
golden flush of perfect mushrooms. I promised myself that as soon
as we had squared away the new hut and otherwise settled in, that
we should again take the mushroom.

However, in all of our recent surge of speculation, our original
ethnobotanical intentions, the search for the elusive *Oo-koo-hé*, had

not been forgotten. Far from it. Our immediate intent was to use *ayahuasca* as a MAO-inhibitor and a problem-solving drug, and to brew and take the *Banisteriopsis caapi* that Ev and I had gotten from Basilio a few days before.

As it happened, Ev and I spent the rest of the day following the move clearing the ground around the hut and pulling large tree roots out of the sandy soil. We stacked them in the sun to dry out so they could serve as fuel for the fire we needed to brew up our *ayahuasca*. We seemed to glory in physical exertion. Energy and light seemed to fill everything. Taking his notebook, Dennis, who had been rather withdrawn and snappish since his experience with inner sound and its mixed reception by us, wandered down the forest trail in the direction of the Witoto village thirteen kilometers away.

In the middle of the afternoon he returned, very excited. He had completed writing out the preliminary notes for what became "the experiment at La Chorrera." It is the only written record of his ideas that was actually made at the time, and as such, it is the only piece of written, primary evidence that we have about how we viewed what we were doing as we were doing it.

These notes do not of course represent the final form of our theorizing about these matters and are not at all to be taken at face value. Refinement of these ideas has been constant since their creation.* But how complete the vision was and how finely worked its detail! The theory that is represented in my brother's notes remains the operational basis for understanding the effect that was triggered on March fifth at the conclusion of the experiment. His notes were our working blueprint, and they were very effective. They are not, however, for the reader of faint heart, since they read like the words of an alchemical text. Alchemy is a test of the limits of language as much as a test of the limits of matter. Alchemical machinery runs smoothest in the imagination. Magicians will wish to linger over these alchemical mutterings, which I will help decipher in the next

---

* The scientific basis of our work is elaborately described in *The Invisible Landscape*. That work represented our considered, composite opinion as of 1975. Since then these ideas have been much revised as the myths and fallacies spun into the fabric of their first conception have been separated out.

chapter. The rest of my readers might wish to skim over them and
hurry on with what is, even without the adumbrations of arcane
theory, a ripping good story:

March 2, 1971

*Further experiments with the psycho-audible warp phenomenon
yesterday raise some interesting new questions and enhance our
ongoing understanding. I chose the term "audible warp" because
my experience thus far, coupled with what I have been told, leads
me to believe that this all has to do with vocally generating a specific kind of energy field which can rupture three dimensional
space. I do not understand if the field is electromagnetic, but it
seems to bend space in such a way as to turn it upon itself through
a higher dimension. Here is how it is done:*

*One must take enough psilocybin to allow the sound to be au-
dible. This sound we understand to be the Electron Spin Resonance (ESR) of the psilocybin alkaloids within the mushroom.
The presence of rapidly metabolizing high-energy tryptamines
within the* ayahuasca *acts as an antenna that sensitizes the
neural matrix to the spin resonance energy of the* Stropharia
*psilocybin. It is this principle that allows the signal to be made
audible. It must then be amplified via the tryptamine admixture
antenna to what is felt to be its fullest amplitude. Then, via vocal
sound, this energy is placed into the harmine complex within the
body and within the mushroom which has been, in some small
part, cooled to absolute zero—the temperature at which molecular vibration ceases, through absorption of the psilocybin ESR
pulses.*

*Once this ESR wave has been detected, it will be possible to
amplify it within the neural circuits by channeling it through the
harmine complex: i.e., by imitating the psilocybin ESR with the
voice, causing the amplified sound to strike a harmonic tone with
the harmine metabolizing in the brain and thereby exciting the
harmine ESR. Since harmine complexes are merely further down
the same bio-synthetic pathway that converts tryptophane into
psilocybin, it is possible to consider the ESR tone of psilocybin as
a harmonic overtone of harmine and vice versa.*

Using harmonic overtones, it is possible to sound a tone which will cancel one or more of its octaves reflected in the harmonic scales above and below it. This is easily demonstrated on a cello: Suppose a tone, say the open string A, is sounded. The sound is a wave-vibration of air molecules caused by the string, which then acts as a resonator. The tone is heard mostly loudly in the key in which it was sounded, but it also sounds every other key of "A" in the octaves above and below it. It is possible to cancel out the original tone by touching the string very lightly at certain harmonic points. When this is done, the overtones in the higher and lower registers become audible. If one understands the theory of harmonic resonators well enough, one can determine which overtones will be resonated if certain points on the string are touched.

When this understanding is applied to molecular ESR resonation, it remains essentially the same in principle. When the ESR tone of the psilocybin is heard via tryptamine antenna, it will strike a harmonic tone in the harmine complexes being metabolized within the system, causing its ESR to begin to resonate at a higher level. According to the principles of tonal physics, this will automatically cancel out the original tone, i.e., the psilocybin ESR, and cause the molecule to cease to vibrate; however, the ESR tone that sustains the molecular coherency is carried for a microsecond on the overtonal ESR of the harmine complex. This leaves the momentarily electrically canceled and superconductive psilocybin suspended in a low energy electromagnetic field generated by the harmine ESR. In so doing, it will regain its original, but now superconductivity amplified, ESR signal, which will permanently lock it into a superconductive state.

As this phenomenon proceeds, it will automatically trigger the inverse of the initial process. The psilocybin, superconductively charged by mind, will harmonically cancel the ESR resonance of the harmine within the brain. The energy of the harmine-psilocybin complex ESR will be absorbed instantly into the matrix of the mushroom. This will cause those molecules metabolizing within the body and bonded to the neural DNA to instantly drop to absolute zero. Clearly this harmine-psilocybin-DNA complex must immediately separate itself from the cellular matrix. There is great danger at this moment, but pathways exist to deal with it. We will find that these molecules condense out of our bodies accompanied by a sound. This sound will be the harmonic ESR tone of this complex amplified superconductively and broadcast and frozen into the superconductive matrix of the mushroom. The superconductively charged psilocybin acts as an antenna which picks up the amplified ESR signals of the complex and condenses vibrational signals into a superconductive matrix.

The opus can now be briefly summarized:

- *The mushroom must be taken and heard.*
- *The* ayahuasca *must be taken and charged with overtonal ESR of the psilocybin via voice-imparted, amplified sound.*
- *The ESR resonance of the psilocybin in the mushrooms will be canceled and will drop into a superconducting state; a small portion of the physical matter of the mushroom will be obliterated.*
- *The superconductively charged psilocybin will pick up the ESR harmonic of the* ayahuasca *complex; this energy will be instantly and completely absorbed by the higher-dimensional tryptamine template. It will be transferred to the mushroom as vocal sound and condensed onto the psilocybin as a bonded complex of superconductive harmine-psilocybin-DNA.*
- *The result will be a molecular aggregate of hyperdimensional, superconducting matter that receives and sends messages transmitted by thought, that stores and retrieves information in a holographic fashion in neural DNA, and that depends on superconductive harmine as a transducer energy source and superconductive RNA as a temporal matrix. This aggregate will be a living and functioning part of the brain of the molecular "singer" who creates it. It will be composed of higher dimensional matter, i.e., matter that has been turned through the higher dimension via the process of canceling its electrical charge with a harmonic vibration, transmitting that vibration across space (from superconductive transmitter to superconductive receiver), and then recondensing that vibration onto a superconductive template (the charged psilocybin in the mushroom), until the harmine-psilocybin-DNA complex condenses into a superconducting molecule. A molecule that is higher dimensional matter would, by*

this theory, be stable as long as it remains in a superconducting
configuration, probably forever, since it is powered by its own
ESR energy. It will then be responsive to command via endoge-
nous tryptamine ESR (thoughts), it will be keyed into our collec-
tive DNA, and it will contain harmine as a superconductive
transceiver and power source.

Talk about a steep learning curve! I had never heard my little
brother carry on so. To the extent that I grasped what Dennis was
saying, he thought, and it seemed a magnificent thought to me, that
the body is like an undiscovered musical and scientific instrument
whose potential lies all around and within us, but of which we are
unaware. He said that the mind, through an act of will, could use
the singing voice to interact with the brain as though it were a color
organ and holographic library all wrapped up into one.

Dennis pointed the way toward a kind of Orphic science where
the great advances would be made by using only the interaction of
the quarternity of singing voice, mind, brain, and imagination.
More, however, than a chant-induced, collective synesthesia was
promised. He was saying that the laws of acoustics and low amper-
age bioelectrical phenomena, and our bodies, could be manipulated
to give the experimenter a doorway into exploring states of matter
and realms of physics involving high energy and low temperature
that are, currently at least, supposed to be the exclusive province of
researchers totally dependent on extremely sophisticated and powerful instruments. It became possible for a moment to dream that
the powers of shamanism, derived from a millennium-old knowledge of microphysics and bioelectronics, was far in advance of our
own. The doorway that seemed to swing open was a doorway out of
historical time, back toward some sort of archaic completion nearly
forgotten.

Perhaps the shamanic traditions of this planet are the keepers
of an understanding that uses the human body/brain/mind as its vehicle, leaving the present state of the art, which our own "scientific
method" has achieved, a very poor second. This is really an old
idea—the siren song of Pythagoras—that the mind is more powerful than any imaginable particle accelerator, more sensitive than

any radio receiver or the largest optical telescope, more complete in its grasp of information than any computer: that the human body— its organs, its voice, its power of locomotion, and its imagination— is a more-than-sufficient means for the exploration of any place, time, or energy level in the universe. It was this idea that Dennis would set out to prove, to realize in the actual hardware of the dimension-roving lenticular vehicle that he was convinced could be generated out of his own DNA and living organisms present at hand in the Amazonian environment—the mushroom and the *ayahuasca*.

CHAPTER NINE

A CONVERSATION OVER
SAUCERS

*In which the details of the plumbing of the
Resurrection Body are rehearsed for each and
all, and a partial test of our theory is made.*

AS I READ DENNIS'S NOTES, I felt that the themes
of the strange place we had come to had crystallized. I felt again the
sense of something in the sky, calmly omniscient but closely observing us. I returned to the beginning and read the notes all over
again, but I had no basis whatsoever to judge what I was reading.
My brother's scientific speculation seemed to have acquired a life
of its own. He was like a great, all-knowing computer.

Around our campfire, we all listened to him explain his idea for
the experiment. He was very deeply involved. Ideas were coming
out of him like spaghetti from a rasher, thousands of words about all
of these strange things. He said, "You know what we could do?"
Then he laid down the rap that is now enshrined as the central doctrine of the opus. He called it hyper-carbolation. According to his
theory, you could use the singing voice and superconductivity (or
the complete disappearance of electrical resistance, usually only
possible with temperatures at absolute zero) to drive the molecules

of psychedelic compounds into states of permanent association—or bonding—with living human DNA.

Dennis's rap drew on the theory of sound. If you pluck a string, it will sound in the octave in which it is struck, but it will also sound in octaves above and below its key. It has what are called harmonic overtones. If you strike the chord and then squelch it, you can still hear the harmonic overtones, a phenomenon that had fascinated Pythagoras. Dennis pointed out to us that one can use two sounds to cancel each other if the two sounds are exactly the same in relation to each other.

The same phenomenon that produces harmonic overtones can be used to still the movements of molecules. In very localized areas, perhaps only a few thousand angstroms across, one can produce low temperatures with audio cancellation. Molecular motion is a type of vibration and in the presence of just the right audio input such molecular motion will cease. Operationally speaking, when molecular motion ceases the molecule has reached a temperature of absolute zero, and superconductivity becomes possible.

Dennis felt he had figured out a way to blow the locked doors of paradise right off their hinges using psychoactive compounds, psilocybin, the tryptamine complex, and the beta-carbolines that occur in *ayahuasca*. He said that if you look at the vibration of molecules in the beta-carboline family, you find that the electron spin resonance of these molecules, moving from one to another, is in fact a series of harmonic overtones. This is interesting because psychiatrist Claudio Naranjo had reported in *The Healing Journey* that 50 percent of his subjects who took harmine, a beta-carboline occuring in *ayahuasca*, reported a buzzing in the head. It was not associated with other kinds of psychedelics; it seemed to be uniquely associated with these harmine compounds. The Jivaro shamans of Ecuador also report a buzzing in the head. Dennis's idea was that when *ayahuasca* is metabolizing through one's neural matrix in the brain, a sound is heard.

Explaining just how this happens is far from simple. Electron spin resonance is a phenomenon of molecular structure in which high frequency energy is put into the molecular system and electron spin resonance signals emerge from the system. But not all compounds have an electron spin resonation; to exhibit ESR activity a molecule must have a ring free of molecular encumbrances. All compounds with a free ring will resonate under certain conditions. The hallucinogens we were interested in have free rings, as does DNA, the molecule at the center of the genetic machinery of all life.

When your body is metabolizing the alkaloids in *ayahuasca*, a relationship is formed with the tryptamine metabolites in the brain. A sound is heard that is characteristic of the interaction. Once the sound is heard, it can be imitated. Then what you have is a vocal sound.

Ordinarily it would not occur to anyone to draw a connection between this sound and the signals produced by the ESR, which occur in the microphysical realm. Here was where Dennis made his leap into delusion or illumination, for he began to insist that he could do things with this sound. By vocalizing, Dennis felt that he would, in effect, be emitting an amplified spin resonance signal, an amplified ESR-modulated sound that would be coming from the psilocybin metabolizing in his brain. Making this sound would set up a series of harmonic vibrations above and below it in other compounds also active in his brain.

Now, from this theoretical basis, we take flight. If he is in the correct spatial orientation to the molecule he is directing sound at, when he stops making the sound he is hearing, the molecule will become superconductive, because its vibration has been canceled. Of the many millions of this kind of molecule struck by this sound, a few dozen or hundreds will be in the correct geometrical orientation and their molecular motion will be stilled almost instantly. Now a peculiar property of low temperatures is that very high bonding energies appear between molecules. A molecule close to absolute zero will bond to anything. It just forces its way into the structure.

Dennis tried to explain:

"The harmine molecule, which is structured like a little bell, gives a bell-like chiming and buzzing sound. If we come on it right and cancel it and there is neural DNA active in the brain, the electrical configuration of harmine is enough like the molecular configuration of adenine, one of the bases in DNA, that it will replace it. It will bond through into the chain. And when it is bonded in, its ring will become activated. It is the same size as adenine, but it's a little more complicated. It has a free resonance ring." Dennis paused and then gathered his thoughts to continue.

"Now the normal ESR of harmine is a simple signal, but the electron spin configuration of DNA is very, very complicated. It is a broad band. When the harmine goes in there it will cease to broadcast its own resonation because it will have become very tightly bonded into the structure of the macro-molecule. It will instead begin to broadcast the ESR resonation of the DNA. That's it. If you have followed it this far, the rest is easy. DNA is what you are. The physical form is just a lot of juicy macro-physical crystals caused by gene expression, you know, the result of enzymes set in motion and coded by DNA. Neural DNA is known to be non-metabolizing. It does not go away. The meat on your body comes and goes every few years. Your skeleton is not the same one you had five years ago, but neural DNA is an exception. It is there for all time. You come into the world with it. It records and it is an antenna for memory. Not only our personal memory, but any entity or organism which has DNA in it; there is a way to find a connection to it. This is how we open a passage to the Divine Imagination, this is how William Blake understood Redemption. This is now within reach.

"This is how it's done. You put a radio into the DNA and this ESR resonation will begin to flood your system because the bond will be permanent; there will be no way to disrupt it. It will tell you everything—everything that can be known in the world of space and time because it contains your own and everyone else's records. We are all connected through this magical substance, which is what makes life possible and which causes it to take on its myriad forms. All DNA is the same. It is the settings that are different; you get butterflies, mastodons, or human beings, depending on the settings."

"Or so you say," was my noncommittal reply. But I had the distinct impression that I did glimpse his meaning. Organisms are complex structures that have emerged and stabilized their forms over millions of years. They are literally shaped by the ebb and flow of time on a vaster scale than any individual lifespan can experience or compare itself to. Organisms have enfolded in their embryology, in their morphology, a message about the structure of the larger universe. Mysticism has always insisted on this. Molecular biology as the inheritor of the theory of evolution seems to confirm it.

Perhaps life is a strategy for amplifying quantum mechanical indeterminacy to a level where a macrophysical chemical system, in effect human beings, can experience and understand it? If one of us could pharmacologically redesign our neurocellular chemistry, there might indeed be strange new realms of perception and understanding to be explored, brave new worlds of the imagination based on new ratios of neurotransmitters in the still-evolving brains of human beings. I thought, "Who am I to judge?"

I was intrigued by his precision in invoking these ideas, but for the moment I simply did not know what to say. He stared at me, clearly expecting more. I believed in the infinite, self-transforming power of the human mind and species, and I could suppose that there were parallel worlds and alternative dimensions. I could imagine any number of science fiction possibilities, provided that I was not asked to believe that I was about to be present personally at their discovery or unleashing. But this is what Dennis was saying: We had somehow stumbled upon or been led to the trigger experience for the entire human world that would transform the ontological basis of reality so that mind and matter everywhere would become the same thing and reflect the human will perfectly.

How could anyone conceive of such a thing? We had come to La Chorrera with a belief that if life and mind are possible, then the mysteries of the universe might well be inexhaustible. Yet something very passive, yet ever present, was there elaborating these ideas in our minds—something that we had thought of for some days as "The Mushroom."

We talked for more than an hour about these ideas and what finally emerged was the need for a test, or at least Dennis maintained that a partial test of the idea could be undertaken to convince me and our companions. He thought that as the superconducting state became stabilized there should be a marked lowering of temperature in the immediate area. In our talking, he and I had left the area of the hut and drifted down the forest path. It would be possible to attempt to generate the effect of coolness right there on the spot, he supposed.

We seated ourselves on the sandy path facing each other, with the afternoon sun on both of us. After a couple of preliminary low, mechanical buzzes, Dennis made a sound very similar to the one he had unleashed in the knoll house three days before. This sound had an extremely peculiar quality and, as it rose in intensity, I looked down at the hair on my arms and saw it rise as goose-flesh formed and a wave of intense shivering swept over me. I yelled at Dennis to stop. He did instantly and seemed much drained by the effort. I was quite disoriented. I frankly could not tell whether a real wave of very cold air had swept over me or whether that particular sound had somehow made my body react as though it was being exposed to cold air. It was not lost on me that if the effect had truly generated a blast of cold air, then it had violated the known laws of physics. But I did not care to experiment further—the whole thing had an eerie aura about it and if the effect was real, who knew what could come of pushing it too far? I was more confused than ever by my enigmatic brother and his burgeoning ideas and abilities. The whole thing seemed absurd and yet very compelling, like a hypnotic game into which one becomes absorbed in spite of oneself.

"Now can we call the press conference?" Dennis asked insistently on our return walk down the trail. But I could barely hear him so lost in delicious anticipation of previously unimaginable futures was I.

We returned to our camp and mentioned to all present that Dennis had generated the wave of cold air that he had predicted from the theory. But it was all sufficiently ambiguous that no one felt drawn to comment. After dinner, Vanessa and Dave returned to the riverside house and Ev, Dennis, and I settled into our first night in the forest since arriving at La Chorrera.

Dennis was in a state of continual activity, amplifying his ideas and trying out new wrinkles on us. That night and the next day, he retired into a world of very intense activity. He wrote his ideas over and over, the steps to do it and the theory of why it should work. He spent lots of time alone writing, then he would come back and talk to us. He was on to something very strange; his word-pictures caused reality to shimmer and crinkle at the edges. He was really in touch with this bubbling obsidian fourth dimensional fluid that we were going to stabilize into a usable tool. And end history. And go to the stars.

My attitude was "Fine, we'll try it." The atmosphere was drenched with the bizarre. Now we had arrived at the center of the Amazon and we could feel something in the sky, watching. At first, we had been happy heads trying to explore one last fairy tale so we could be rationalists forever, and instead we encountered something enormous. Something alive and very old and very strange. Something peculiar in every extreme.

I was quite uncreative in this period. I had taken the mushroom and was ecstatic all the time. It was the only time in my life when I was truly content simply to *be*. I had quite effortlessly formed the assumption, which I assumed was shared by all, that we would never leave La Chorrera. Leaving seemed unimaginable since all things seemed to be perfectly present there. The sense of homecoming and of being at last where one was supposed to be was at times overwhelming. As for the future, I imagined that I would simply listen to Dennis rave. His vision into which my credulity was dissolving went beyond anything that anyone I knew had ever dreamed of.

We had set the following evening, that of March 4, as the day we would test the full theory of the harmine-DNA bond. I noted with unusual satisfaction that this day corresponded with an idiotic pun that had stuck with me since earliest childhood: "What day of the year is a command?" Answer: "March fourth."

"How fitting then," I ranted and raved. "How fitting that we will attempt to concretize the soul on that day." Absurdly, the coincidence of the date with that pun seemed part of a universal secret plan unraveling to bring us to the history-culminating moment when humanity would march into a higher dimension. My own thoughts seemed to me to be nothing like the super-scientific theory formation that my brother was involved in. I was baffled by much of what was going on. That day, March 3, I amused myself constructing a pipe out of the strange, heart-shaped *Macoubea* fruits that we had otherwise given up on as inedible. From one of those fruits and a hollow reed and a bit of river clay, I constructed a water pipe that gave me great satisfaction.

While the jargon of the ESR biophysicist whirled around me, I contemplated what I had achieved with two plants and a bit of

mud. It seemed to me a marvel of ingenuity, and because the fruit
was so strange, there was something about it vaguely unearthly.
This pipe might have been fashioned from one of the fruits that
gentle Weena offered the Time Traveler in Wells's epic. My pipe
was a weird and haunting object, and when it was smoked the
bubbling of the water beneath the thick rind sounded very like
the beating of some great mammalian heart. Even Dennis paused
to admire this pipe, and we determined that it would be used in
our experiment when the moment came to smoke some of the
ayahuasca bark to boost the harmine levels in our blood. We were operating in a world where scientific method, ritual, and participation
mystique were inseparably intertwined. Our own minds and bodies
were to be the retorts, the vessels, of the psycho-alchemical transformation that we were experimenting with.

That afternoon we all pulled roots and stacked them in the
sun. It seemed the most satisfying activity imaginable. Nothing
could have seemed more right. That evening we made a tape of our
intentions, but unfortunately our tape recorder was not in good
working order and that tape has proven impossible to salvage. I
greatly regret this loss, since the emotional content of what we were
experiencing would come across most clearly from our own words.
The taping session ranged over a number of themes:

Hyper-carbolation: This is what we had named the process of
altering the neural DNA and changing man into an eternal hyperdimensional being. It was a process we imagined to be intimately
akin to sexual generation. We spoke of it as the "birth of an idea" in
a sense whose literalness is not easy to convey to minds that have
not brushed with schizophrenia. We hoped that mind, driven by a
will to the good, could control the process of generation and guide
this process toward the production of the imagination-modulated
resurrection body so dear to the Patristic Fathers, sixteenth-century
alchemists, and modern UFO enthusiasts. In this notion we were
following Jung, who early on realized that the flying saucer is an
image of the self, the suppressed psychic totality that lurks behind
the apparent dualism of mind and nature. We thought that the field
of mind and its will toward the good could be templated onto the genetic engines of life. The hope was that out of biology, Tantra could

summon the reality of the living stone, the chimerical unicorn of the alchemical quest made at last to lay his head in the maiden's lap. We dreamed, in short, of a union of Spirit and Matter.

The dead: We believed that hyper-carbolation was to be the shamanic defeat of death, that those doorways through which the dead enter daily were to be finally thrown open to a hyper-carbolated humanity, which would then have freedom of movement to and from an eternity in which all the members of the species existed as a living reality. The presence of giants from the human past—Carl Jung, Newton and Nabokov, Bruno, Pythagoras, and Heraclitus—was an overwhelming and all-inclusive intuition that we shared and could not ignore.

There seemed to be an ideological lineage, the golden chain, whose collective task was the shattering of the historical continuum through the generation of the living philosophical lapis of hyper-carbolated humanity. All these visionary thinkers had performed their part in this project. Now, as the secret work of human history, the generation of Adam's cosmic body, lost since paradise, neared completion, these shades stirred and pressed near to our Amazonian campsite. Our destiny was apparently to be the human atoms critical to the transformation of *Homo sapiens* into galaxy-roving bodhisattvas, the culmination and quintessence of the highest aspirations of star-coveting humanity.

The psychologically minded will recognize this as a description of messianic ego inflation. Such it is, but we felt these things as anyone would feel them if they truly believed they were at such a point in history. We wondered, "Why? Why us?"

To such questions the mushroom spoke in my mind without hesitation: "Because you have diligently sought the good and because you trusted no human being more than yourself."

The emotional impact of these sorts of inner exchanges was intense beyond anything I have ever experienced. I felt humbly grateful to the point of tears. I felt exalted. We wanted to salvage paradise for humanity, and we thanked all gods and nature that our eccentric quest, out of all the lives and paths being lived out on earth, was placed by fate so near the cutting edge. Where the elder shamanism had failed, we would succeed. The rescue of the timeless pearl of human immortality from the well of death would, through the act of hyper-carbolation, become a living reality for every person who had ever lived. All the pain and suffering and war and desperation would somehow be repaid and made right through the intercession of the mystery of higher dimensions and a backward flowing logic of time that somehow undoes what has already happened. The wave of understanding that had been gaining strength since the twenty-seventh of February was so strong as to be nearly visible in everything around me. The lenticular shape of the approaching philosopher's stone seemed to be everywhere that I looked. Every shape and form around me was pregnant with its unearthly, opalescent depths.

CHAPTER TEN

MORE ON THE OPUS

*In which we refine the theory and begin
preparations for experimental test flights
of the Sophic Aerolith.*

THE NEXT DAY WAS the much-anticipated fourth
of March. After we made breakfast we did not tear down our fire as
we normally would have done. Instead we began to brew the carefully shredded *Banisteriopsis caapi* vines in several gallons of spring
water. The fire made of the gnarled and now sun-baked roots burned
furiously. The pot responded with an even, rolling boil that is the
correct condition for making the brew.

All afternoon long we three cooked and said little. Dave and
Vanessa used this time to visit and photograph the old village of La
Chorrera across the lake. That evening they were to join us for a
light meal, after which they had agreed to withdraw from the group
and allow the *ayahuasca*-taking and the experimental test of hyper-
carbolation to go on without them. I am sure that Dennis's mind, far
more than my own, was preoccupied with the details of the test.
During the days preceding, he had been often irritable, and this I
took to be a part of the spectrum of effects accompanying whatever
odd sort of mental unfoldment he was experiencing. While he was
thus preoccupied with interior issues and vistas, I was the hawk-
eyed guardian of the shamanic fires and procedures.

There recently had been much discussion of fire and the role it must have played in forming the mental world of archaic human beings. Once, as we sat staring into the camp fire, Dennis had remarked to me that, "People have been looking into fires like this for thousands and thousands of years. The squeal of these coals is the release of ionized plasma and in the flickering waves of free electrons thus created, one can see into the past and the future. The fire is the place where the ideas come from."

I was silent. I felt our ancestors then, seemingly present on the other side of the interface represented by the flame. "What is happening to us?" I again asked myself, but said nothing, silence seeming more eloquent.

Dennis, completely occupied with creating a test that would reveal the phenomenon in such a way as to overturn skepticism, spent part of the day writing furiously:

March 4, 1971

It is now possible to reconstruct the physical-chemical idea that has evolved in the process of understanding this phenomenon: i.e., the fourth-dimensional rotation of matter. I understand from examining the linguistic model we have constructed that the waveform ESR interference that will accomplish the work operates in a somewhat different manner than I had thought. It can be explained thus: The psilocybin that occurs in the mushroom acts as an antenna for picking up and amplifying the harmonic ESR tones of all tryptophane-derived compounds of all living organisms within its range. Since the psilocybin undergoing metabolism is superconductive, this means that its range of reception is theoretically infinite. The antenna does, to some degree, pick up a signal whose ultimate origin is the totality of living creatures; but since the psilocybin metabolism is carried on within the brain (or mushroom) at a very low voltage level, the antenna behaves as though its range was limited, even though it is superconductive.

I see this notion as an effort to explain the very real sense of informational interconnectedness that pervaded our experience, which occurred in one of the densest tropical forests on the planet. We did seem to be in touch with the living mind of the tropical forest. Perhaps tryptamine compounds are the mediators of the signaling mechanisms of the command-and-control structure that regulates and integrates whole ecosystems.

More Dennis:

> It seems clear, therefore, that the signal, which when we are intoxicated on the mushroom in this ecologically dense area can be discerned so clearly, originates in the ESR resonation of the ayahuasca *plant, though perhaps all the biosphere is picked up and broadcast, amplified via the* ayahuasca *superconductive transducer. This understanding will clarify precisely what will occur at the moment of fourth-dimensional warp. Ingesting the* ayahuasca *harmine will speed up the process of metabolism enough to amplify its ESR tone to an audible level; this ESR tone will harmonically cancel out the ESR tone of the psilocybin within the mushroom, causing it to lose its electric field and snap into a superconducting configuration. The* ayahuasca *ESR signal will have keyed the mushroom psilocybin into a superconducting antenna; it is then ready to have the psilocybin- harmine-DNA compound being metabolized within the body condensed onto its charged template. A microsecond after the mushroom psilocybin has been superconductively charged, its amplified ESR wave will then cancel out the ESR signals of the tryptamines and harmine metabolizing in the body, as well as the genetic material. This will cause these compounds to drop into superconductive configuration and bond together at the exact moment that they bond to the waiting mushroom template.*
>
> This transfer of superconductive compounds charged within the body to a superconductive template prepared within the mushroom will not occur in three-dimensional space; no actual physical transfer will be visible, as the organically processed superconductive material will bond itself to the mushroom template through a higher spatial dimension.

It is at this point that the rationalist will despair, for indeed what abyss of untested theoretical and perhaps fanciful assumptions hides behind the phrase "through a higher spatial dimension"? Nevertheless, and like the alchemists of old, Dennis seemed to act from the assumption that the experiment, once successful, would sanction the theory. Like the vocabulary of alchemy, his words are a blend of modern scientific formalisms and Hermetic aspiration. He had created a new alchemical dispensation and raised the specter of alchemical hope, phoenix-like, from the ashes of modernity.

> The result will be the work of works—that wonder which cannot be told—four dimensions captured and delineated in three. The stone will be all things; but the elements which are bound together in hyperspace to form it are among the most common natural products, and the function and place of each in the stone can be understood. The stone is a solid-state hyperdimensional circuit that is quadripartite in structure:
>
> First, psilocybin, charged in the mushroom to act as a template on which the rest of the circuit is condensed. In the final state the psilocybin acts as a superconducting antenna to pick up on information diffused through space and time.
>
> Second, the superconductively charged harmine complex within the stone will act as its transmitter and energy source. It is interesting to note that the same energy that sustains the antenna circuits in superconductivity will sustain the whole of the device.
>
> The third component of the stone is the DNA bonded to and resonating through the harmine. It will constitute the hyperdimensional, holographic memory of the device and will contain and explicate the genetic history of all species. It will be the collective memory of the device, and all times and places and conceivable forms will be accessible within its matrix.
>
> The fourth part of the circuit will be the RNA, which will also be superconductively charged. [Normally the function of RNA is to "read" the molecular code of DNA and to transcribe its genes into usable protein molecules.] Through its function of self-replication turned through hyperspace, the RNA will be able to project a wave form, a three-dimensional holographic image, and thus it will give form instantly to any idea. It will perform the same function it has always had—the process of replication through time. But henceforth replication will be subject, in part, to the whim of consciousness.
>
> Why I and my companions have been selected to understand and trigger the gestalt wave of understanding that will be

the unleashing of the hyperspatial zeitgeist is becoming more clear to me each moment, though I know I won't understand our mission fully until the work is complete. We will be instructed in the use of the stone by some infinitely wise, infinitely adept fellow member of the hyperspatial community; of that I feel sure. It will be the taking of the keys to galactarian citizenship. I speculate that we will be the first five human beings to be instructed in its use— our mission will be to selectively disseminate it to the rest of humanity, but slowly, and in such a way as to ease the cultural shock. It is also somehow appropriate that at least some segment of the species have an intimation of the implications and possibilities of this, the last cultural artifact.

And so now, against all probabilities and chance and circumstance, my companions and I have been given the peculiar privilege of knowing history will end. It would be a strange position to find oneself in if being in that position did not bring with it a full understanding of the forces that brought one there. Fortunately, as the phenomenon is an acceleration of understanding, one gains clearer insight into the forces that have bent space and time, thought and culture back upon themselves to focus at this point.

As this monumentally inscrutable statement intimates, Dennis was in the process of turning some sort of corner. Under the influence of his ideas and images, our lives had become pure science fiction. This entire transformation had been achieved through the opening of our collective imagination. But what had really changed? Were we about to take the tiller of history into our hands, or was this one more sadly misguided reach for the power of an archetype that must always slide though one's fingers?

Now I can look upon my life as spread before the scanner of memory and understand all those moments that foreshadowed this one. It is easy to look beyond the personal history to the events of human history and discern therein the prefiguration of this last moment. As a phenomenon it has always existed and it will continue, for it is the moving edge of phenomenal understanding that was generated in the era before physics and it has gathered momentum—a constant acceleration ever since. What we are moving

*toward in three dimensions is the passing of this wave of under-
standing into a higher dimension, the realm of the atemporal. As
it happens, it will make this transition through one of us. But
there will be no change in this cosmic order or even a blip on the
cosmic circuits, for the phenomenon has gathered constant momentum from the beginning and it will flow through and beyond
all dimensions with the same smoothness with which it entered
until finally it has moved through all beings in all dimensions. Its
joy will then be complete when in a vast amount of time it has
constellated full understanding throughout creation.*

*If we trigger the eschatology, we will appear to act in the
role of the Anti-Christ, but the real Anti-Christ is history's dis-
torted reflection of the Christ at the end of time—the cosmic
Adam-anthropos. The eschatological Christ is Anti-Christ only
from a historical perspective. It is interesting that among Maza-
tecans and other tribal groups of the Central Mexican highlands
the idea of Christ is linked to the mushrooms—is this syncretism
or prophecy?*

That evening's collective meal with Dave and Vanessa at our
camp, with the *ayahuasca* infusion cooling in the background, was
less than successful. By now positions relative to "the phenomenon" had polarized us into irreconcilability. Dave and Vanessa did
not arrive till the close of day, but they joined us in the hut for a
smoke. Discussion led to an update and final outline of the experiment proposed for the evening. Dennis spoke:

"We will obtain a metabolizing, living mushroom. Dig up the
shit around it and physically move the whole thing to the hut. We
want to do the bonding in the mushroom because we don't know
what it would be like if it were done in our own bodies. It is wide
open. With your voice, your mind, and a mushroom, these things can
be done. That is all one needs. Particle accelerators, all of that, no!
With the energy that is hundreds of times less than the energy in an
ordinary flashlight battery, one can probably rend space/time apart."

The air was heavy with charged ions. Dave was full of doubts; as
he talked, there was the grumble of distant thunder far off over the
jungle. Dave's objections to what we were doing were emotional

and fearful, along the lines of "Man was not meant to know these things." Hardly what we expected from a colleague. We tried to be reassuring, but he became agitated and rushed out of the hut, perhaps, we thought, intending to walk back to the river house.

Instead we heard an exclamation of fear and a kind of moan, a yell of amazement. We all clambered out of the hut to find Dave, white-faced and staring at the sky, pointing. The light of a first-quarter moon revealed the tattered sky and, directly above the path returning to the river, an enormous black thunderhead rearing its twisting and writhing form up through thousands of feet of moisture- and electricity-saturated air. It looked like an enormous centipede with broad strokes of lightning flickering out of its lower portions, stroking the tops of the jungle canopy with a roar that, when it broke over us, was as deafening as field artillery. Over the howl of the wind now whipping into a wild frenzy the jungle all around us, I heard Dennis yell:

"It's a backwash from the approaching breakthrough. It says to me there is now no doubt that we'll succeed!"

Dave moaned as he sank, unbelieving, to the sandy soil while the first huge drops began to fall. I thought of Ahab saying, "I'd strike out the sun if it insulted me. For could it do that then could I do the other, since there is ever a sort of fair play." In the wake of an ear-splitting blast we all fell back to the hut, during which Vanessa sprained her ankle slipping from the notched log that served as a step-ladder. In a few minutes the giant storm moved on, leaving only a chaotic and churning sunset.

The sudden electrical storm and its impact on us was taken as an omen by both points of view. Dennis, Ev, and I assumed it was associated with a feedback of effects from the experiment whose performance was only a few hours ahead of us. Dave and Vanessa thought it a light dose of the wrath of God for having such Promethean aspirations. The possibility that it had nothing to do with us at all went unexamined.

"Is this the healing of my split-T that my astrologer predicted for this time?" Scorpio Vanessa asked of no one in particular.

Ev and I shared a light meal with our guests while Dennis ate nothing. Dave and Vanessa wished us goodnight and good luck, and then hobbled away toward the river. The three of us were left alone, and there remained nothing but to make the test that Dennis had devised and whose anticipation had caused such strain on our expedition.

The *ayahuasca* had been brewed. Since then, having seen *ayahuasca* brewed professionally by shamans in Peru, I am sure that our brew was too weak to have had any major role in what followed. It was the mushroom that was the causal agent, if a causal agent could be isolated. And mushrooms we had, both ones we had picked as well as a specimen moved into the hut, *in situ* in its manure base. Dennis confidently stated that living, metabolizing psilocybin should be present. We had hung the chrysalis of a *Morpho* near the mushroom so that animal tissue undergoing metamorphosis would also be represented in the target area tableau. What was science and what ritual? We did not know and could not tell. All bets were covered. Poetic inspiration and scientific insight had become fused.

CHAPTER ELEVEN

THE EXPERIMENT AT
LA CHORRERA

*In which the experiment is attempted and the
brothers McKenna are driven mad by its
unexpected aftermath.*

THE NIGHT OF MARCH 4 was absolutely black. A low-lying cloud bank had appeared, muffling the small world of La Chorrera and wrapping it in a bowl of all-absorbing velvet darkness. Following the storm we had rebuilt our fire and boiled off several liters of water from our infusion of *Banisteriopsis caapi,* so that it was much stronger than it had been before. We then added crushed leaves, which Dennis had gathered that day near the *chorro* and which we were using as DMT admixture plants. It was the admixture plants that we hoped would provide the DMT necessary to drive the intense hallucinations for which the brew is famous. We had tentatively identified these plants as *Justicia pectoralis var. stenophylla*—a plant thought to be used as an admixture of *ayahuasca* in the Vaupes drainage north of us. Now, years after that evening, not only do I question the concentration at which we brewed the *Banisteriopsis* but also our identification of the admixture plant.

There is no doubt that there was considerable harmine alkaloid in the infusion, but as I later learned not as much as is necessary to provoke an unambiguous intoxication. The harmine alkaloids present were, in my opinion, boosted by the psilocybin that had accumulated in our systems, or rather the MAO-inhibiting effect of these beta-carbolines caused the residual psilocybin to emerge into consciousness as a deep hallucinogenic experience.

While I completed the boiling, Ev and Dennis went to their hammocks and lay down to await the completion of the preparations. We laughed together and talked softly. Yet in spite of this there was an undercurrent of tension as we approached the experiment into which we had poured so much of our energy. As we neared the critical moment, Ev and Dennis became unaccountably clumsy and seemed to find their bodies hard to handle; it was that which had sent them to their hammocks. I seemed unaffected and was able to look after whatever needed attention. Lying in his hammock, Dennis ate two mushrooms to launch the beginning of the experiment; Ev and I did the same.

Our little thatched hut on its stilt legs looked in the flickering firelight like a small spaceship dropped into the howling jungles of an alien world. We all felt as if we were approaching hyperspatial overdrive. There was a sense of immense energies accumulating. The effect was reinforced by the hammocks hanging like acceleration slings ready to receive a starship's crew. Dennis lay in his hammock nearly unable to hold a pencil, but writing furiously in tight, operational terms about the experiment just ahead:

> *The mushroom is presently metabolizing within our bodies; this has keyed in on the tryptamine template in the living mushroom and it has been sensitized for the condensation of the harmine-psilocybin-DNA molecule. When the* ayahuasca *is ingested the harmine analog will start to metabolize within the body. The ESR of the presensitized psilocybin circuit will immediately cancel the ESR of the harmine and cause it to bond superconductively to the DNA-RNA complex both in our bodies and in the mushroom simultaneously in a higher dimension. The bonding completed, the harmine-DNA memory bank and drive unit will condense into the waiting, charged psilocybin circuit in the mushroom. We will see this condensation, as it will appear in the*

mushroom at the same instant that the bond is completed in a
higher dimension.

I had no notion of what this all meant or was leading to. I took
the attitude that I must simply be a good witness. Surely nothing at
all would happen, or something wonderful was in store.

Dennis explained that he was unable to move about very well
because of something having to do with the backward flow of time.
The ever-increasing constraints on the set of possible futures had
rendered him nearly immobile; only the mind, planning and com-
puting, was free.

We finished boiling the *ayahuasca*. I ground the admixture
plants and added them to the cooling brew. I moved the *ayahuasca*
into the hut, then the mushroom. With those things in place, we
were ready to begin.

Dennis began narrating our countdown toward an Omega that
none of us could really understand; we were completely transformed by the expectation that we might witness the outbreak of
the millennium. He said that time was appearing to slow down as
we approached this point. Prior to this, we had taken no hallucinogens for several days, so the effects we were experiencing were not
arising from that source. Something else was happening. As proof of
this amazing assertion, he called our attention to the candle that I
had set upon a small shelf jutting from the wall of the hut. Unattended, its slight tilt had become slowly exaggerated so that now it
hung at a crazy angle, defying gravity because, he said, time was
passing so slowly that we could not see that it was actually in the act
of falling.

I walked closer to this apparition and bent toward the flame.
The fire appeared still, absolutely frozen. My mind shot back to the
moment above the river when it too had seemed stilled forever.
The flame was uncanny. As deeply as I cared to look into it I could
see no movement of particles or gas. I seemed to have my usual
freedom of movement, but the world around me was coming to a
crystalline and eerie halt.

It was Dennis who finally spoke: "A series of discreet energy
levels must be broken through in order to bond this thing. It is part

mythology, part psychology, part applied physics. Who knows? We will make three attempts before we break out of the experimental mode."

We all drank the *ayahuasca*. The taste was sharp and astringent, like a sauce of leather and molé, but it faded quickly as the liquid went churning through our guts. Dennis took only one more mushroom to help him hear the tone. The darkness outside was utter and we had no clock; it seemed hours since Dave and Vanessa had left us. All was finally in readiness: the living mushroom, the harmine brew, and a harmine smoking mixture, "just in case." After we each had about a half-cup of the *ayahuasca* infusion, we settled down to wait.

For the past several days, Dennis had been hearing the ESR tone that he deemed the *sine qua non* of what we were attempting. After about fifteen minutes, he announced that he could hear it more clearly and that it was gathering strength. He felt prepared to attempt the experiment at any time, he said.

We agreed that each time during the actual making of the sound we would extinguish the candle so that our minds would not be burdened by the sight of any tryptamine-induced facial distortions that the odd yelling might cause. Years before, during peak episodes of DMT among our old Berkeley gang, we had witnessed spasms of facial musculature that were completely hair-raising, invoking as they did the entities of Tantric Buddhism—the bulging eyes, the impossibly long, rolling tongue, that sort of thing.

Dennis then sat up in his hammock. I put out the candle, and he sounded his first howl of hyper-carbolation. It was mechanical and loud, like a bull roarer, and it ended with a convulsive spasm that traveled throughout his body and landed him out of his hammock and onto the floor.

We lit the candle again only long enough to determine that everyone wanted to continue, and we agreed that Dennis's next attempt should be made from a sitting position on the floor of the hut. This was done. Again a long, whirring yodel ensued, strange and unexpectedly mechanical each time it was sounded.

I suggested a break before the third attempt, but Dennis was quite agitated and eager to "bring it through," as he put it. We settled in for the third yell, and when it came it was like the others but lasted much longer and became much louder. Like an electric siren wailing over the still, jungle night, it went on and on, and when it finally died away, that too was like the dying away of a siren. Then, in the absolute darkness of our Amazon hut, there was silence, the silence of the transition from one world to another; the silence of the Ginnunga gap, that pivotal, yawning hesitation between one world age and the next of Norse mythology.

In that gap came the sound of the cock crowing at the mission. Three times his call came, clear but from afar, seeming to confirm us as actors on a stage, part of a dramatic contrivance. Dennis had said that if the experiment were successful the mushroom would be obliterated. The low temperature phenomena would explode the cellular material and what would be left would be a standing wave, a violet ring of light the size of the mushroom cap. That would be the holding mode of the lens, or the philosopher's stone, or whatever it was. Then someone would take command of it—whose DNA it was, they would be it. It would be as if one had given birth to one's own soul, one's own DNA exteriorized as a kind of living fluid made of language. It would be a mind that could be seen and held in one's hand. Indestructible. It would be a miniature universe, a monad, a part of space and time that magically has all of space and time condensed in it, including one's own mind, a map of the cosmos so real that it somehow *is* the cosmos, that was the rabbit he hoped to pull out of his hat that morning.

Dennis leaned toward the still whole mushroom standing on the raised experiment area.

"Look!"

As I followed his gaze, he raised his arm and across the fully expanded cap of the mushroom fell the shadow of his *ruana*. Clearly, but only for a moment, as the shadow bisected the glowing mushroom cap, I saw not a mature mushroom but a planet, the earth, lustrous and alive, blue and tan and dazzling white.

"It is our world." Dennis's voice was full of unfathomable emotions. I could only nod. I did not understand, but I saw it clearly, although my vision was only a thing of the moment.

"We have succeeded." Dennis proclaimed.

"I don't understand," and I did not. "Let's walk to the pasture. I need to think."

Ev was exhausted by the night's activities and probably glad to have us leave her in the hut with the encroaching dawn promising some sort of new day. As we let ourselves down the log ladder to the ground, I was struck by the scene of utter confusion our activities had left behind during the last frantic hours of brewing. Our huge fire was now only white ashes. The waste from the *ayahuasca*-making was piled beside it, looking like a mound of beached seaweed. Everything was strewn about. We walked through all this, shaking the stiffness out of our bodies and stopping at the small stream that crossed the path to splash water in our faces.

We had not spoken. It was Dennis who broke the silence.

"You are wondering if we succeeded?"

"Yes. What happened? You're riding herd on this effect, so what is going on?"

"Well, I am not sure how, but I know we have succeeded. Let me try to understand this."

Though the mushrooms and *ayahuasca* of the night before seemed to have worn off, my own mind was racing with questions. As we walked along, Dennis would make occasional comments that were, it burst over me, answers to things I was thinking but not articulating. I stopped in my tracks. I clearly formed a question in my mind. Dennis, head bent beside me, began to answer without waiting for me to speak my thought aloud. I was dumbfounded. Was this it then? I asked. Had he somehow acquired telepathic powers? No, he replied, there was more to it than that.

According to Dennis, the bonding of the harmine into his DNA had given him immediate access to an enormous, cybernetically stored fund of information. And this information was freely available to anyone in the world who looked into their mind and prefaced their question with the word "Dennis." The absurdity of the second half of this proposition struck me as utterly too much. But naturally, at his insistence, I made the test. I picked up a small plant growing at my feet, closed my eyes and asked:

"Dennis, what is the name of this plant?"

Immediately and without any effort of my own that I was aware of, a scientific name, now forgotten, popped into my head. I tried the same thing again with a different plant and to my amazement received a different answer. The experiment seemed to secure that something was giving answers in my head, but I could not tell if they were correct or not. I was shaken. When we left the hut I was sure we had failed and that we had to talk over revising our approach. I was even relieved since the obsessive nature of it all had been a strain. But now as we walked along and I could hear a voice in my head that was answering, however inanely or inaccurately, any question put to it, I was less sure.

Dennis was oddly preoccupied, yet he assured me that his effort had succeeded and that all over the world the wave of hypercarbolation was sweeping through the human race, eliminating the distinction between the individual and the community as everyone discovered themselves spontaneously pushing off into a telepathic ocean whose name was that of its discoverer: Dennis McKenna.

As I watched my mind and listened to my brother rave, I began to realize that the experiment had indeed unleashed some sort of bizarre effect. I ask myself now why it was so easy for me to make the leap from assuming that we were having a peculiar localized experience to the idea that we were key parts of a planet-wide phenomenon? It is an important, unanswered question that speaks volumes about my susceptibility to inflation and suggestion at that moment. I was quite simply the victim of a cognitive hallucination; that is, rather than a visual experience of something not actually present, a cognitive hallucination is a total shift of the highest levels of our intellectual relationship to the world. The psilocybin-induced cognitive hallucination made the impossible and unlikely seem probable and reasonable. I became flooded with ecstasy as the realization passed over me that we had passed the omega point, that we were now operating in the first few moments of the millennium. Both of us felt our excitement rising as we became convinced that somehow the world was now radically, fundamentally different.

"So this must be it," Dennis said. "We have not condensed the stone into visible space, but we have generated it in our heads. It does not immediately appear as a visible vehicle, but first as a teaching—the teaching we are hearing in our heads right now. Later, the words will be made flesh."

I could only stare at my brother. Who was he and how was he able to know and do these things? I could only wonder.

"Now Mother and possibly lots of dead people will be showing up soon. Jung will doubtless come and, by god, I want to hear what he has to say." Dennis, saying this, gazed over my shoulder as if craning his neck to see who approached our hammock-hung hut. "Is that Nabokov, Sunny Jim that nice Joyce boy, or is it that pesky Nick Cusa?"

We embraced each other, laughing. I felt as though I was being led like a little child. For no reason, I had ceased to question; rather, I felt an urge to see other people and to feel their immersion in the new heaven and the new earth. Dennis agreed I would go to the river and get Dave and Vanessa and return with them to the forest. Dennis would return to the camp and explain to Ev what was happening.

As I set out toward the river, I seemed to be nearly weightless. I felt reborn, full of energy, and bursting with good health and vitality. Over a period of a few minutes, I had passed from weary, disgruntled skeptic to ecstatic believer. Looking back on it, I believe that, for me, this was the critical juncture. Why did I not question Dennis more closely? Was I somehow self-hypnotized? Did the unfamiliar setting, the restricted diet, the strain and expectations push me into a place where I was unable to resist participation in the world of my brother's bizarre ideation? Why was I unable to maintain my detached and skeptical viewpoint? In some sense this willing suspension of disbelief is the crux of the matter—and, I believe, of many a "close encounter" situation.

The Other plays with us and approaches us through the imagination and then a critical juncture is reached. To go beyond this juncture requires abandonment of old and ingrained habits of thinking and seeing. At that moment the world turns lazily inside out and what was hidden is revealed: a magical modality, a different mental landscape than one has ever known, and the landscape becomes real. This is the realm of the cosmic giggle. UFOs, elves, and the teeming pantheons of all religions are the denizens of this previously invisible landscape. One reaches through to the continents and oceans of the imagination, worlds able to sustain anyone who will but play, and then one lets the play deepen and deepen until it is a reality that few would even dare to entertain.

As I walked along that perfect morning no such soothingly objective thoughts came to me. Instead I assumed that my body was metabolizing its way toward the resurrection body, the "soul made visible" of Christian hermeneutics, that we had expected to be part of the success of our experiment. I did not know what was happening in the world or far away, but I did know that since the moment Dennis had pronounced the experiment finished, I had felt an expanding and ever-increasing wave of energy and understanding unfold through my being. As I walked along, what seemed to be a profound realization came over me. The understanding bloomed in my mind that we are all enlightened beings and that only our inability to see and feel ourselves and others as we really are keeps us from shedding our guilt and experiencing ourselves as truly enlightened. I have never been a psychedelic bliss bunny, yet there I was suspended somewhere between cliché and archetype.

I felt beatific, yet I couldn't believe what seemed to be happening. The walk to Dave and Vanessa's place took about ten or fifteen minutes. By now it was about 7:00 A.M. The sun was well up in the sky and it was a beautiful day. As I walked across the pasture I would stop and say, "Dennis," and the response would be instantaneous, just like thought. It confused me. I kept stopping and asking questions. Sitting down on the grass. "Is it all right? What is it? I don't know. Is it safe? I can't understand what this means."

I walked on toward the river. As I walked, I did some experiments. I said "Terence. Terence." It was very much like talking to myself. Then I said "Dennis," and the thing was instantly there, ready to do business. Then I said "McKenna, McKenna," and it was still there. I realized that I couldn't reach it with my first name, but I could reach it with my last name. I felt simultaneously enlightened and bewildered, I could *not* understand what was going on.

I was pondering these sorts of things when I arrived at the riverside house of Vanessa and Dave. They were still asleep in their hammocks, but crowded around the door, even this early in the morning, was a group of wide-eyed Witoto children. As I pushed my way through them, my gaze fell on each and I thought: "You are enlightened, and you . . . and you . . ."

My arrival was the first event of the day for Dave and Vanessa. I told them that we had succeeded and that the fruit of our success was not a condensed hyper-object, but a teaching. I asked them to dress and come with me. While they were gathering their hammocks, they told me that during the darkest part of the night Dave had awakened hysterical, in a state not unlike the condition induced in him by the electrical storm the evening before. They had been very agitated and could only attribute this to what we had been doing.

I was interested in all of this but seemed to hear it as from a long distance. I wanted to return to the forest and see what would unfold there. In my mind I was recalling something Dennis had said a few minutes before in the pasture. He had said that the demarcation between day and night, the dawn line, was now making a twenty-four hour sweep around the world, a sweep that began at the dawn moment when the experiment at La Chorrera was finished. Throughout the world, traffic and factories were coming to a halt. People were leaving their homes and schools to stare into the sky, realizing that someone, somewhere, had broken through, that it was not a day like any other day. Dave and Vanessa followed me back to the forest. Vanessa's ankle had made little improvement overnight and they grumbled a good part of the way.

When we had gone slightly past the place where Dennis and I had parted, we came upon something that could not be fit into any set of expectations. This was Dennis's *ruana*, a short blanket worn by South American peasants, and his shirt discarded in the middle of the path. Next came a pair of pants and then further on two sweat socks. And, though I was to learn this only later, his glasses and his boots had also been hurled away. We followed this trail of cast-off garments back to the hut in the forest. There we found Ev and Dennis, both naked and sitting on the floor of the hut, discussing and doing the "ask Dennis" meditation.

With the instruction that you could not receive a proper initiation unless you were naked, Dennis insisted that we take off our clothes. Vanessa peeled and Dave and I followed. Even their skepticism seemed to have been put aside. The presence of the mushroom was palpable and it seemed to be saying, "Take off your clothes. Throw everything away. Everything is breaking. All objects are no good to you now. Throw everything away. You do not need it any more."

We all looked at each other, glossy pubic hair and secret genitals now resplendent in the sunshine. I rolled a joint and we sat in a circle and smoked. We told Dave and Vanessa about the teaching and they tried it—with varying degrees of success. Dave seemed to think it worked, skeptical Vanessa was not so sure. I was not surprised at this result since a voice in the head is a very slippery and subjective thing. If one has it, there is no doubt; if one does not have it, it seems a very murky matter.

Everyone was very amiable, except that Dennis was showing a tendency to talk right through other people's comments as though they were not present. It seemed as if he were on a different time-track from the rest of us, since he really seemed unable to realize when someone else was talking.

We thought that it was logical to untie our hammocks from the house, to take them and nothing else, and to go naked into the jungle. We would tie the hammocks in a tree and get in. Then we would explore the mode, because clearly you could do more than ask questions. The door was standing open. Experiment alone would show what one could do. Once we had moved, I asked the thing in my head what should be done and received instructions that we should visualize our lives starting from the present, and then move back through our entire life, encountering and setting things right with every sentient creature that we had ever wronged. When we reached the end of this process, we would leave our bodies and somehow enter into the dimension of absolute freedom, which now seemed so near. I conceived of this as though it were a fast rewind of the recording of karmic activity. Once one's karma was rewound a state of original innocence would naturally flower.

Lying in our hammocks, we set out to meditate our way into hyperspace. In my mind's eye, I could see myself at La Chorrera and then going down the trail to El Encanto, up the river to Leguizamo and back to Bogotá, back to Canada. At each point I would meet the people that I had lived my life with and I would say, "We got it! I'm sorry. I hope I didn't offend you too much back in 3-D. It's all over now. Just all over."

I could see people. Immediately, I reached out for all of them. "We're on the Amazon," I explained to each. "And now we are going home. Or some place." The vision had an utterly bizarre, real quality. Tears welled up behind my closed eyelids. It was very peculiar.

The voice of the teacher spoke in my mind. "You've found it. This is it. It's all over now. There is no more. Within a few hours, the superstructure of earthbound, human civilization is going to collapse and your species will depart. First you will go to Jupiter and then to Alpha in Sagittarius. A day of high adventure dawns at last for the human beings."

At first the images seemed to be deepening and growing more intense, but after an hour it was clear that they were actually fading. One by one we pulled ourselves out of the stupor that the morning heat and being in our hammocks had induced. We began talking and talking, analyzing and analyzing. Dennis seemed the most out of it. Dave and Vanessa were uncertain that anything at all had "really" happened. Ev was distant, and I was feeling definitely stoned and immersed in the surreal perception that had been mine since the chaotic opening of the day.

Then I realized that something was wrong. Apprehension was outrunning reality, as it always does. For everyone else, nothing had happened. As we talked, it came out that no one could hear Dennis in their mind except me. And actually, they were all wondering what was going on, growing more alarmed as they couldn't help but conclude that I was losing my mind. We were entering what I later came to view as the next phase, which was a period of confusion for all. Dennis was definitely disengaged from reality. I would talk to him and he wouldn't know he was being spoken to. He broke into conversations because he didn't know anyone else was speaking. As the gulf between our perceptions became clear, we all felt the need to return to normal, to touch the basics; a visit to the priest's outdoor shower was suggested and seized upon, since we were all filthy and covered with the grime of the night's fire tending.

We gathered up our scattered clothing. During this effort, we discovered that Dennis had thrown his glasses away along with his boots and everything else. Disheveled and disoriented, we retraced the path to the mission, searching unsuccessfully for the lost pair of glasses.

A group of Witoto gazed at us as we passed and then roared with appreciative laughter. "They know. They know what has been done," the voice in my head assured me. They were certainly beaming and chortling about something. On we walked toward the mission and its shower in the sunshine.

Dennis wouldn't stop talking, and it was really no longer possible to communicate with him. Consensus among the others was building that we had a crisis on our hands, but it wasn't out of control yet. I agreed with them that *ayahuasca* was very peculiar, and they thought that the passage of a few hours would smooth everything out. My conclusion was that something real and unanticipated had happened, that Dennis had done something, and that some kind of odd pharmacological effect had been unwittingly manipulated. But the effect had behaved only in part as we had expected, and so we were cast we knew not where. I was calm and could at least participate in the social situation. Though I was moved by emotions that sent tears of joy streaming down my face, I wasn't out of touch with reality.

"We'll wait for tomorrow. Dennis will come down," I tried to reassure the rest of the group.

Everyone seemed to be finding their way back to their normal psychic equilibrium save Dennis and myself. While I was burdened with odd but wonderfully expanded perceptions, his wandering ideas and wild eyes indicated that he was having real difficulty getting his feet on the ground. After our shower, on the way back to the forest, I mentioned all of these things to him, but acting as sly as Hamlet in his madness, he replied in riddles and with the mimicry of dead relatives. I could get nothing out of him; I continued to assume that a night's sleep would set him right. When we returned to camp, I insisted that he lie down, which he did.

"Now can we call the press conference?" he inquired from his hammock, as the rest of us moved about trying to reestablish order.

CHAPTER TWELVE

IN THE VORTEX

*In which we discover that the Universe is
stranger than we can suppose, Dennis makes a
shamanic journey, and our group is polarized
and divided.*

To SPARE VANESSA THE WALK back to the river
we decided that she and Dave would stay the night at our hut.
Their two hammocks were hung next to our three. It was crowded,
but we dined well that evening, and except for the occasional
oblique or incomprehensible comment from Dennis, the surface of
things seemed to have been restored. Vanessa's ankle remained
bad, and much attention was directed toward this difficulty, perhaps due to its palpable nature in contrast to most of what was
going on. I still felt utterly changed and made new, both removed
from everyone and content to let events unfold as they would. I was
assured by the new thing inside of me that however odd things appeared all was very, very well.

The last rave of this long, amazing day came after dinner in the
firelight. From his hammock Dennis broke the silence to explain
that this night in our dreams we would learn a series of things that
would end with us severing our connection to our bodies long before morning. We would reassemble in our perfected, virtual bodies

on the bridge of a starship that was in geo-synchronous orbit twenty-two thousand miles above the Amazon Basin.

This was the second self-limiting prophecy that had been made since the experiment, the first being that morning's effort to meditate backward to one's birth. In retrospect I now see that this "eschatological hysteria" was one of the chief ways in which my thinking seemed radically different. Over the next weeks and years there would be many more of these self-testing prophecies, many scenarios of the possible way the world might undergo final, total, and complete eschatological transformation. Like Old Testament prophets or Hellenistic alchemists, we felt that we were caught up in a cosmic drama of fall and redemption.

Four days from the experiment, five, seven, ten, sixteen, twenty-one, forty, sixty-four—all were times awaited with hope and willful suspension of disbelief and all came and went with the eschaton still all-pervading, yet still very elusive. The idea of a dimension-roving lens vehicle, once articulated, was never far away. It haunted Dennis's and my waking fantasy, our secret hopes, and our nightly dreams.

Dennis's statement about the awaiting starship was also the first appearance of the UFO image in his thought since the experiment, a theme to be articulated in a thousand ways in the days that followed. The equation lapis = self = UFO was the operating assumption of Dennis's long voyage of self-discovery and return. With these images of death-in-sleep and rebirth-inside-a-starship ringing in our minds, we turned in, thoroughly exhausted.

I stress that the hut was crowded, with hammocks strung from every available beam. It was difficult to move about without jostling one's neighbors through the tugging and twisting of the many ropes. We must have retired around ten o'clock. I slept soundly until sometime many hours later, which I took to be after two or so. I rose to take the traditional middle of the night piss that the use of condensed milk induces in explorers. Sitting up in my hammock, I struggled for matches and lit a candle. In the silent night I heard the inrush of my own exclamation of amazement. An intense, triple-layered corona of light was shimmering out from the candle flame for a distance of about four feet. A deep, iridescent blue alternated with an equally pure orange. I was immediately reminded of the aura of light that surrounds the body of the resurrected Christ in the painting by Matthias Grünewald. I understood that Grünewald must have seen the same thing that I was seeing now and later incorporated it into his "resurrection."

Simultaneously, as though I was having a yet deeper thought, I somehow intuitively "understood" that the distortion or polarizing of the light of the flame was an effect caused by the distortion of psychic space-time induced by our experiment and the nearby, ubiquitous presence of the lapis. This thought was followed by another: Perhaps the temporal and spatial distance from the stone could be gauged by the intensity of the colors in the aura of light around a simple candle. The distortion of light from a candle might act as a detector of the philosopher's stone. I recalled Diogenes prospecting for the good with a lantern. Was that what he was doing? I thought of the phrase, "It is better to light one candle than to curse the darkness," and laughed.

I awakened Ev and she sleepily confirmed the colors around the candle, but it communicated nothing to her of what it communicated to me. She rolled over, and when I returned from going outside, she was snoring softly. As I climbed back into my hammock, I counted heads and noted that everyone was present and asleep. I lay awake a long time, thinking. All seemed still.

As breakfast unfolded the following morning, the sixth of March, it became clear that the restful sleep I had imagined we had all shared had been anything but that. From Dennis, still disorganized but expansive, comments emerged that he had, or imagined he had, a *very* active night. Upon close questioning, it came out that he was completely convinced that sometime during the night he had arisen and dressed and then had a series of nocturnal adventures. These involved going alone in the darkness to the thundering immensity of the *chorro* over a mile away, then returning to climb and spend some time in a large tree near the edge of the mission, then making his way back across the pasture and returning to his hammock, strung among all the others. The thought of him wandering around during the night on those trails, without his glasses, falling in and out of shamanic ecstasy, perhaps howling and otherwise paleolithically comporting himself, was too much for me. It was a breech of the collective cool. Even though I was 90 percent

certain that it had never really happened, I was determined to eliminate all possibility of such rambles in the future.

Dennis's story was the classic description of a shamanic night
journey. He said that he had gone to the *chorro* and had meditated
in the mission cemetery we had visited before. He had begun to return to camp when he confronted a particularly large *Inga* tree near
where the path skirted the edge of the mission. On impulse, he had
climbed it, aware as he did that the ascent of the world tree is the
central motif of the Siberian shamanic journey. As he climbed the
tree, he felt the flickering polarities of many archetypes, and as he
reached the highest point in his ascent, something that he called
"the vortex" opened ahead of him—a swirling, enormous doorway
into time. He could see the Cyclopean megaliths of Stonehenge
and beyond them, revolving at a different speed and at a higher
plane, the outlines of the pyramids, gleaming and marble-faceted
as they have not been since the days of pharaonic Egypt. And yet
farther into the turbulent maw of the vortex, he saw mysteries that
were ancient long before the advent of man—titanic archetypal
forms on worlds unimagined by us, the arcane machineries of sentient agencies that swept through this part of the galaxy when our
planet was young and its surface barely cooled. This machinery,
these gibbering abysses, touched with the cold of interstellar space
and aeon-consuming time, rushed down upon him. He fainted, and
time—who can say how much time—passed by him.

He next found himself in the pasture a few hundred feet from
his newly discovered *axis mundi*. If he fell from the tree, it did not
seem to have hurt him. Amazement, exaltation, fear, and confusion
were all present in his thoughts. The continuum seemed to be
shredding and ripping itself to pieces before his eyes, time and
space swirling the artifacts of twenty-thousand years of human
striving into a vortex of apocalyptic contradictions. In that state of
fear and exultation, at the depth of the revelation of humanity's
destiny among the stars, Dennis returned to our camp and noise-
lessly returned to his hammock, or awakened there from a dream of
the same thing.

Twenty-four hours had passed since the attempt to hyper-
carbolate human DNA. It was apparent that Dennis was not pulling
out of the induced state of shamanic excitement as quickly as we

had hoped. This was too long to be considered a normal reaction to mushrooms or *ayahuasca*. Two choices presented themselves to explain the situation:

The first was the position that Vanessa and Dave leaned toward, and it said that the strain of the journey and the recent psilocybin tripping had contributed to activate a shamanic archetype in Dennis that had been latent all along. This was now overt and carrying a strong transference potential to which I was succumbing by being unable to recognize my brother's condition as a potentially pathological state. This was the source of much of our differences of opinion on how to proceed.

A second explanation, the one Ev and I leaned toward, took a biochemical rather than a psychological approach. It said that Dennis, through his unusual diet of alkaloids and the experiment he performed, had inhibited some enzyme system that would normally return one from the heights of a hallucinogenic trip, but in this case had somehow become inoperative. The most likely candidate for this would be the monoamine oxidase (or MAO) system, which is responsible for rendering many hallucinogens into inoperative byproducts. The phenomenon of irreversible MAO inhibition is known to occur with some drugs and is a condition that takes nearly two weeks to correct itself. Though the compounds in *Banisteriopsis caapi* are known to usually reverse their MAO inhibition in four to six hours, as subsequent events show, this explanation was doubtless some part of the story, since Dennis was to be in the grip of his shamanic ravings for nearly two weeks.

After years of thought, my own explanation continues to lean heavily on the second idea for an operational explanation. I do not believe that Dennis was predisposed to an archetypal submergence. I believe that somehow, in a single moment, he bound up all the MAO in his body, and his derangement was due to the lag time that was required to rebuild his MAO level from a complete and sudden inhibition. I believe that this sudden depletion was caused by his experiment and that vocally induced, resonance canceling of the forces that normally operate in these molecules caused major changes in his body chemistry. In short, I believe that he induced an irreversible MAO inhibition in his body through the use of psilocybin and his voice and will.

If this is true, then the implication for humankind may be every
bit as great as we, in our inflated state of mind, supposed, since it
hints at a pharmacological technology by which humankind might
explore the parallel continuum whose interaction with our own existence is signified by the visionary experience. We had brushed
against an effect that someday may open a door to all the worlds
teeming in our dreams and imaginations. Certainly it is an effect to
be studied and learned from. Today, years after the experiment, it
still seems full of great promise. My continued interest in these matters is based on the personal belief that some unusual and still unconfirmed effect was at work in our experiment, something like the
principle of resonance-canceling that Dennis was so intrigued by.

Breakfast on March 7, the second day following the experiment, was closed with a hot discussion of whether Dennis had really gone to the *chorro* or only dreamed that he had. As the
rhetoric exhausted itself, Vanessa drew me away from the hut, and
we walked along as I went to the spring for water. She wanted to
have a talk, the gist of which was that since there were wide differences in diagnosis of what was going on, so there were wide
differences concerning what should be done.

"But since Dennis is your brother and you have strong opinions on this subject, I will defer in favor of what you think should
be done here. At least for the moment."

I was grateful for the margin of time contained in Vanessa's
chosen course. The whole question revolving around Dennis's state
of mind concerned how and especially *when* he would pull out of it.
Any diagnosis had to come forth with an operational prediction on
that vital point. I was assured by the inner voice that all was well,
but I wanted Vanessa to understand that I appreciated her approach
even if I did not agree with it.

I understood from Vanessa's demeanor that we would be left
pretty much to ourselves in the forest house. We could expect her
and Dave only as visitors, and already the possibility of retreat
from the jungle isolation was becoming a faint but growing theme.

Thus the stage was set for the next five days of chaos at La
Chorrera, from the seventh to the twelfth of March. From that day
onward, Ev became a kind of liaison with the rest of the world of
the mission. She arrived in the late afternoon and departed each

morning, cooking an evening and morning meal and being very game about it all, considering that she had only fallen in with our little group three weeks before.

During this time, Dennis very slowly got better. His mind seemed to have been quite literally turned inside out. During certain times each day when he became more coherent he said that the experience had catapulted him to the edge of the Riemannian pseudosphere that is the universe, in which even parallel lines intersect. He claimed he had to come back into ordinary space and was regressing inward through level after level after level. Very strange things went on during this period. He could hear my mind working. He was telepathic; of this I have no doubt. He could do perfect voice imitations of our mother and father. He became many people, imitating them perfectly. He saw me as a kind of shaman or messiah. He referred to me as "The Teach," not teacher or teaching but The Teach, a kind of personified alien ambassador empowered to negotiate the entry of the human species into the councils of higher intelligence.

And there was much more; a vision of twentieth-century history, building the lens, and the end of time. He said that the discovery of a higher physical dimension was a few years ahead of us, but somehow linked up to Egypt, to *Acacia* tryptamine cults, to Tibet eight thousand years ago, to *Bön-po* shamanic magic and the *I Ching*. All these ideas were in constant circulation while he talked and performed incessantly.

No notes exist from this period. So filled was I with the assumption that we were abiding in eternity that I felt no need to write at all. As the world seemed to me to grow more perfect, I determined at some point that I would write a poem, but that moment never came. Nothing is coherent or remains connected from those five days. I remember it as the most intense time that I have ever gone through. There was not an emotional or intellectual chord in the human register that was not rung again and again in a thousand variations.

In the notes made weeks after those times I could only summarize those five days by labeling them, absurdly: fire, water, earth, man, peace. I sat and Dennis raved. Without his glasses, his eyes were wild, piercing, and unsettling to look into. Since the night of his shamanic ramble, I had formed the intention not to sleep but to stand watch constantly with him day and night. For the next nine days I neither slept nor needed sleep. Though I know that such cases are on record, for years afterward I took my lack of a need for sleep for nine days as the most solid argument for the reality of the forces with which we experimented. Not only did I not need to sleep, but I was constantly thinking in a rich, calm, image-filled way that made my normal thought process seem a pale and jerkily animated shadow. This mental power continued throughout the sleepless period and long afterward.

The time that we were moving through seemed made of the reflections of what had preceded it and what was to follow. The first night of my decision not to sleep, March 6, was passed in deep reverie and a growing amazement that I was actually functioning without any apparent need of sleep. In the last of the darkness before dawn, at a time I felt matched exactly the time when we performed the experiment two days before, I heard Dennis stir in his hammock inside the hut. Then I heard him make, low but strong and clear, the same undulating howl that had catapulted us into a new world forty-eight hours before. Three times it sounded, just as something in my mind assured me that it would.

The last howl was drawn out as before; it rose and fell for perhaps a minute. Then, as it faded away, I again heard the cock's crow drifting across the whitening air from the mission. Why did things happen with such symmetry, as though a huge, ordered form was trying to surface in the very organization of the reality around us? Sunrise flamed across the sky and another of those titanic days began. The thing in my mind stirred to meet the challenges to reason that charged each new moment. All that remains of those times are images and incidents, only metaphors acting as sustained themes. All was myth-making and image-making, mercurial, meta-leveled, ever-flowing.

CHAPTER THIRTEEN

AT PLAY IN THE FIELDS
OF THE LORD

In which Dennis and I explore the contents of
our mutual illusions and illuminations.

THE MORNING OF THE SEVENTH, Ev returned
with Dave and Vanessa to the river, and for the first time in two
days Dennis and I were alone. The atmosphere was one of calm. I
busied myself sorting through and arranging the equipment. Our
campsite was again spic and span. Dennis alternated between calm-
ness and long harangues on a supra-cosmic scale as in *The Starmaker*
of Olaf Stapleton. He imitated, personified, described, and otherwise invoked immense Gnostic and Manichaean entities that were
struggling on a cosmic scale. The ageless struggle between good
and evil was being enacted as a fourth dimensional comic book in
the labyrinth of his mind. But he was not without humor, occasionally moaning out that he felt "like an old Mandaean," then collaps-
ing with laughter at this cleverness.

I sat in my hammock and verbally participated as much as I
could in all of this, though it was clear that Dennis had no difficulty
in maintaining the conversation on his own. In fact, he seemed to
have hit the main vein of the fountain of sprung verse.

I closed my eyes for a moment and there, fully formed beneath my eyelids, was the first of what I considered to be teachings or messages. It was a beautiful, recursive geometric form with four "petals." The voice in my mind informed me that this was "the valentine curve." Obviously the four petals of the curve looked somewhat like a valentine or a bleeding heart. I thought for an instant of the heart-shaped fruit I had fashioned into a water pipe. No obvious connection . . . the image slid. I got my notebook and drew the valentine curve, at first crudely, later much more smoothly. It made me think of Basil Valentine, a fifteenth-century alchemist and author of *The Triumphal Chariot of Antimony*. I had read the book, but could remember virtually nothing about it. I thought too of Valentinius, the Alexandrian Gnostic of the second century, and his doctrine that the material world was the condensed emotion of the errant Sophia, who had selfishly created a universe without undergoing any union except with herself. The concrescence of the anguish of the Sophia, the lowest of the Archons, into the physical world was an idea closely related to our own alchemical efforts. The condensation of emotion into matter; that theme was hair-raising. It was the theme that had brought us to the Amazon. Alchemy was the gnosis of material transformation. Clues seemed everywhere; everything was webbed together in a magical fabric of meaning and affirmation and mystery.

During that day and the days that followed, thoughts and ideas of all sorts formed in my mind unbidden and would lead inevitably to some further expansion of the set of themes that we had organized our lives around. One of those themes that was seized upon and amplified, at first slowly and then more rapidly, radically and inclusively, was the set of ideas and relationships contained in the *I Ching*, the Chinese oracle. These ancient and fragmentary commentaries on a still more ancient set of sixty-four oracular ideograms, called hexagrams, had long been of interest to me as part of my general interest in non-causal forms of logic. In fact, I had first learned of the *I Ching* from reading Jung, who suggested that the meaningful juxtaposition of a hexagram with a situation in the outer world, the juxtaposition that allows the *I Ching* to be used as a fortune-telling device, hinted at a noncausal connection between the inner mental world and objective exterior reality. Jung named this phenomenon synchronicity.

For several years it had been my habit to throw the *I Ching*, which consists of manipulating forty-nine stalks of yarrow or in my case bamboo skewers whose configurations create the hexagrams, at each new and full moon and to record the throws on a slip of paper, which I kept inside the back cover of my copy of the book. The first day following the experiment the voice inside my head suggested that I get out my record of the hexagrams that I had thrown. I could hardly then imagine the insights and conclusions to which this simple suggestion would eventually lead. I went through this record of throws looking for an instance when I had thrown the first of the sixty-four hexagrams; upon finding that, I returned to the beginning of the list and looked for a record of the second hexagram being thrown, and so on. My list of throws covered three years and contained about eighty throws and their changes.

After a half-hour of the exercise I determined that, according to my record, I had thrown each of the sixty-four hexagrams at least once in the three years leading up to that moment. This mildly improbable fact seemed charged with significance to me. The likelihood of occurrence for each hexagram is not equal, and the odds of getting all the hexagrams in so few throws seemed unusual. It felt to me as if I had a kind of secret identity that I was in the process of uncovering. It proved that I was somehow a reflection of the microcosm and had been chosen somehow to be in precisely the situation in which I found myself. Tears came easily at this personal verification of the ordered pattern of life whose designs I was discovering everywhere. I composed myself and then, at the strong prompting of the inner wave of understanding, I quietly burned the record of my *I Ching* throws. It was a very uncharacteristic thing for me to do.

Dennis watched all of this and then delivered himself of one of the many riddles that he was to propound over the next few days. "What can you do with a hole in a stick that you can't do with a stick in a hole?," he bellowed across the sandy expanse to where I stood by the fire. I assumed that this answer involved a dig at the cheerful and steamy assumptions of Tantra in favor of the idea that a pipe was the superior vehicle of inter-dimensional travel and *that* was what you could do.

An hour or so later and after a long silence that was uncharacteristic of his new condition, Dennis looked up from his meditations and announced that he had just realized that he could cause any telephone to ring by simply concentrating on an image that he refused to divulge. He went further than that and claimed that he could make phones ring at anytime in the past during which telephones existed. To demonstrate this ability he dialed Mother sometime in the fall of 1953. He caught her in the act of listening to Dizzy Dean call a World Series game. And according to Dennis she refused to believe that he was on the phone, since she could see his three-year-old form asleep in front of her. He told her he would call back earlier and then spent the rest of the afternoon calling everyone he could think of at various times in the past, carrying on animated conversations and chortling to himself about the minds he was blowing and the wonders of what he called "Ma Bell." And thus did the afternoon of March 6 pass.

A reasonable conclusion would have been to suppose that Dennis was toxically schizophrenic and that we should leave the Amazon. What muddied the water considerably was me. I was comparatively normal except for one thing: I insisted that everything was all right and that Dennis knew exactly what he was doing.

"It's okay," I attempted to assure the others. "He has done what he set out to do and now people should try to relax until this all plays out."

I felt this way although I knew nothing about how he had performed the experiment or discovered the theory. I knew only that from that dawn moment when we looked at the mushroom immediately after the experiment something very bizarre had happened to me.

I was in a very strange place. I felt as though I had become myself. My contact with the voice was like that of a student to a teacher. It let me know things. Beyond any possibility of argument I knew things that I couldn't ordinarily know. Ev had gone through the experiment, but nothing at all had happened to her. My other friends seemed very distant. They couldn't understand what was happening and preferred to reject us. Everyone thought that everyone else was crazy. In fact, relative to their normal behavior everyone did behave very oddly.

The main thing the unseen teacher said was, "Do not worry. Do not worry, because there is something that you *have* to get straight about. Your brother will recover. Your companions will take care of him. Do not worry, but listen. You have to get this down." Within hours after the experiment this started impinging on me— something that I must figure out.

This morning, the seventh, Dennis seemed to me to be more down to earth, but to such a slight degree that it was a matter of opinion whether he had made any improvement at all. I noticed with interest that while he seemed disoriented and his ideation was structurally as wild and woolly as ever, in content there had been a definite sort of improvement. On the day before, he had seemed to be spread over so vast an amount of time and space that there was little to be identified out of the cosmic churning that he was undergoing. On that day, to find even our own galaxy in his mind had been impossible. On the second day, he awoke within the galaxy and his visions and fantasies remained within it. Had that been the only instance of his telescoping back into himself, it would not have been worth noting, but the fact was that each step of his return to a normal state of mind was accomplished this way. The day after he reached the confines of the galaxy, he entered the solar system, condensing through its planets over several days until he identified only with Earth. Coalescing and condensing through the ecology of his home world, he came to think of himself as all humanity and was able to vividly relive all of its history. Later still, he became the embodiment of all the members of our vast and peculiar Irish family stretching back till before Judges had given us Numbers or Leviticus committed Deuteronomy, as James Joyce put it. They were of all kinds and he played them all: hard-rock miners, a seventeenth-century cleric sweating beneath a burden of lust, bombastic patriarchs and thin-faced women one generation, and women with shoulders like field hands and tongues like hedgeclippers the next. After a good bit of lolling around in those environs he was finally resolved down into our immediate family and progressed from there to confront and resolve the question of whether he was Dennis or Terence. Finally and thankfully, he came to rest with the realization that *he* was Dennis, returned from the edge of the universe of mind, restored and reborn, a shaman in the fullest sense of the word.

But that reintegration and recovery was still twenty days in the future as we walked to the pasture the morning of March 7, just as we had on the morning after the experiment. We walked to the top of a small rise on which grew a young tree. *Ama*, the Witoto word for "brother," had become one of the many new forms of address that Dennis had created for me. Now as we walked along, we kept our eyes open for mushrooms, as had become our habit even though all thought of eating mushrooms was behind us now.

Dennis strode ahead of me and made his way to the tree. Bending down and parting the grasses at the base of the tree, he pointed to the letters A M A carved in the bark. It was a carving at least several years old. The incident was confusing. How had Dennis known the carving was there and what did it mean anyhow? He answered my questions by sweeping his hand toward the dawn horizon and announcing that this was the planet Venus, or the archetypal world of Venus, I have no idea which. These assertions that flew completely in the face of reason were very hard to take and enkindled in me brief stabs of despair for his state of mind, though most of the time I was able to convince myself that he was improving and returning from the unseen worlds that were so vivid to him that he could see nothing else.

I tried directing the developing fantasy of my brother—I used the idea that the re-creation of the scattered self was as an alchemical act with immense personal and historical significance. Each morning for several days after the fifth of March we would walk to the pasture and I would demand of him "the stone." Neither of us perceived these goings on through anything like the light of normal consciousness. The world seemed filled with a near-bending wonder and power that assured me that all things were possible and that the course of things *in the light of this* was moving in the right direction.

"Be amazed at nothing; you are to receive the kingship of the father," spoke the quiet voice from hyperspace. "The Mystery of the wellspring and the datepalm will unfold."

I watched my own understanding of the connections between what we were doing and classical alchemy move by vast intuitive leaps to implicate Gerhard Dorn, Robert Fludd, and Count Michael Maier, names associated with the finest literary flowering of the alchemical mind. And equally associated with a view of man and nature that had perished with the rise of modern chemistry.

Yet I was haunted by their alchemical imagery. The thirty-sixth emblem of Maier's *Atlanta Fugiens* is a wonderful visual pun that connects the cube of *Stropharia cubensis* with the UFO, the hyperobject seen in the sky. It was an image that was constantly before me through those times. John Dee, with his angel-haunted skrying stone and the occult geometry of his cryptic opus *The Hieroglyphic Monad*, is mixed up in the same set of images. Why? Did this circle of alchemical adepts penetrate the mystery to a secret undreamed of by their contemporaries and competition?

Images flashed before my mind's eye: Nicholas Flamel and his wife, Pernelle, their legendary love affair and their unknown end. *Mutus Liber* ("the silent book") depicts a couple working at a furnace; it almost looks as though they are drying mushrooms. How sophisticated did alchemy become before Enlightenment science scattered the adepts and rendered their control language inoperable?

In the pasture each foggy morning, when I demanded of Dennis that he give me the philosopher's stone, it was both pressure upon him to reformulate his consciousness into a unity and something that served to focus the transference potential that was so intense as to again and again threaten to engulf us. Not sleeping, being awake constantly, I was both in the world of the developing situation at La Chorrera and also in the world into which my brother had become psycho-topologically enmeshed—a dimensional vortex beyond which seemed to be eternity, the land of the dead, all human history, and the UFOs. It was a world whose unseen, cybernetic chroniclers spoke to us telepathically in our minds and revealed that we and all humanity were in the act of once again becoming able to go between these alien dimensions and our own to re-establish the eschatological shamanism lost scores of millennia ago.

At one point I picked up a stick and in the sandy soil of our living area I scratched the shorthand symbol for "and." I called it "the ampersand." I found its binding fold in one corner of a quaternary structure to be very satisfying. I began to imagine this symbol as the symbol of the condensation of the alchemical lapis. To me it appeared to be the natural symbol for a four-dimensional universe somehow bound into a 3-D matrix. I spoke of it as the ampersand for several days, then I called it "the eschaton." This I imagined as a basic unit of time; the combination and resonance among the set of eschatons in the universe determined which of the possible worlds allowed by physics would actually undergo the formality of occurring. "The formality of actually occurring" was a phrase from Whitehead that kept echoing through my thoughts like the refrain of a half-forgotten song. I imagined that at the end of time all the eschatons would resonate together as a unity and thereby create an ontological transformation of reality—the end of time as a kind of garden of earthly delights.*

Occasionally I would seem to catch the mechanics of what was happening to us in action. Lines from half-forgotten movies and snippets of old science fiction, once consumed like popcorn, reappeared in collages of half-understood associations. Punch lines from old jokes and vaguely remembered dreams spiraled in a slow galaxy of interleaved memories and anticipations. From such experiences I concluded that whatever was happening, part of it involved all the information that we had ever accumulated, down to the most trivial details. The overwhelming impression was that something possibly from outer space or from another dimension was contacting us. It was doing so through the peculiar means of using every thought in our heads to lead us into telepathically induced scenarios of extravagant imaginings, or deep theoretical understandings, or in-depth

---

*These were the first faint stirrings of thoughts that were to lead eventually to the development of my own theory of time described in *The Invisible Landscape*. These early intuitions bore no resemblance to the final theory; and it is just as well that they did not, for at that time I would have been completely unable to understand the theory that I was finally to develop. It took years of reading and self-education to keep track of the things that the internal voice was saying. Its presence and persistence over the years since La Chorrera has been amazing. That day at La Chorrera, the voice had a holistic and systems-oriented approach to things that did seem to be slightly of another order—not enough to be alarming, but enough to repeatedly remind me that the ideas I was producing were coming fully organized from somewhere else, and I was nothing more than a message decipherer, hard-pressed to keep up with a difficult, incoming code.

scannings of strange times, places, and worlds. The source of this unearthly contact was the *Stropharia cubensis* and our experiment.

Our collective intelligence was not compromised, but what was compromised was the ability of reason to give a coherent account of what was going on, as paradox, coincidence, and general synchronistic strangeness began to increase exponentially. Into the vacuum left by the collapse of reason rushed a staggering array of exotic intuitions about why things were as they were.

🍄 🍄 🍄

Shortly after breakfast on the morning of the seventh, the third day following the experiment, Dennis announced a new teaching. He said that one could see any point in time by closing one's eyes, visualizing an eight, turning it on its side so that it approximated the sign for infinity, and then mentally sliding the two closed rings over each other to form a circle, shrinking the circle to a dot, and thinking the word "please" and the target point in space-time. Usually I knew not whence these images came to him; however, this time I was amazed. I recalled with perfect clarity that six weeks before, shortly before I left Vancouver, British Columbia, I had gone to a dentist as part of the standard pre-travel tune-up. While in the waiting room, I had read a several-months-old journal of some Canadian education association. In that journal, which I had not discussed with anyone, was a very short article about teaching-machines and very young children. The "Picture This" scenario with which the article opened was of a child looking at a figure-eight on a television screen, rolling it on its side, squeezing it together, etc., etc. It was a bit of media flotsam that my brother, or something working through my brother, was able to lift right out of my mind weeks after I had forgotten it. Something was able to refashion and use our memories in whatever absurd way that it wished.

"Now can we call that press conference, Bro?" Dennis inquired again from his hammock swinging hypnotically in the shadows.

CHAPTER FOURTEEN

LOOKING BACKWARD

*In which several miracles are recounted, not the
least of which is the appearance of James and
Nora Joyce disguised as poultry.*

TWO MONTHS AFTER ALL of these experiences,
around mid-May of 1971, I was moved to try to sum up the particularly bizarre and possibly physics-compromising incidents that I
could then recall. Here is what I wrote at that time—a time when
I was concerned to refute the idea that schizophrenia was a magic
word explaining all that we had undergone:

> *May 12, 1971*
>
> *I have almost two months' perspective on the events surrounding
> our experience at La Chorrera, and I can clearly recognize that
> both my brother and I evinced the classic symptoms of the two gen-
> erally distinguished categories of process schizophrenia. He ap-
> peared to manifest the withdrawn characteristics of essential
> schizophrenia while my behavior was of a more outward and
> paranoid sort. Nevertheless, I am unable to make the assumption
> that our experiment was therefore "nothing but" two simultane-
> ously occurring cases of schizophrenia. With the full knowledge that
> such a position argues that I may still be experiencing residual*

symptoms of the illness, I maintain that we were in fact dealing with an objective phenomenon that, though of a highly peculiar nature inexorably bound up with psychic processes, does have its basis in the molecular ideas we were in the process of investigating. As empirical evidence of this viewpoint, I mention the following points, which seem to me to set our experience outside the realm of mental illness:

The suddenness with which the symptoms developed following our actual experiment: Within a few minutes after we completed our pre-planned experimental procedures, my brother began to disengage himself from the continuum of shared perceptions and at this same time I underwent a willing suspension of disbelief and began to experience the cybernetic unit that we had predicted would be a part of the effect we would cause if we were successful in our attempt to generate a superconducting genetic matrix and harmine bond.

The integrated or dovetail aspect of our shared disassociation: meaning that though both of us were exhibiting the symptoms of types of schizophrenia, the fantasy, the ideas, and the understanding which we were experiencing was shared. While my brother thought of me as the shaman messiah in all manifestations, I perceived him as the condensed mind-lens making a return journey across the universe that might have been one logical outcome of our experiment. Each of us alone would have given the clear appearance of being deluded; however, each of us seemed to offer elusive proof of the correctness of the other's position. I might add that though no one else could understand my brother's peculiar mental processes, I believed I could discern depth and an integrated understanding which seemed to be behind them—but at the same time I understood that his apparent lack of integration was due to the fact that his thinking was moving backward in some fundamental way. In the same way that a film running in reverse seems to present a spectacle of wild and irrational confusion, yet manages in the end to have things in their proper places, my brother's ideas and physical movement seemed to me to be simply the exact reverse of logical expectations.

Dennis felt confident that the brain operates on the principle of a hologram. This was an idea originated by Karl Pribram, a neurophysiologist at Stanford, that was very much in vogue in our circles then. It neatly explains the fact that a large percentage of the physical brain can be damaged or removed with no impairment of memory, since a portion of a hologram contains all the information embedded in the larger whole from which it has been taken. Dennis had speculated before our experiment that he might receive a reverse image of my brain/mind organization for a brief time during the experiment. In listening to his free associations after the reversal, I became certain that this had in fact occurred—but for a much longer time than we had anticipated. In fact, I still believe that our only error throughout this entire experiment and the events following it has been our inability to correctly predict the duration of the process. I believe that our understanding of the mechanics of the process, aside from its duration, has been correct, though still incomplete. Time is still, in other words, the crux of this matter. At times my brother's free associations consisted of incidents which I had experienced more than a year previously and more than ten thousand miles from where Dennis was then living—incidents about which I had spoken to no one.

Dennis seemed to possess the ability to hear my mind working during the period immediately after the experiment. I illustrate by recalling an incident when I was sitting outside of our jungle hut listening to his free association, having noticed a few moments before that his muscles were almost rigid with the enormous physical energy associated with some types of schizophrenia. I worried that he might at some future time resist my efforts to keep him from wandering away on the archetypal errands that constantly motivated him to try to leave our immediate living area. It occurred to me that with such strength he could easily injure me or perhaps escape. While mulling over this disturbing possibility for the first time, I noticed that Dennis had left his hammock and was standing in the doorway of the hut; in a perfect imitation of our father's voice, he consoled me with the spoken thought that "Dennis is a good lad and would never do a thing like that."

Another incident occurred seven days after the reversal began, on March 12. Dennis announced that at eleven o'clock that night the "good shit" would appear. This was a reference to a kind of psilocybin-enriched hashish that Dennis claimed he had encountered a few months before leaving the States, but which would be impossible to find in the Amazon. This prediction of a material transmutation is not so odd when the alchemical concerns and ideas that led us into this experiment are recalled. After all, we had been reading and discussing alchemical ideas ever since I had discovered Jung's *Psychology and Alchemy*, at age fourteen. It had seemed to us then that in the projection of the phantasms of the unconscious onto matter, the alchemists were achieving a kind of psychedelic state of understanding. And, after all, isn't the alchemical faith really a faith that the world is made of language? That poetry can somehow be the final arbiter of authentic being?

After this conversation, Ev and I returned through rainy darkness to the forest house for the night and Dennis stayed at the river house with Vanessa and Dave, where he had moved by this time. As was our custom, we smoked a bit of our Santa Marta Gold before turning in. During this process, a small fragment fell, still burning, from the pipe. As I picked it up to return it to the pipe, the characteristic odor of Asian hashish was very noticeable. I examined the pipe's bowl very carefully and, though no change in the physical appearance of the smoking mixture had occurred, it was now definitely, to my own satisfaction and to that of skeptical Ev, behaving exactly like hashish—a luxury absolutely unknown in the Amazon in 1971.

This phenomenon persisted for about five minutes and then slowly faded, returning to the rational continuum of normal behavior for materials. It is to be regretted that this transmutation occurred with a substance where any skeptic will be at ease in venting his or her scorn. We are all familiar with the facile view that "potheads can't think straight," but to anyone who has in-depth involvement with these two substances the difference is unmistakable. This experience contained a number of parallels to the *Nijuli* movement among the Lawangan people of Borneo, who in the early 1920s promulgated ideas centering around the claim that a piece of resin had suddenly become longer through the influence of a flute played nearby, and that the lengthening of the resin foreshadowed human immortality.

Equally absurd and even more inexplicable was an incident that occurred on the morning of the fifth day, or the ninth of March. Dennis was sitting and raving to no one in particular with the normal camp life going on around him. I was sitting near the cooking fire sharpening the expedition's buck knife. I listened while Dennis raved, scanning his ramblings for a hint of a message. Suddenly I stopped my work.

"Are you my tailor?" He demanded, in a strong English accent. That seemed familiar to me from somewhere.

"All these reflections. See. It's me. Uh, but where is my tailor, my silly? Look, look at you, cor, why you've got my knickers on!"

I blushed deeply. I looked at the ground and said nothing. I felt very boxed in. Dennis was imitating the conversation that I had had with my English friend in Nepal, after I had come looking for her and had returned with her delirious to my room during our LSD and DMT trip more than a year before! This crazy conversation, which I had never discussed with anyone save her, was now booming out over our Amazon clearing in the mad voice of my brother.

It was hardly the sort of situation in which I wanted to exalt my brother's prowess as a telepath. I said nothing and waited, squirming, for his raving to drift off into incoherence. But I was impressed and convinced that he had somehow penetrated not only my immediate thoughts but my private memories.

Most important among the factors arguing for more than a simple case of simultaneous schizophrenia is the surprising durability of the model we have created out of the careful observation of the things that happened to us. No one can deny that the theory of the hyperspatial nature of hallucinogenic drug states, and the experiment my brother devised to test that theory, yielded spectacular results. But I have taken the fruits of the visionary revelation and carried them further, deconstructing them to discover a very elegant wave/particle theory of the nature of time. Quite unexpectedly, what I now propose, based on those initial experiences, is a revision of the mathematical description of time used in physics. According to this theory, the old notion of time as pure duration, visualized as a smooth plane or straight line, is to be replaced by the idea that time is a very complex fractal phenomenon with many ups and downs of many sizes over which the probabilistic universe

of becoming must flow like water over a boulder-strewn riverbed.
I had discovered the fractal dimension of time itself, a mathematical constant that replaces probability theory with a complex, but
elegant—indeed an almost magical—set of constraints on the expression of novelty.

After the first mushroom experience at La Chorrera, Dennis
and I were involved with two ideas in particular. These were the
motifs of the "teacher" and the insect. We could feel the overwhelming presence of some unseen, intelligent entity that seemed
to be observing and sometimes exerting influence to keep us moving gently toward a breakthrough. Because of the bizarre nature of
the DMT flash, with its seeming stress upon themes alien, insec-
tile, and interstellar, we were led to speculate that this teacher was
somehow a diplomat-anthropologist, come to give us the keys to
galactarian citizenship. We discussed this entity in terms of a giant
insect and through the insect trill of the Amazon jungle at midday
we seemed to be able to discern a deeper harmonic buzz that was
the signal keying us to the entity in hyperspace.

This sense of the presence of an alien third party was sometimes very intense, especially from March fifth to the tenth, after
which it faded off gradually. The image of the insect teacher gave
rise to numerous entomological speculations:

We thought at the time that the process we were involved with
was akin to giving birth to a child, but also much like the metamorphosis that occurs in the life cycle of insects, especially beetles,
moths, and butterflies. We "knew" that tryptamine was somehow
a major part of the solution to the enzyme mysteries surrounding
metamorphosis. We recalled certain unconfirmed reports of the
grub of a beetle eaten by Indians in Eastern Brazil for its hallucinatory effect.

The diffraction of light that occurs in natural phenomena such
as rainbows, peacock feathers, certain insects, and the colors that
appear on the surfaces of some metals during heating are persistent
motifs within a particular stage of the alchemical opus. The *cauda
pavonis* (the peacock's tail) is the brief stage that heralds the final

whitening; by exotic intuition I "knew" that the occurrence of such iridescence in nature indicated the presence of tryptamine-related compounds. Going further, I "knew" that the New World butterfly genus *Morphoea*, which is characterized by a large wing area usually entirely expressed in brilliant blue iridescence, would be an ideal group upon which to conduct research to illuminate this unstudied field.

I "knew" that the enzymes active in insect metamorphosis received molecular tuning and control through resonation induced by the harmonic strum of those forest insects with psychoactive tryptamine in their bodies. The tryptamine acted for them as an antenna to the electron spin resonance signal of the collective DNA, just as it did for us in the experiment. This signal is somehow keeping the entire class *Insecta* keyed into a point of stable equilibrium in the evolutionary stream. This odd notion explained the remarkable durability of insect adaptation, which, it is true, stabilized its basic evolutionary strategy some hundreds of millions of years ago. Such improbable insights into nature were delivered quite conversationally by the voice in my mind.

During this time, an iridescent black sheen from the mushrooms particularly caught my eye. This effect occurred when *Stropharia cubensis* grew in clumps, and larger mushrooms shed spores on the caps of smaller companions. Interestingly enough, this same metallic blue-black sheen was quite noticeably present on the carapace of a large and shrill beetle, a member of the genus *Buprestidae* that I had captured in the forest in the heat of the afternoon. It is known that the chitinous material that forms the outer covering of insects and spores is one of the most electron-dense materials in organic nature, being, in this property, similar to metal. The inner teacher urged that this specimen be analyzed for the presence of psychoactive tryptamines. If they were found, it would tend to confirm the idea that some species responsible for the buzz of the forest would be discovered to contain tryptamines. The tryptamines are the antenna of a bioelectronic system that allows the insects to key in on harmine present in local *Banisteriopsis* lianas and through them to key on the collective DNA network. I supposed that if a few of these species resonated, then other shrilling species could tune themselves to the molecular signal—

thus amplifying it and sustaining it through the forest for some hours of every day. Acoustically driven chemical reactions are well known; I felt sure that some of the life processes of the *Insecta* must be acoustically regulated by a few species in this way.

These unlikely and bizarre ideas unfolded themselves over those long, hot days, while Dennis lay confined to his hammock and I squatted on the earth nearby. By the third or fourth day following the experiment, I had learned enough of the new and peculiarly symbolic language that he was speaking that I was increasingly convinced that through it I could observe him achieving a gradual but progressive integration. Often, then, long silences would fall between the raves, and we would each drift off into a world of private reveries. Several times on such occasions I looked down and noticed with a weird thrill that my unconscious fingers had been engaged in gathering small twigs and arranging them in patterns as though they were to be miniature fires. This unconscious laying of small fires by my busy fingers seemed to me most extraordinary— I interpreted it then as a literal overflowing of the organizing energies that were being poured into me from some unknown source, the same source that was supplying me with energy so that I could matter of factly go without sleep.

Occasionally Dennis would interrupt me to ask that I or Ev smoke a cigarette for him. Questioning uncovered his belief that in hyperspace the topology of all human bodies is continuous and so he could effortlessly absorb what he needed directly out of our bodies. For five days life went on in that mode, a waking dream of overkill by palindrome and pun. We sent amazingly few waves of interaction out into the "real world" around us. No one stopped to stare at us or our camp; we seemed to have become invisible. The morning of the tenth of March changed that.

I had hardly been away from the hut and the short stretch of trail that separated it from the edge of the pasture for five days; so after breakfast on that particularly flawless morning I chatted with Dennis and found him calmer and more lucid than he had been at any time since the experiment. So composed and relaxed did he seem that I made the inevitable mistake of taking the situation for granted. I slipped away with Ev and the butterfly net for a relaxed stroll down the trail and deeper into the jungle.

The trail was of washed, white sand, inches deep in places and soft and inviting. We had walked hardly a quarter of a mile when lust overtook our interest in lepidoptera. Adding to our thrill was the risk of discovery by Witoto trail users. We tossed caution to the winds and were soon lost in each other. Pleasant it was in that verdant setting to part and defile the shaggy, slippery riches of Ev's sex. I thought of it as "Doing it for Vladimir." Verdant lust and butterflies were always entwined in Nabokov's enviable mind.

We were gone scarcely forty minutes, but returned to the hut and clearing to find it humming with a deserted, heart-sinking air of emptiness. I was no longer afraid that Dennis would wander into the forest and become lost. I was convinced that whatever his state of mind it did not include that sort of thing. What I did fear was that he might focus others' attention on us and the borderline area that we were investigating.

Leaving Ev at the camp in case Dennis should turn up, I ran to the pasture and across it to the mission on the far side. As I ran I was busy telling myself that he had probably just gone down to see Dave and Vanessa and that I would find him there. I was too preoccupied to notice that the bells of the mission, silent normally except on Sundays, had been pealing for some time. As I came over the rise that gave me a clear view of the river house and the lake below the *chorro*, I saw Vanessa leading Dennis toward the river house. I could sense as I arrived that the situation was more difficult than I had hoped.

Vanessa was angry and had seized the situation to drive home her point. It seemed that Dennis must have bolted from his hammock the moment Ev and I had passed out of sight. He had gone straight to the mission, located the bell rope of the bell used to call the people to Mass, and had rung it furiously until the priest found Vanessa and Dave and they had none too gently persuaded Dennis to desist from his hijinks. Nevertheless, the already circulating rumor that one member of our expedition had gone a bit off the deep end was not eroded by this sudden and totally public outrage. The delicate political balance I had established allowing me to have my way in the matter of how to treat Dennis was now destroyed. Vanessa's idea that he should be moved to the river house was brought forth and endorsed by the priests and, I was told, by the police. Riding on the inner assurance that worry would be preposterous and acknowledging that I had completely lost control of the situation, I agreed to all suggestions.

Vanessa had more news. An airplane was coming. It was not coming to take us out, but it would enable us to begin our withdrawal, since it would allow one of us to get a lift over a hundred kilometers of jungle to San Raphael, where we had left the cache of equipment before making the overland march to La Chorrera. This was the only opportunity to fly rather than walk back to those supplies, and Vanessa pressed that we should take advantage of it. I agreed with everything. I assumed that the eruption of the millennium would soon obviate all such mundane concerns, but that was a fact that I would let others discover for themselves as they made their way into the ever-deepening dimension of the future.

Dave volunteered to go on the airplane—the decision was made almost at a moment's notice. He would reach our supplies and single-handedly undertake to have them and himself shipped up the Rio Putumayo and then back to Bogotá. We would meet him back there when and if we got out by some means not yet clear. A bag was hastily packed. The airplane came skimming in, and then it was gone again, and with shocking suddenness we were four.

Dennis was moved to the river house, and Vanessa and Ev became his nurses. I preferred to continue to live at the jungle house to avoid crowding. The debate continued as to whether the direction in his raving was toward improvement or whether he was only drifting further into the world in which he had become lost. As residents of Berkeley, we had all encountered acid casualties; comparison of Dennis's state with those lost souls was not reassuring. Dennis's move to the river was a turning point, for from then hence the effects the phenomenon unleashed were less in our minds and more in the world.

Through it all, even after the move, he and I were still after the lens-shaped object. What the teacher told me in the first few days after the experiment was, "You almost got it; you didn't quite get it." Or rather it used the metaphor of condensation: "It is condensing."

It was like a perfect alchemical metaphor. The stone is everywhere. It is here.

Dennis would say, "I can see the lapis. It is two hundred and fifty feet away to the left; it's down near the waterhole, hovering above the water." I continued to ask him each day for the stone, and each day the Sophic hydrolith—a.k.a., the universal panacea—would get closer in. There were freak lightning storms. Slowly I noticed that meteorological phenomena tended to concentrate in the southeast. I began to look there and whenever I did, I would see rainbows.

Our intuitions concerning what was going on ranged from the religiously profound to the utterly absurd. On the afternoon of the twelfth of March, Dennis underwent a few hours when he was able to respond, however cryptically, to the questions we put to him concerning how things appeared to him. This conversation went on at the river house underneath which a handsome rooster and his mate were living. He was perhaps the very cock that I heard crow at dawn on the day of the experiment and again two days later. There was a perky alertness about this cock and hen that had received comment among us before. This particular afternoon, Dennis called our attention to the little hen, saying that if one thought of her as art, then the achievement she represented was immense. Who could make such a hen? Only the one who could have fashioned the peculiar world that we had fallen into. And that was? He looked around expectantly, but finding no takers he delivered his own punch line:

"James Joyce."

Over the next few minutes he proceeded to make his case: that *Finnegans Wake* represented the most complete understanding yet achieved of the relation of the human mind to time and space and that therefore Joyce, at his death, had somehow been shouldered with the responsibilities of overseeing this corner of God's universe. In this Dennis was only following Wyndham Lewis, who made Joyce's ascent to eminence in the afterworld the subject of his novel *The Human Age*.

"Jim and Nora," as Dennis called the newly revealed deity and his consort, were both in and acting through everything at La Chorrera, particularly in the things that Joyce had loved. The little hen as the symbol of Anna Livia Plurabelle of the *Wake* was one of these things. It was Joyceaen humor that radiated outward from everything in our jungle Eden. These ideas were absurd but delightful, and they led me eventually to reread Joyce and to accept him as one of the true pioneers in the mapping of hyperspace. They did not, however, shed much light on our predicament at the time.

From the view of life as literature Dennis moved on. He reminded me that one of our alchemical analogues for the philosopher's stone, which we shared in our private code of associations as children, was a certain, small, silver key to a box of inlaid wood with a secret compartment that had belonged to our grandfather. I reminded him that the key had been lost since our childhood. I said that the ability to produce that key right then would prove the reality of Dennis's shamanic powers and ability to transcend normal space and time. The conversation took the form of a question-and-answer session that ended with Dennis demanding that I hold out my hand, and then, slapping his closed hand into my open one, letting out a loud, ludicrous squawk, and depositing in my palm a small, silver key.

At the time I was thunderstruck. We were hundreds of miles from anywhere. He was practically naked, yet the key before me was indistinguishable from the key of my childhood memories. Had he saved that key over all those years to produce it now, in the middle of the Amazon, to completely distort my notion of reality? Or was this only a similar key that Dennis had been carrying when he arrived in South America, but that I had somehow not noticed until he produced it? This seemed unlikely. He was confined to a room far from our stored equipment, and it was difficult to conceive of him becoming calm and organized enough to go to the baggage and carefully sort through it to find the secreted key. And anyway, it was I who had conceived of asking for the key; had he somehow tricked me into asking for the one object that he had brought with him to deceive me? This matter of the silver key, whether it was the original key or not, has never been satisfactorily settled. The original box was lost long ago, so the key was never tested. A final ironic note is added to the episode by the fact that both Dennis and I are fans of the stories of H. P. Lovecraft and so were aware of his story "Through the Gates of the Silver Key," a tale seething with many dimensions, strange beings, a cosmic time scale, and reckless, oddball adventurers like ourselves.

After Dennis was moved to the river house, there was no longer any need for my sleepless watch at night. But the lack of a need to sleep prevailed. I actually looked forward each night to the time when everyone would retire and I would have before me long hours of delicious, silent thought. Like the fox spirit of the *I Ching* who wanders eternally among the jeweled, night grasses, I wandered in the pastures and on the trails around La Chorrera. Sometimes I would sit beneath the AMA-initialed tree for hours, watching vast mandalas of time and space turn and glisten around me. At times I would walk with long strides, nearly loping, head thrown back, gazing at the every-colored stars. Effortlessly, the deeper something that shared my mind connected up the constellations for me and showed me the enormous Zodiacal machine of stellar fate that must have come to the ancients with the same suggestive force.

I immersed myself in millions of images of humankind in all times and places, understanding and yet struggling with the insoluble enigmas of being and human destiny. It was during those velvet, star-strewn, jungle nights that I felt closest to understanding the tripartite mystery of the philosopher's stone, the Alien Other, and the human soul. There is something human that transcends the individual and that transcends life and death as well. It has will, motive, and enormous power. And it is with us now.

I have come to believe that under certain conditions the manipulative power of consciousness moves beyond the body and into the world. The world then obeys the will of consciousness to the degree that the inertia of pre-existing physical laws can be overcome. This inertia is overcome by consciousness determining the outcome of the normally random, micro-physical events. Over time the deflection of micro-events from randomness is cumulative so that eventually the effects of such deflections is to shift the course of events in larger physical systems as well. Apparently, when wanting wishes to come true, patience is everything.

Is this just a fantasy, a grown man trying to explain to himself how wishes can come true? I don't think so. I have lived it and know that the greater the amount of time that consciousness has in which to make its effects felt, the greater the possibility becomes that the desired event will come to pass. It is as though subtle pressure toward a given end accomplishes a series of micro-deviations leading to a non-random and anti-entropic situation—a wish come true. And I confess the desire to make wishes come true was a wind ever blowing at my back. I remember being so small that my mother could cradle me in her arms, and she would lean over me and whisper the old nursery rhyme, "If wishes were horses, beggars would ride." I could say it before I could understand it. In fact I am still trying to understand it.

Now it seems to me that this must be how consciousness works within the brain, where matter and energy are in a more unbound and dynamic state than throughout the rest of nature. It is easy for consciousness to direct the electrical flow in the central nervous system (though we have no idea how this is done); it is less easy for it to move, not electrons, but the whole atomic system spread far and wide in time and space. This may explain why it is easy to form a thought, but having one's wishes come true takes longer.

I pondered these things during the long, starry nights at La Chorrera when the very heart of the mystery of being seemed about to give itself to me. Alchemical gold was ever flowing through my fingers; I was certain that if I could alloy it with hope and imagination it would not pass away.

I saw that there is an interphase between consciousness active in the world and consciousness active in the central nervous system, whose intermediary is the body. That interphase is language. To use language, consciousness informs the brain to inform the body to impart coherency to the random motion of the air molecules near but outside the body. This coherency is supplied by consciousness in the form of a word. None of the physical laws operating on the air molecules have been violated, because the coherent pattern of behavior of the molecules is due to an input of energy—an input of energy whose release was initiated by an act of conscious will. Will is not an item in the toolkit of scientific explanation.

Language is thereby seen to be a kind of parapsychological ability since it involves action at a distance and telekinesis, albeit voice-transduced. Perhaps under the influence of psilocybin an immense energizing of will could be vocally transduced into the world where it might do more than imprint a signal onto the random motion of air molecules. Perhaps instead a word, visibly beheld, might be transduced and appear through appropriate shifts of refraction in those same nearby air molecules.

Normal speech itself is sometimes seen to effect the refractive index of the air in front of the speaker's mouth. Viewed in profile a speaker is sometimes seen to generate a wavering of the air in front of the mouth that is like the shimmer of a mirage above a hot highway. Perhaps this is an indication of the hidden potential of speech to go beyond its normal function of symbolizing reality to actually signifying it. A more perfect Logos would seem to be the result—a Logos able to regulate the activity of the ego as it exists in the sum total of individuals living at any time. It is like a god; it is the human god. It is something that will happen to human destiny sometime in the future, and because it will happen, it is happening. Nothing is unannounced. The ontological mode of the higher dimensions into which humanity is being propelled is being anticipated by the singularity that we call the wholly Other or the alien. The alien is teaching something through its reinforcement schedule: It is preparing us to confront the God facet of ourselves that our explorations into the nature of life and matter are about to reveal.

Such was the table talk of our distressed band of adventurers. How long ago our arrival at La Chorrera then seemed!

CHAPTER FIFTEEN

A SAUCER FULL OF
SECRETS

*In which we plan our departure, I encounter
a flying saucer, and theories sprout like
mushrooms as we return to Berkeley.*

THE ELEVENTH OF MARCH was a full moon. It
passed uneventfully enough after the adventure of Dennis and the
mission bell, meaning that I can now recollect little of what happened. I remained ecstatic, certain that all was for the best, certain
that some definitive tipping of the hand by the thing we were dealing with was about to occur.

The next day, in the late afternoon, Ev walked out from the
river house to see me. She invited me to return with her to the river
and for all of us to have dinner together. She showed the strain of
what we had all been going through. There was no doubt that whatever had happened was pushing us to the limit of what we could assimilate without wanting to move against it. As we walked back
across the pasture, the atmosphere seemed to be even more alive
and active than usual, with spawning clouds and drifting mist. Ev
pointed to the southeast, where a black, stratocumulus mass was
seething and boiling up to great altitudes. We watched for a few

moments, and it became like a vast mushroom cloud—the aftermath of a thermonuclear blast. The impression was very startling, and Ev recalled to me Dennis's words with regard to *Stropharia cubensis*. He said that it was the mushroom at the end of history. To him the shape of the atomic cloud was a physical and biophysical pun on the transformative powers of the *Strophariad* and its eruption into human history.

As we watched, suddenly Ev gasped. From the seething base of the cloud what looked like a column of light emerged. The column was sustained, not merely a bolt of lightning. It was hard to see how it could be a shaft of sunlight, since it was late afternoon and the sun was in the west, while the cloud was in the southeast. We watched it for perhaps a minute. Then it stopped abruptly. Ev was quite shaken. Even more than the frozen appearance of the river, this occurrence was of an empirical order different than anything that she had experienced at La Chorrera.

Arriving at the riverside campfire we learned that Vanessa had been up at the mission with Father José Maria talking on the radio to the bush pilot who had whisked Dave from our midst. The pilot was willing to follow Vanessa's intent and think of us as a low-grade emergency. He promised to return in a few days to fly us out. I was unhappy with these arrangements. I knew that we, the *gringo* strangers, would lose face with the local people when our need for this airlift became known. Also, I did not have Vanessa's faith that all Dennis needed to return to normal was to check into the world of modern psychiatry. But there was nothing to be done for it, and so we dined in silence, each lost in unshared thoughts.

The next day we were to pack all our equipment and move it to the river in preparation for a flight that could come unannounced at any time. Already we were preparing to withdraw from the vortex at La Chorrera.

The evening's only moment of humor was provided by Ev's animated description of Dennis evading Vanessa's wardenship and slipping away from the river house sometime during the previous night to go and sit quietly in the house of some Colombian *colonistas*, who awoke to find him there as unassuming as a piece of furniture. As the story died away, the unspoken dimensions of it returned to move in each of our minds.

The next day was March 13. The camp in the forest, the hallowed-seeming spot where the transforming experiment had occurred, was dismantled. All the artifacts that set it apart from dozens of other Witoto huts were tucked away, and it was returned to its native anonymity. Outside, in a pile, we left quite a cargo trove behind us, for our forced evacuation by airplane left precious little room for any gear; some insect and plant specimens would leave with us, the cameras, the notebooks on the experiment—that was it. The things that we left would be swiftly assimilated by the tolerant Witotos who owned the site of our attempted probe of hyperspace.

We were all installed in the river house ready to go with the airplane whenever it should appear. Everything seemed to be moving forward of its own accord. We swam in the river and sat on the rocks, scanning the sky and listening for the drone of the little amphibian. Thus the afternoon passed, with even Dennis quiet after an episode in the early morning in which he had methodically thrown the contents of his room out the window to the point of ripping out the window frame and hurling it after everything else.

Around four o'clock, I was lying on the river bank about twenty feet back from the river's edge. I was thinking about a walk to the river I had taken two days before, when each step nearer the water seemed to bring more rhyme and rhythm into my thoughts. From out of nowhere I remembered an old Celtic saying that Robert Graves discusses: "Poetry is made at the edge of running water." My recent experience at water's edge had something to do with that, I believed, and I was pondering it. Vanessa and Ev were washing in front of me at the river bank. Directly across the river from us was the southeastern sky in which Ev and I had seen the cloud with the shaft of light just twenty-four hours earlier.

I was gazing in that direction when I noticed what I thought was the weak beginning of a rainbow, a place low in the sky near the horizon where there seemed to be the faint touch of a spectrum. After a few seconds, I called down to the two women and asked if they saw a rainbow across the river. They glanced across the river for only a moment and said that they saw nothing. I did not persist, but instead watched the sky in that spot. By this time, I had stopped forcing my opinions on people. I was already regarded as nuts, not incoherent exactly, but not to be trusted or relied upon because I believed such odd things. That was my flaw.

I kept watching across the river and I saw the thing intensify. I became extraordinarily interested. In this pastoral setting, it seemed to me that a great revelation was brewing. I watched and I saw the colors deepen; the bow of a rainbow never formed, but the deepening of the colors in one spot was very definite. Again I inquired of the women if they saw the rainbow across the river. Again the light glance. And? Wonderful!

"Yes, we see it. Not much of one is it?"

The clue-scanning part of my hyperactive imagination was upon this detail in an instant. Yes, first a cloud with a shaft of light; now a spot of spectrogrammatic color in the same spot in the sky. I had the strong sense of the eye-in-the-sky drawing close to my thoughts and watching with satisfaction as I understood the importance of the southeast, and of watching and focusing my attention on that spot. In my mind, the teacher said, "This is the place. This is the sign. Watch here."

I said nothing to anyone, but I formed the resolve to not spend that sleepless night as I had spent the others: wandering the fields like the fox-spirit or meditating at the *chorro*. Rather I would sit here where the lake emptied and the Igara-Parana resumed its languid course. Here at the boat landing, seventy feet down a steep mud bank from the river house, I would sit through the night and watch.

🍄 🍄 🍄

And so, all night long, I sat reviewing the things that had passed, seeming to divide my consciousness and send it both backward through my family tree and forward into the future. I seemed to see all the years still ahead; I saw some technique emerging from this contact, our careers pursued across space and time, and finally vindication as the world realized the truth of the transdimensional nature of the *Stropharia* visions and the true nearness of the worlds that they had thrown open. For it had become my belief that the contact with an intelligent and utterly alien species was beginning for humanity. It seemed that out of the long night of cosmic time the novelty of novelties, the moment of contact between minds on utterly different planes, was beginning.

We were among the first to achieve contact with this Other species. It was the real thing. We had come to the equatorial jungle to explore the dimensions glimpsed in tryptamine ecstasy, and there, in the darkness of the heart of the Amazon, we had been found and touched by this bizarre and ancient life form that was now awakening to the global potential of a symbiotic relationship with technical humanity. All night long strange vistas and insights poured through me. I saw gigantic machineries and worlds of vegetable and mechanical forms on scales inconceivably vast. Time, agatized and glittering, seemed to pour by me like living super-fluids inhabiting dream regions of terrible pressure and super cold. And I saw the plan, the mighty plan. At last. It was an ecstasy, an *ecstasis* that lasted hours and placed the seal of completion on all of my previous life. At the end I felt reborn, but as what I knew not.

In the gray of a false dawn, the wave of internal imagery faded away. I rose from where I had been sitting for hours and stretched. The sky was clear, but it was still very early and stars were still shining dimly in the west. In the southeast, the direction toward which my attention had been focused, the sky was clear except for a line of fog or ground mist lying parallel to the horizon only a few feet above the tree tops on the other side of the river, perhaps a half mile away. As I stretched and stood up on the flat stone where I had been sitting, I noticed that the line of fog seemed to have grown darker, and now seemed to be churning or rolling in place. I watched very carefully as the rolling line of darkening mist split into two parts and each of these smaller clouds also divided apart. It took only a minute or so for these changes to be executed, and I was now looking at four lens-shaped clouds of the same size lying in a row and slightly above the horizon, only a half mile or so away. A wave of excitement swept through me followed by a wave of definite fear. I was glued to the spot, unable to move, as in a dream.

As I watched, the clouds recoalesced in the same way that they had divided apart, taking another few minutes. The symmetry of this dividing and rejoining, and the fact that the smaller clouds were all the same size, lent the performance an eerie air, as if nature herself were suddenly the tool of some unseen organizing agency. As the clouds recoalesced, they seemed to grow even darker and more opaque. As they all became one, the cloud seemed to swirl inward like a tornado or waterspout, and it flashed into my mind that perhaps it was a waterspout—something I still have never seen. But even as the thought formed, I heard a high-pitched, ululating whine come drifting over the jungle tree tops, obviously from the direction of the thing I was watching.

I turned and gave one glance at the river house seventy feet behind me and up the steep hill, gauging whether I had time to run and awaken someone to get confirmation of what was happening. To arouse someone I would have had to go hand-over-hand up the slope and consequently take my eyes off the thing I was watching. In the space of an instant, I decided that I could not cease observing. I tried a shout, but no sound came from my fear-constricted throat.

The siren sound was rapidly gaining pitch, and in fact, everything seemed to be speeding up. The moving cloud was definitely growing larger rapidly, moving straight toward the place where I was. I felt my legs turn to water and sat down, shaking terribly. For the first time, I truly believed in all that had happened to us, and I knew that the flying concrescence was now about to take me. Its details seemed to solidify as it approached. Then it passed directly overhead at an altitude of about two hundred feet, banked steeply upward, and was lost from sight over the edge of the slope behind me.

In the last moment before it was lost, I completely threw open my senses to it and saw it very clearly. It was a saucer-shaped machine rotating slowly, with unobtrusive, soft, blue and orange lights. As it passed over me I could see symmetrical indentations on the underside. It was making the whee, whee, whee sound of science fiction flying saucers.

My emotions were all in a jumble. At first I was terrified, but the moment I knew that whatever was in the sky was not going to take me, I felt disappointment. I was amazed and I was trying to remember what I had seen as clearly as possible. Was it real in the naive sense in which that question is asked of UFOs and tables and chairs? No one else saw this thing as far as I know. I alone was its observer. I believe that had there been other observers, they would have seen essentially what I have reported, but as for "real," who can say? I saw this thing go from being a bit of cloud to being a rivet-studded aircraft of some kind. Was it more true to itself as cloud or aircraft? Was it a hallucination? Against my testimony can be put my admitted lack of sleep and our involvement with psychedelic plants. Yet curiously this last point can be interpreted in my favor. I am familiar through direct experience with every known class of hallucinogen. What I saw that morning did not fall into any of the categories of hallucinated imagery I am familiar with.

Yet also against my testimony is the inevitable incongruous detail that seems to render the whole incident absurd. It is that as the saucer passed overhead, I saw it clearly enough to judge that it was identical with the UFO, with three half-spheres on its underside, that appears in an infamous photo by George Adamski widely assumed to be a hoax. I had not closely followed the matter, but I accepted the expert opinion that what Adamski had photographed was a rigged up end-cap of a Hoover vacuum cleaner. But I saw this same object in the sky above La Chorrera. Was it a fact picked up as a boyhood UFO enthusiast? Something as easily picked out of my mind as other memories seem to have been? My stereotyped, but already debunked, notion of a UFO suddenly appears in the sky. By appearing in a form that casts doubt on itself, it achieves a more complete cognitive dissonance than if its seeming alienness were completely convincing.

It was, if you ask me—and there is no one else really that one can ask—either a holographic mirage of a technical perfection impossible on earth today or it was the manifestation of something which in that instance chose to begin as mist and end as machine, but which could have appeared in any form, a manifestation of a humorous something's omniscient control over the world of form and matter.

It was not a mirage of the conventional sort. Years later it occurs to me that perhaps it was a kind of mirage still unknown to us—a temporal mirage. The ordinary mirage is an inverted image of water or a distant place. The cause is the distortion of light by alternate levels of hot and cold air. Outside Benares, in India, I saw a triple image of the city suspended over the surface of the Ganges River. But a temporal mirage is another matter; it is a lenticular image of a distant time and place. Cause unknown. What makes the ordinary and temporal mirages members of the same class is that both types of mirages require the intercession of the human mind in order to exist. Certain areas of the world have local conditions which make them mirage prone; might the same be true of temporal mirages? Or perhaps the temporal mirage is a natural phenomenon, and the UFO is an artifact resulting from the temporal mirage being used or experimented with by some future technology?

I believe that this latter comes close to the mark. The UFO is a reflection of a future event that promises humanity's eventual mastery over time, space, and matter. We, in our clumsy attempt to probe these mysteries, were able to coax nature into throwing out this great, burning scintilla of pure contradiction from the dark retort where she labors over the chemistry of the millennium. That we were able to do this is full of import. It meant to me that we were on the right track; the *Stropharia cubensis* mushroom is a memory bank of galactic history. Alien, but full of promise, it throws open a potential for understanding that will sweep away the petty concerns of earth and history-bound humanity.

At La Chorrera I had only the isolated personal conviction that our approach would be vindicated; now, as our ideas are finding a small community that share these intuitions, I am yet more sure that the answer to all of the mysteries that disequilibrate our view of the world are to be understood by looking within ourselves. When we look within ourselves with psilocybin, we discover that we do not have to look outward toward the futile promise of life that circles distant stars in order to still our cosmic loneliness. We should look within; the paths of the heart lead to nearby universes full of life and affection for humanity.

The UFO encounter marked for me the culmination of our work at La Chorrera. My contact with the saucer took place at dawn on the fourteenth of March. The following morning at eleven, March 15, the airplane arrived, unannounced but not unexpected. Vanessa had been anticipating it for three days. It was a matter of a few moments to clamber aboard after saying farewell to the priests and the police, all of whom had been most patient with our colorful party and its unusual preoccupations. Only in visions had my eyes recently rested on stuff such as the little airplane was made of—the highly polished, acrylic surfaces of machines and things impervious to hard, ultraviolet radiation; what the people of Amazonas call "machete skin." It was a reminder of all that we were returning to.

Dennis was on his best behavior. Beyond his commenting as we got aboard that an airplane was a partial condensation of a flying saucer, he said little. A roar of the engine, a hard pull back on the stick, and we and our legendary bush pilot were airborne. We circled the mission once before settling down to follow the Rio Igara-Parana back to the Rio Putumayo and the version of civilization that the town of Leticia would afford. What a tiny world La Chorrera is, left behind in the trackless jungle after only a glimpse of buildings and Zebu cattle resting in the green pastures, looking like lumps of melting, vanilla ice cream. I imagined that whatever we had touched and been touched by, it was now falling behind us.

We stayed two days in Leticia, days in which Dennis showed marked improvement while the rest of us drifted into various stances of distance with regard to each other. This seemed to be compensation for the excessive intimacy our isolated expedition had made necessary. The oddest thing about Leticia was that we were hardly off the plane before we ran into Jack and Ruby, an American couple who had rented Ev's apartment in Bogotá for a few weeks. I had thought the name combination weird when I met them six weeks before, and now the fact that they were practically awaiting us in Leticia heightened the strangeness. I could not quite get my mind around it.

By the time we reached Bogotá, Dennis had almost completely returned to normal, lending weight to the idea that some form of temporary chemical imbalance had been responsible for his reaction rather than the emergence of a chronically unbalanced personality structure. He was very shaky and very bummed by any mention of fourth-dimensional superconducting bonds, *ayahuasca*, or shamanism. He said, "Look, I have had it." He had, too.

He was nearly normal, but I was just at the beginning of a years-long period of unusual ideation—the state of suspended disbelief that gave birth to the ideas concerning time set out in *The Invisible Landscape*.

On the twentieth of March, there was general agreement that Dennis was totally back with us. It was an occasion of great happiness and we celebrated at one of Bogotá's finest restaurants. It was an immense accomplishment to have been able to allow the reversal to work itself out without the aggravating influence of modern mental health care procedures. The ordeal in the wilderness that all shamans must face had been endured. A step on the path to knowledge had been taken.

On March 21, I made a journal entry—the first in weeks and the only one that I was able to make for another couple of months. I said this:

March 21, 1971

It is now seventeen days since March fourth and the concretizing of the ampersand. If I have more or less correctly understood this phenomenon, then tomorrow, the eighteenth day, will mark some sort of half-way point in this experience. I predict that tomorrow Dennis will return to the psychological set he experienced prior to March first, though it is possible that rather than a residual amnesia concerning events at La Chorrera he will have instead a growing understanding of the experiment of which he was the creator. The past weeks have been harrowing and seemingly made of so many times, places, and minds that a rational chronicle has been impossible. Only Finnegans Wake *gives some idea of the reality of the paradoxicum as we experienced it by virtue of being able to pierce beyond time's double face. In spite of earlier misunderstandings and mis-projections concerning the cycles of time and number operating within the phenomenon, I now believe that in these seventeen days we have experienced, albeit sometimes running backwards and certainly enormously condensed, enough of a full cycle to begin to foresee in some dim sense the events of the next twenty or so days and have some idea of the approximate nature and direction of the opus.*

This journal entry makes clear that while Dennis was recovering from his submergence in the titanic struggle I was quite in the grip of a struggle of my own. I was caught up in an obsessive immersion, almost an enforced meditation, on the nature of time. The ordinary concerns of ordinary life ceased to matter to me. My attention was entirely claimed by my efforts to build a new model of what time really is. Resonances, recurrences, and the idea that events were interference patterns caused by other events temporally and causally distant claimed my attention. In those early speculations I imagined a mythic cycle needing forty days to be brought to completion. It was only later, when I began to be impressed with the DNA-related and calendrical nature of the temporal cycles, that I turned my attention to cycles of sixty-four days duration. This speculation eventually led me to turn to the *I Ching*. In those early notions of a forty-day cycle of alchemical redemption there is only the slightest hint of the eventual theory in its operational details; yet the intent is clearly the same. Resonances, interference patterns, and fractal regresses of times within times—these were the materials that I began to build with. Eventually, after some years of work, the result would have a certain elegance. However, that elegance was reserved for the future; the early conception was crude, self-referential, and idiosyncratic. It was only my faith that it could be made coherent and rational to others that kept me at it for those several years, transforming the original intuition into a set of formal propositions.

The end of March was mostly spent in Bogotá, a dreary time. The urban frenzy of a teeming, modern city did not rest lightly on our jungle-sensitive perceptions. Dennis seemed quite normal, though weakened and sobered. There were no messages from Dave, and Vanessa finally returned to the States. On the twenty-ninth, Dennis followed her example and flew to Colorado. I insisted that Ev and I go to southern Colombia so that I could have some time to reflect. This we did. I reviewed the whole incident at La Chorrera with no new insights and concluded that some sort of psychic gravity was pulling us home. On the thirteenth of April, one day short of a month after my encounter with the UFO, we arrived in Berkeley.

It was a short and difficult visit. I was beginning to see the dim outlines of what would become the *I Ching* time-wave theory. The first maps of the *I Ching* hexagram hierarchy, which was eventually turned into a computer software program I called *Timewave Zero*, were done at that time. I kept myself away from people. I was totally immersed in my work; I had no interest or patience for anything else. I was in the grip of a creative mania more extreme than any I had thought possible. Each conversation with someone on these matters seemed to open vast gulfs of misunderstanding.

The most grotesque of these incidents involved my effort to obtain feedback concerning our ideas from what I thought of as "real experts." This misguided notion found me, one perfect day in May, inside the Donnor Laboratory of Virology and Bacteriology on the University of California campus at Berkeley. Earlier I had made an appointment to see Dr. Gunther Stent, the world-class molecular geneticist and author of the *The Molecular Chemistry of the Gene*. I didn't know at the time that Stent was a legend for his Scandinavian rectitude or that he fancied himself quite the Renaissance man and social philosopher. A year or two later he would publish a book advocating a reform of global society with the traditional social models of Samoa as an ideal goal.

I found the great man in his lab whites in a room filled with bubbling glassware and adoring grad students. I was shooed out of the lab, and an underling ushered me into his private office looking west over the campus toward the Golden Gate Bridge miles away. From that ninth-floor vantage point, the spring crop of students were reduced to ant-like scurryings on the greensward below. Gunther Stent joined me a few minutes later.

Austere and balding, he settled back in his chair while I launched into the ideas behind the experiment at La Chorrera. I tried to begin gently, but I was overawed and very nervous. After a few minutes, I sensed that he might be calculating the odds of whether I would physically attack him. To his credit, he seemed to fight back this alarming swarm of thoughts, allowing me to ramble on and on. His face became utterly impassive as I became more and more uncertain of the direction in which the conversation was headed. Finally, after a particularly long and outlandish burst of speculation through which he remained utterly unreadable, I decided to try to bring the matter to a head.

"Dr. Stent, my concern in coming here to discuss this with you is simply that I would like to know whether this theory has any validity or is simply fallacious."

He seemed to soften slightly and left his position behind the desk to join me in looking westward through the thick, tinted glass. With a sigh of resignation that was heart sinking to his visitor he turned to me and spoke.

"My dear young friend, these ideas are not *even* fallacious."

My chagrin was bottomless and I fled, dizzy with embarrassment. So much for my bridge building efforts toward normal science.

Encounters such as that convinced me that I had to relearn epistemology, genetics, philosophy of science—the entire gamut of subjects necessary to discuss the areas for which I now had such compelling concern. As my study of the *I Ching*, or *Book of Change*, advanced, I had refined the idea that its structure was the basis of a timewave or waves. These waves are discrete periods of change that follow each other as well as enclose each other. I came to realize that the internal logic of the timewaves strongly implied a termination of normal time and an end to ordinary history. At that point, the idea of concrescent psycho-matter and the UFO that I had encountered at La Chorrera became identified in my mind with each other and with the end of time scenarios of the Western religious traditions.

The early unquantified time chart was full of coincidences relative to my own personal life. In particular, the termination points of each component section of the wave seemed to have special meaning for me. Positioning one of these points on the experiment at La Chorrera seemed to make other points in the past (the death of my mother and my meeting with Ev), and points then in the future (my twenty-fifth birthday), especially important. I saw that important events in my own life seemed to be occurring every sixty-four days with eerie regularity. It was necessary to work these ideas out alone, since my intensity concerning them and their paradoxical nature looked absurd in the eyes of other people. I understood that whether or not the effect I was exploring was a general phenomenon in nature or a unique idiosyncrasy, it was obviously vitally important for me, personally, to let the forces I had become entangled with play themselves out to the end.

Bizarre as the plan seemed to others, I resolved to return to La Chorrera, to its solitude and its strangeness, and to spend time there simply and calmly observing the thing that had come over me. Ev and I had bought emeralds as one of our last acts before leaving Colombia and the sale of these was more than enough to finance our return to the surreal domain of sunlight, forests, and rivers that had spawned my obsession. Once back at La Chorrera, I was determined to write down all that had overtaken us; that was my resolve, and much of the early draft of *The Invisible Landscape* was the result. This decision to depart California was hailed by my circle in Berkeley. Concern for my mental state was rife among my friends, and rumor had reached us that the FBI was aware that I was somewhere back inside the country and had begun looking for me. The Bombay-to-Aspen hashish blues were catching up with me. It was, as they say, time to make a move.

CHAPTER SIXTEEN

RETURN

*In which Ev and I return alone to La Chorrera
and a new comet heads toward the earth.*

ON THE FIFTEENTH of July, Ev and I again stood
on the edge of the Amazon interior. My intention to return to La
Chorrera was fast becoming fact. My journal takes up again as we
started down the Rio Putumayo, a name that by then suggested to
me an etymology like "the whore of illusion":

July 15, 1971

    *Having left the vicinity of Puerto Leguizamo a few hours ago
with our cargo of beer and cattle, Ev and I are once again enclosed by and moving through the dream that is the forests and
rivers of the Amazon Basin. This return to continue the contemplation of the phenomenon in the pure medium of tropical nature
in which we discovered it marks a dedication to and an immersion in the phenomenon that, I imagine, anyone familiar with the
events which overtook us in March finds incredible and even perhaps not without an element of risk.*

    *I refer not to danger inherent in the jungle or to the inevitable
hardships attendant upon travel in remote areas, but rather to the
psychological stress inherent in confronting the phenomenon—*

167

strangely so much a part of one's self and yet vast and other—
away from the mitigating world of friends and a world that is
unaware or skeptical concerning our encounter with the phenom-
enon and the subsequent understanding which we derived from it.
My first consideration in this area is to do all in my ability to
eliminate the unexpected. My brother's crypto-schizophrenic re-
versal is ever in my mind in this regard. I believe we are dealing
with something to which no vagueness or uncertainty of inner dy-
namics adheres. Careful thought and study can eliminate the pos-
sibility of the contact phenomenon suddenly "turning on us" or
otherwise behaving unexpectedly.

The right approach to these things remains elusive. Again
and again the "inner voice" of the phenomenon has insisted that
since my brother's opus of hyper-carbolation nothing at all re-
mains to be done, and that if something is required in the way of
activity, then by virtue of the very nature of the contact, that some-
thing will be precisely what we are doing.

Ev and I lived quietly at La Chorrera from August until mid-
November of 1971. There were moments of frequent high hilarity.
And during that time I was able to completely indulge my submer-
sion in the interior processes that I was experiencing. My days were
filled with long, thoughtful walks on the trails around La Chorrera
and by hours crouched over the tablets of graph paper that I had
brought with me. There in the center of the Amazon greenery I
elaborated my theories of time and covered sheet after sheet of
paper with my wave mechanical fantasies. When not reading or
daydreaming, Ev and I indulged ourselves in long conversations in
which the new view of being in the world seemed almost within
reach.

During this second residency at La Chorrera, the theme of *oo-*
koo-hé recurred. We made the acquaintance of several of the Witoto
people who regularly walked the path near our own hut, which was
a few hundred yards down the same trail where the original experiment had taken place. Among those Witoto who stopped to ex-
change a word or watch me collecting insects was a sturdy older
man named Demetrius. He was a cloudy-eyed old weasel who pos-
itively exuded the stench of the cosmic gatekeeper. In my excited

state of mind, the letters D, M, T seemed to stand out in his name
like a beacon. As soon as I could get him alone I haltingly put the
question to him.

"*Oo-koo-hé?*"

"*Oo-koo-hé!*" He was barely able to believe his ears. It must
have been incredible to him that this strange, weak creature, like
something from another world, should directly inquire after a secret
tradition of his people. I have no idea how many cultural conven-
tions were overlooked, but after a bit more conversation, or what
passes for conversation between people who share no common language, I was sure that he would try to help me. Days later, on my
twenty-fifth birthday, I was brought a tarry goo wrapped into little
leaf packets. I was never able to obtain a hallucinogenic experience from this material, but later analysis by the chemists of the
Karolinska Institute in Stockholm confirmed the presence of di-
methyltryptamine. Demetrius had been as good as his name.

The important thing about the second trip to La Chorrera was
that the teaching of the Logos was more or less continuous. And
what it taught during those months and afterward was an idea about
time. It is an idea that is very concrete and has mathematical rigor.
The Logos taught me how to do something with the *I Ching* that
perhaps no one knew how to do before. Perhaps the Chinese knew
how to do it once and then lost it thousands of years ago. It taught
me a hyper-temporal way of seeing. My books, my public life, my
private dreams have all become a part of the effort to feel and understand the new time that was revealed at La Chorrera. A revolution in human understanding is not something that can be corralled
within the confines of a conversation.

This new model of time enables one to have as much of a certain
kind of knowledge about the future as it is possible to have. The future is not absolutely determined; there is not, in other words, a future to "see" in which every event has already been determined.
That isn't how the universe is put together. The future is not yet
completed, but it is conditioned. Mysteriously, out of the set of all
possible events, certain events are selected, in Whitehead's phrase,
to undergo the formality of actually occurring. The Logos was concerned to reveal the mechanics of this process and did reveal it as the
idea of the timewave.

What had originally gotten me looking at the *I Ching* was the odd way in which my early, simplistic notion of sixty-four day cycles worked very well in my own life at the time. My mother's death was the first of these points in time that I isolated. Then I noted that my chance-formed relationship with Ev had begun sixty-four days after that, and that the culmination of the experiment at La Chorrera had occurred another sixty-four days later. The notion of a hexagram-based lunar year grew out of the idea of six cycles of sixty-four days each, a year of six parts, just as an *I Ching* hexagram has six lines.

The personal worth of the idea was confirmed for me when I noticed that such a year of three hundred and eighty-four days, if begun at the time of my mother's death, would end on my own twenty-fifth birthday on November 16, 1971. I saw then that there were cycles and there were cycles of cycles: I imagined a three-hundred-and-eighty-four day lunar year and then the larger thing of which it was a part, a cycle of sixty-four times three hundred and eight-four days, and so on. The maps that I constructed and the eventual qualification of them that I achieved are described in *The Invisible Landscape*. But what was not told there were the experiences at La Chorrera and the way in which these coincidences and my unconscious mind—or something in my mind—guided me to discover these long hidden properties of the *I Ching*.

What to make of the ocean of resonances that the timewave seemed to show connecting every moment of time to every other moment through a scheme of connection that knew nothing of randomness or causality? And what to make of the fact that certain details in the mathematics of the wave seemed to imply that the time in which we live was the focus of an ages-long and terribly important effort? These were inflationary images—and I recognized them as such—but the power and allure of them as a form of private entertainment was frankly irresistible.

The timewave seemed to be an image from the collective unconscious that sought to prove, at least in its own terms, that the culmination of all the processes in the universe would occur within our lifetimes. For each of us this is obviously true: our own lives do seem to us, embedded as we are in our bodies and our historical milieus, to be somehow the expression of the final purpose of things.

The timewave predicted its own end within our lifetimes; actually only a decade after the turn of the century, a time of such novelty that beyond it there could be nothing less than the end of time itself. This was the most puzzling of all, more puzzling than its personal, idiosyncratic side, this implicit "end of time": a period when a transition of regimes would take place that would completely transform the modalities of reality.

I was familiar with the idea of eschatology—the end of time— in a religious context, but it had never before occurred to me that regimes in nature might undergo sudden shifts that would reshuffle natural laws. There is nothing against it really. It is simply that science, in order to function, must assume that physical laws are not dependent on the time and the context in which they are tested. If this were not so, the idea of the experiment would have no meaning, since experiments performed at different times might then give different results.

For years I continued to elaborate this theory and to clarify my own understanding of the theory-forming enterprise generally. I succeeded finally in 1974 in achieving a completely formal, mathematical quantification of the fractal structure that I had unearthed inside the structure of the *I Ching*. Throughout the eighties I worked, first with Peter Broadwell and then with Peter Meyer, to create personal computer software, which I called *Timewave Zero*, that allowed careful study of this wave. The computer is a powerful tool that made it possible to greatly refine my notions of what constituted proof or disconfirmation of the theory. Today my conclusion regarding these matters is that the theory of the fractal and cyclical nature of novelty's ingression into the world is a truly self-consistent and completely mathematical theory. It is true to itself. And it returns the human drama and our own lives to the very center of the universal stage.

It is possible, in a certain sense, that all states of liberation are nothing more than perfect knowledge of the contents of eternity. If one knows what is contained in time from its beginning to its end you are somehow no longer in time. Even though you still have a body and still eat and do what you do, you have discovered something that liberates you into a satisfying all-at-onceness. There are other satisfactions that arise out of the theory that are not touched on in this formulation. Times are related to each other—things happen for a reason and the reason is not a causal one. Resonance, that mysterious phenomenon in which a vibrating string seems magically to invoke a similar vibration in another string or object that is physically unconnected, suggested itself as a model for the mysterious property that related one time to another even though they may be separated by days, years, or even millennia. I became convinced that there is a wave, or a system of resonances, that conditions events on all levels. This wave is fractal and self-referential, much like many of the most interesting new curves and objects being described at the frontiers of research mathematics. This timewave is expressed throughout the universe on a number of extremely discrete levels. It causes atoms to be atoms, cells to be cells, minds to be minds, and stars to be stars. What I am suggesting is a new metaphysics, a metaphysics with mathematical rigor; something that is not simply a new belief or new religious conviction. Rather this insight takes the form of a formal proposition.

I would be the first to admit that it has not been possible to find a bridge between this theory and normal physics. Such a bridge may be neither possible nor necessary. We may find that normal science indicates what is possible, while the time theory I propose offers an explanation for what is. It is a theory that seems to explain how, of the class of all things possible, some events and things undergo the formality of actually occurring. It is clear to me that the theory cannot be disproven from without; it can only be disproven by being found inconsistent within itself. Anyone is welcome to dismantle it if they are able; this is what I have attempted to do and failed.

By November 16, 1971, I had begun to realize that the chart had too many variables to ever function as a predictive map of the future. It would be necessary, I realized then, to quantify somehow the various parameters of the wave so that judgments concerning it could be less subject to personal bias. My last piece of writing at La Chorrera was done on the morning of the sixteenth, my twenty-fifth birthday. It was a kind of fable:

November 16, 1971

Two old friends, Arabian somehow, yet more ancient, sit in a palace far older than themselves, set on a mountainside surrounded by vineyards, date palms, and citrus orchards. Insomniac and affable, they pass the long starry hours preceding dawn in the smoking of hashish and the propounding of riddles.

"Share my pleasure at this puzzle and its resolution," said the darker to the older, and he passed his hand across his companion's eyes. The older man then stood in the dream and watched the puzzle—a world of form and law, interlocking wheels and passion and intellect—unfold. He passed into its species and empires, dynastic families and individual men of genius, he became its philosophers and weathered its catastrophes. He felt the texture and tone of all the beings in the world his friend had created. He sought the secret pattern his friend, he knew, had surely hidden in his creation, for this was a game that they often played.

Finally, in a great despotism, in an age of brash science and bright decadence, he saw himself divided into the persons of two brothers—and through them, through their wanderings and lifetimes which passed before him in a moment, he perceived the intricate and pleasing nature of the riddle. Understanding at last, he dissolved the mists and wheels of the dream fable with a laugh—a laugh they shared. And then once more they passed their pipe before strolling into the azure garden where dawn would find them conversing among the peacocks, beneath the pomegranates and bending acacias.

Are we to be left then with nothing but fable? Or is there more here? Tropical gardens that I have planted have in them small acacias straining toward maturity. Perhaps there is still time for them to grow into shade for philosophical rambles. Life is stranger than even the strangest among us *can* suppose.

The work at La Chorrera felt finished then. We folded our camp and retraced trails and rivers. It took time, there were books to write, loose ends to a life too loosely lived to be tidied and trimmed. We lived for a time in Florencia at the *finca* of a friend. There I wrote some of the early chapters of *The Invisible Landscape*. We went through the Christmas holidays of 1971 there, but the writing was slow, the lack of reference materials frustrating. We returned to the States and lived in Boulder with Dennis for a few months, during which I worked in the local hot house rose industry. It was a series of mundane American adventures. Eventually though we found ourselves back in Berkeley.

🍄   🍄   🍄

Until the *I Ching* timewave was quantified with more data, its way of integrating seemingly meaningless and unrelated factors made it very easy to become psychologically entangled within. It seemed to operate like a kind of bottomless inkblot test; one could see whatever one wished to see in it. Even though my twenty-fifth birthday came and went with very little shift toward the novel, either in my own life or in the world, I continued to propagate the cycles of the chart forward into the future. I felt that the idea of a hidden structure of time was correct but that this could not be argued for until the correct alignment between that structure and human history had been found and confirmed. I began looking for a date with special features related to the wave, a date that would be a good candidate for the emergence of a special event.

Here is a part of my story that I found most puzzling: After the seeming disconfirmation of the cycles by my birthday, I looked at other future dates on which the three-hundred-and-eighty-four day cycles would end if I continued to assume that the sixteenth of November, 1971, was the end of one such cycle. That meant that the next ending date of the three hundred and eighty-four day cycle would be the fourth of December, 1972. I consulted several astronomical tables, but the date seemed unpromising. The closing date of the next three hundred and eighty-four cycle was immediately more interesting, as it fell on the twenty-second day of December, 1973.

I noticed this was the winter solstice. Here was a clue. The winter solstice is traditionally the time of the rebirth of the savior messiah. It is a time of pause when there is a shifting of the cosmic machinery. It is also the time of the transition of the sun from Sagittarius to Capricorn. I put no particular stock in astrology, but I noted that Dennis is a Sagittarius and Ev a Capricorn. I consulted my star maps and added another coincidence: where the ecliptic crosses the cusp of Sagittarius and Capricorn, at 23 degrees Sagittarius, is the very spot to within one or two degrees where the galactic center is presently located. Over twenty-six thousand years the galactic center, like all points on the ecliptic, slowly moves through the signs, but now it was on the cusp of Sagittarius and Capricorn on the winter solstice day.

This seemed an unusual number of coincidences and so I pressed my search. Consultation with the almanac of the Naval Observatory brought a real surprise. On the very day that I was researching, December 22, 1973, a total, annular eclipse of the sun would occur and the path of totality would sweep directly across La Chorrera and the Amazon Basin. I was dumbfounded. I felt like a person in a novel; this string of clues was actually real! I researched the eclipse to determine exactly where it would achieve totality. This would occur, I learned, almost directly over the city of Belem in Brazil, in the delta of the Amazon River. The vertiginous elf chatter of hyperspace rose squealing in my ears. Was it mocking me or egging me on?

Meditation on this eclipse data carried my mind out of the realm of astronomical coincidence and back to the motifs of the trances at La Chorrera. Belem means Bethlehem in Portuguese. My perceptions, sensitive to any messianic possibility, seized on this. Belem is Bethlehem; it lies at the delta of the Amazon. Delta is the symbol for change in time; delta in Joyce's fiction and among graffiti artists throughout history represents the vagina. Dennis was born in Delta, Colorado. Was it possible that all of our experiences could have been a premonition of an event at a time and place two years hence in Brazil? Was this why, absurdly, at the conclusion of the experiment at La Chorrera, the strains of "Oh Little Town of Bethlehem" had come echoing through my mind? By late spring of 1972, I knew everything that I have just mentioned. Why did the wave point to December 22, 1973? And why was there such a stream of coincidence pointing to that time? Had I known of the impending eclipse on some unconscious level? Had I known it would achieve totality over Belem? Why did the dates that were important to my life line up with that date according to the wave I had learned to construct in the wake of the UFO encounter at La Chorrera? To me it seemed impossible that I had somehow known these things and manipulated my conscious self to imagine that it was "discovering" these things. I was like a snow-blind traveler caught in a blizzard of coincidence.

Finally, in the early spring of 1973, an event occurred that offered perfect proof that something larger than my unconscious, seemingly larger even than the total collective consciousness of the human race, was at work. This was the discovery of the comet Kohotek, heralded as the largest comet in human history, dwarfing even Halley's Comet.

"Brightest Comet Ever Headed Toward Earth" was the headline in the *San Francisco Chronicle*. As I scanned the article, I actually let out a yell of amazement. The comet would make its nearest approach to the sun on the twenty-third of December! A non-periodic comet, unknown to anyone on earth until March of 1973, was hurtling toward a rendezvous with the sun within a hundred hours of the solstice and the eclipse over the Amazon. It was a large coincidence, if we define a coincidence as an improbability that deeply impresses its observer. This coincidence is not diminished by the fact that Kohotek never really lived up to expectations, for the expectations alone became a wave of millenarianism and apocalyptic restlessness among the fringes of the population that would die only as the comet returned to the darkness out of which it emerged. Did anything happen in Belem on the day of the eclipse? I do not know; I was not there. I was by then a prisoner of mundane obligation. But I do know that the compression of events that occurred around that date, and the way in which the charts predicted this, were uncanny.

Only with the development of personal computers was I able to understand the way that the timewave describes the ebb and flow of novelty in time over many different spans of time: some last scant minutes, others endure for centuries. Now anyone who becomes operationally familiar with the theory can join me in this intellectual adventure and see for themselves the immense challenge involved in predicting a concrescence. I have not been content to merely understand the theory: I have continued efforts to apply it specifically to predicting the course of future events. If over years of study one becomes convinced that the wave does show the future course of novelty, then the ordinary anticipation of the future is gradually replaced with an almost Zen-like appreciation and understanding of the complete pattern.

Was the above series of events the first intimation that I had that something of importance was connected with a specific date in time and the city of Belem? Strangely, no; it was not. I must mention the following incident in order to connect the history of my own unconscious processes with the curiously specific and puzzling piece of information that was seeking to emerge from me.

In the spring of 1970, I had been in Taipai, Taiwan, readjusting to city life after a long, butterfly-collecting ramble through the outback of Indonesia. I was killing time awaiting a traveling companion, who I had last seen in Bali several months before. One night, I had a very peculiar dream. It occurred, though I did not know it, on the very day that my father and Dennis were told that our mother was dying of cancer. That was something that I would not learn until nearly a week later. My journal records the dream as follows:

May 24, 1970

Dhyanna and I were walking up a gentle, grassy slope. Below us on all sides the valleys were filled with scudding white clouds, tops brilliantly reflecting the sun back into the depthless azure. Ahead of us the steeply rolling hills ascended—many miles away, as I remarked, into the main range of the Rockies. We were in dream geography, somewhere in Western Colorado [where I was born and lived until I was sixteen]. As we continued upward, Herr B. [an Indonesian acquaintance], came to meet us wearing white tennis shorts and drew our attention to several small meteorological balloons whose dangling nylon cords had caught in nearby wind-bent trees. To our left, upon a crest, deeply dimpled, blazing white, and perhaps thirty feet high, was a large balloon perhaps three-quarters filled with gas. The ropes enclosing the gas bag cut deeply into it, sectioning it as though it were a great, bleached orange. As we gazed, Herr B. depressed a lever that had appeared from nowhere and the apparatus rose simultaneously with my query: Would not the wind whipping over the hill cause it to falter? Its white bulk rushed over us, perhaps only twenty feet above our heads and then, passing higher, it met the wind and the fate I had anticipated. Turning on its side, it gently came to earth. We ran toward it and other people [the impression was of children], appeared from the opposite direction, also running toward the rippling white of the now deflated machine.

Amid our laughing examination of the balloon, we were invited into B's home, now visible as a sprawling, "ranch style" house nearby. [This was a house not unlike the house in which I spent my childhood.] As we entered the house I paused to examine a large map of the Amazon Delta on the wall—published, the legend informed me, to commemorate a conference of a French archaeological society which convened on a small island there in 1948. When I rejoined Dhyanna, she informed me that the children of B. had told her that one of the densest rain forests in the world was nearby. I, familiar as only a native can be with Colorado geography, was incredulous. I returned to the bookcase under the map and, taking out a large atlas, sought the rainfall and forest map of Colorado, opening instead upon Assam— while first rejecting a topological rendering of Bengal. I heard myself say that Shalimar was the logical jumping off place—then all faded.

The meaning of this dream was far from clear at the time, and even now it remains obscure. What is clear is that at a given date an event of importance was to be expected in the delta of the Amazon. I hoped then that the total eclipse of the sun was that long-anticipated event, and that its totality over the vagina of the world mother anticipated an event of great import for everyone.

CHAPTER SEVENTEEN

WALTZING THE ENIGMA

*In which I flash back to my near recruitment by
a band of renegade Nazi scientists while visiting
Timor.*

A FEW MONTHS BEFORE that precursive dream a
strange incident occurred that I now look back on as further proof
that I was destined to travel to the Amazon, and that somehow I
had come under the spell of the cosmic giggle:

In February of 1970, a year before I arrived at La Chorrera, my
fugitive wanderings had taken me to the island of Timor in Eastern
Indonesia. Under indictment in the States for the heinous crime of
importing hashish, I traveled and lived under the dramatic assumption that international police agencies were combing the
globe looking for me. My cover, that of a graduate student in ento-
mology doing field work for a degree—a butterfly collector—had
worked well over the previous six months as I had made my way
slowly through Malaysia, Sumatra, Java, and a host of other less familiar but equally exotic insular backwaters.

A particularly muggy and showery afternoon found me smoking
ganja in my room at the Rama, the best and only hotel in Kupang,
Timor. Until that moment, I had been the hotel's only guest for ten
days and had pretty much had the run of the place. Not that it was
palatial. The Rama was constructed of cinder block, and the walls of

its eight identical rooms stopped well short of the ceiling. With concert walls and drains installed at the converging slopes of the floors, it had the cheerful ambience of a new and unused slaughterhouse. However, it was clean, as the manager would hurriedly point out.

As I smoked, sitting cross-legged on my steel cot and reviewing the morning's collecting in the jungle, I became aware of the arrival of other guests. I could hear what seemed like half a dozen people speaking German and moving luggage about in the lobby, a central space with four rattan chairs facing each other over a threadbare rug. I presumed that these were travelers off the afternoon plane from Darwin and that they would presumably fly on to Bali on the next day's regular noon flight out of Timor. What was obviously a couple, to judge by their voices, had occupied the room next to mine. I recognized some German and the women seemed to speak some other language, one I could not place.

When I went out for dinner the new arrivals were nowhere to be seen. The next morning I was up at dawn to catch an Indonesian Air Force plane that took me to Flores, the next island on my butterfly itinerary, and I thought no more about the unseen guests in a now-distant hotel I expected never to see again. I spent a week in the cloud forests on Flores, staying with an alcoholic Dutch priest with a club foot who ran a mission in the forested interior of the island. Then I returned to the steamy coastal capital, Maumere, a small town down the center of whose unpaved main street were piles of Macadamia nuts drying in the sun, waiting to be bagged for export. Maumere had a two-room Chinese hotel in which I expected to stay one night before returning to Bali.

Then the fog closed in. It was a soupy, ground-hugging tropical fog that my Chinese host assured me was known to last for weeks this time of year. I visited the airport the next day but it was clearly a futile gesture. The Bali plane circled the field four times looking for a hole in the cloud cover before giving up and flying on. I was no stranger to delay. Travel in Asia is made of delay. I returned to the hotel for another round of chess with the local chess fiends and assumed that the next day would be clear.

Five days later I was still on Flores. I had played chess with all comers, I was running out of dope, and the specter of staying forever in Maumere seemed too real to be a joke. I thought it over, decided to forget Bali, and put out the word that I would take the next plane out to anywhere.

That decision seemed to be all that was necessary for the weather to clear off long enough for a plane to get in under the clouds. It was the weekly Garuda flight to Kupang. Before I had time to reconsider my decision, I was on the plane and headed back to Timor.

The town was unchanged and my earlier visit had put me on a first-name basis with the rickshaw boys. I felt almost like I was home. "Rama Hotel," I told my favorite driver, and before I knew it I was back in room number one, and the fog-bound chess tournaments on Flores seemed no more than a half-remembered dream.

As I lay on the bed watching the ceiling fan idle against a background of spider-webbed corrugated metal, I became aware of voices in the next room. German and something else, which was softened by a women's voice and more exotic, not Indonesian, maybe Pashtun, I thought. Apparently the travelers who had checked in the night before my departure nearly two weeks ago were still there. That meant they were certainly not tourists; nobody without a good reason lingered long in Kupang.

I am not big on chance meetings. In those days I always tried to avoid having anything to do with what I considered "non-freaks." However, that evening as I let myself out of my room to go to dinner, the door of the next room opened and I was face to face with its occupants.

"Herr McKenna, is it not?"

As I turned to face my questioner, the uneasiness that I felt being addressed by my name must have shown in my face.

"The manager here has told me of your biological researches on Timor. Allow me to introduce myself. I am Dr. Karl Heintz of Far Eastern Mining and Minerals, Inc."

My relief was immediate. Obviously this guy wasn't some kind of Interpol porker come to track me down. But he had the look. He was powerfully built with swept-back, iron-grey hair and strikingly intense eyes of glacial blue. He sported a schmiss on his left cheek, a long, thin scar. I had never seen a schmiss before but the crossword puzzle term sprang into my mind unbidden. I wondered if he had received it in the traditional manner, in a sword duel that is part of the hazings that used to go on in the university fraternities of Prussia.

"As we are the only guests here at Rama Hotel, may I invite you to join my wife and me for some schnapps? I am keen to hear your perceptions concerning Timor."

The town was too small for me to refuse gracefully. Had I said no we would have ended up at separate tables in the same five-table restaurant. I hated the idea of spending time with straight people but there seemed no decent way to escape.

Hearing him speak brought his wife into the small foyer to join us. She made the decision easier, though I was careful to guard my reaction of amazement. Only a year or two older than myself, maybe twenty five, she was stunningly beautiful, dark, sari-clad with huge fawn-like eyes, a gold nose ring, and many bracelets. In that tropical backwater her appearance was as unlikely as a flying saucer; she was a vision of overdressed Brahmanic perfection. Her name was Rani, and when she spoke her voice was cultivated and musical. Though she rarely spoke, her English was better than his. This was no girl from the villages. I confess that I was intrigued. What could I do but accompany this pair? It wasn't as though I had something better to do.

Once we were seated at the restaurant with our quart bottles of Bintang beer in front of us, the conversation began to flow and I started to form an impression of my companions.

Dr. Heintz was, he said, a geologist with an outfit in Singapore. The year before, a survey team had found evidence of a large deposit of nickel that straddled the border between Indonesian and Portuguese Timor. He was there to confirm their findings and to estimate the feasibility of a mining operation. That seemed straightforward enough, although there were references to a set of instruments that could somehow determine the true size of the deposit. I knew very little of prospecting technology, but a device that could see hundreds of feet into the ground sounded far-fetched to me.

I gently inquired about the language that I had heard them both speaking, thinking this would lead him on to discussing his wife. It turned out to be a favorite subject of his. She was, he told me while she merely sat and watched us both, a granddaughter of the Maharani of Maharashtra. It seemed that Heintz had been in the market for a few hundred acres of prime Maharashtran agricultural land and the old Maharani had a parcel that she was willing to cut loose. This had lead to Heintz meeting Rani. Before the deal was closed, it was clear that a wedding would soon follow. He waxed eloquent over the joys of tractor farming in India, how he was really a very simple man, the joys of watching the growth of a new crop, and so on. He was quite a raver, and I was content to let him spin it all out. It seemed that he was a kind of vice-president in charge of operations for the mining concern, a kind of trouble shooter really. He ordered another beer and told a story about being ambushed by guerrillas during the start up of a big tin extraction operation in northern Thailand. At the story's climax he stood and lifted his shirt to display for my edification three neat scars across his chest. From a machine gun, he said.

"Any one of them could have killed me outright. But no! I was preserved, and the triumph of our company's project was complete." Describing the start up of a tin mine as a triumph seemed a bit overblown to me, but it was clear that I was in the presence of one intense dude.

Hardly pausing he moved on to the time in Tanzania when he alone, bare chested and unarmed except for an axe, had strode into a crowd of six thousand angry workers during a strike at a bauxite operation. Modest he was not, but the stories were well told and compelling. And standards for dinner conversation in the warm tropics leave room for the self-aggrandizing traveler's tale.

Eventually he turned his attention to the company that he worked for. "FEMMI is no ordinary company, Herr McKenna, please be assured of that. No. We are like a family. This is the source of our strength. And we have plans for the future. Very big plans." I only nodded, thinking it best not to inform him that I considered large mining corporations the scourge of the earth. But this devotion to his corporation was no casual matter, and he seemed unable to leave the subject alone.

"Nowhere on earth is there a more closely knit and dedicated group than are we. We are bound like comrades in arms. Each member of the core management group is a genius in his or her own right." He pronounced genius like "tchenius." "And why is that you must wonder? Ach, I am telling you why. It is because we, each one of us, has known the horror of privation, the depths of despair, and the glorious feeling that comes from overcoming these things. We are united in our triumph, Herr McKenna, and the sense of inevitable conquest of difficulty has made us invincible!" At this last word, his voice rose and his fist descended to the flimsy table with such force that our quart bottles of Bintang jumped in reply.

Seeing my uncertain response, he continued. "You are amazed to hear this, I see. Maybe you are asking what privations, what difficulties? It is like this: we all lived through the Hitler times and the war. Germany was nothing after the war. There was not one stone upon another in my Berlin. In the ruins of Europe we were like cockroaches. May I tell you that the bank accounts of all the SS families were frozen. My mother, my poor aristocratic mother, was reduced to selling paintings from our estate in order to buy potatoes to feed herself and my younger sister. Imagine this!"

"Oh no," I thought, "Not Nazis. Is this guy telling me he was a Nazi?" I fought to get my look of horror under control, but now he was on a roll and seemed to take no notice.

"My father was captured by the Russians during the battle for Berlin. He was hung like a dog in Moscow for war crimes. Can you imagine? Verdammen Russian schweinen talking about war crimes? For all the SS it was like that."

This conversation was like a bad dream or a B-movie. I looked over at his companion who returned my gaze with utter impassivity. It seemed important to deflect the conversation if only even slightly. "And you, Herr Heintz, what of your role in all of this?"

He shrugged. "I was a mere nothing. A Messerschmidt pilot in the Luftwaffe. A good German only." This last was said without a trace of irony. "Before the war I was a young engineering student. The war changed everything. After the war, a few of us, my fellow, young scholars from the Max Planck Institute, gathered in the ruins of Berlin. We were finished with ideology, with the grand political dreams."

This was the first good news in a while. I gratefully signaled the Indonesian waiter for another round of beer while Heintz continued: "We were a small group, pitiful really, but united by our

revulsion at the horror all around us. We determined to build a new
world for ourselves, a world based on two principles, two great powers, the power of capital and the power of science. We began slowly,
with patents, processes that had been discovered at the Planck Institute during the war, trade secrets really. Carefully we expanded
on this, we established ourselves in Singapore. There was not a
shoemaker among us. Each member of our small team was a genius. Our *fürher* was a professor who had trained us all, a true genius. His name was Max Bockermann. It was he who held us
together; it was his faith and strength that made it all possible."

The schmiss on his cheek had turned bright red at this turn of
the conversation. I had hoped that there were no further depths of
discomfiture to be plumbed in this conversation but I was wrong,
for now I saw that he was moving, perhaps under the influence of
the third quart of Bintang, from passionate intensity to outright
maudlin sentimentality. "No man has ever loved another as Bockermann loved us. We are his kinder, his little birds, ja. When it
seemed that there was no hope he inspired us; he made us believe
in ourselves."

Tears rose in his eyes at this, then he seemed to regain his self
control and continued. "And what is the result? FEMMI, Herr
McKenna, Far East Mining and Minerals Incorporated. We have
grown and prospered. From our offices in Singapore we control projects in eleven countries. Oil, nickel, tin, bauxite, uranium—we
have it all. But we have more, we have love, companionship, community, and the power to make our dreams come true." At this he
broke stride and reached over to put his hand on the thigh of the
woman beside him. I looked away.

When I returned to his depthless blue gaze his mood had
changed. "But what about yourself, Herr McKenna. It is clear that
you are leading the gypsy life." He pronounced the word gypsy like
chipsy. "And we gypsies always have our stories to tell. So what
about you?"

I swallowed hard. He didn't look like the sort of person who
would appreciate my stories of fighting the police at the Berkeley
barricades shoulder-to-shoulder with affinity groups like the Per-
sian Fuckers and the Acid Anarchists. Nor did my participation in
the Human Be-In or the rolling orgies of the Summer of Love in

the Haight-Ashbury seem appropriate to mention. And my recent stint as a hashish smuggler in India and my subsequent move undercover to avoid capture by Interpol also seemed out of place in this particular interview.

I decided to go with the usual half-truth reserved for straight people. "I am an art historian turned biologist. I went to Nepal to study Tibetan but found that I am no linguist when it comes to Asian languages. I have returned to biology, my first love. Specifically, I am an entomologist. I am collecting butterflies here in Indonesia retracing the route of Alfred Russell Wallace. Wallace was the real discoverer of the theory of natural selection, but Darwin got all the credit. I identify with his underdog status. Wallace was shafted by Victorian science because he was of the wrong class and didn't know how to play politics the way Darwin did. Wallace explored the Amazon Basin as well and if all goes well, I hope to travel and collect there too. Eventually I will write a monograph on speciation among the butterflies of Amazonas and Eastern Indonesia, which will get me a degree. Then, who knows. Teaching perhaps. Hard to say."

"So you are a real gypsy, then. And an outsider by your dress and beard. I like this. We like this young man, don't we, Rani?" It was the first time that he had addressed his companion during the entire conversation. She replied with a nod, never taking her eyes off me. "Ja, good. So now we eat. And tomorrow we talk more. I will expect you to join us here at breakfast." And with that he applied himself to his water buffalo steak with a ferocious intensity.

Later we returned to the hotel together, but by then the electricity had been turned off in that part of town and we had to give our slightly sloshed attention to picking our way along the muddy, rutted streets. There was no further serious conversation. As we parted in the atrium of the hotel he turned to me. "You must call me Karl. *Jetzt wir sind freunden.* You understand?" I nodded yes and we parted.

Breakfast was another story. Whatever contribution the beer had made to the evening's conversation it must have been minimal, because within a few minutes of sitting down to breakfast he was fully wound up all over again.

"Last night you spoke of your ambitions to visit the Amazon. This is a commendable dream. But believe me, I know the Amazon well, a jungle the size of a continent; it is not like these islands here. Here you do well to stay with the priests and to make your expeditions, one week, two weeks into the forest. But in Amazonas to do serious work you will have sustain yourself in the field for perhaps months. You will need a boat, equipment, bearers. Believe me, I know. It is not for shoemakers. Therefore I make you a proposal. You have said your work is nearly completed here, that you are going soon to Japan to earn money for South America. Give up this plan and do instead the following. FEMMI, as it turns out, has a deep interest in the Brazilian Amazon. Two years ago I was part of a resource assessment team that made some interesting discoveries. As it happens we are sending our people back for a serious second look. Our teams are thirteen in number and some of these are natural scientists such as yourself. The new team is nearly formed but Bockermann, if he approves of you, would accept my recommendation that you join the team as the thirteenth member. You will be well paid, and our expectations are only that you would complete the monograph that you have already planned. You see, by having scientists with us we can write off part of our tax liability, and anyhow we are believers in the worth of pure science. This plan must be cleared with Singapore, but if they agree then you would go there nearly immediately. You would meet Bockermann. We give you dental check up, complete physical, new eyeglasses, two weeks of tennis to get you physically in shape. The cruise liner *Rotterdam* will call in Singapore in one month. We will ship three speedboats specially outfitted, all our equipment, and the team on the *Rotterdam*. In Rio you will continue training two weeks at the Krosnopolski Hotel, where they have excellent tennis courts. And I tell you something else, my father's old cook is the chef there! We fatten you up some and then we give you your dream of the Amazon. Well, what do you say?" He sat back, evidently very pleased with himself.

I was caught completely off-guard. He was right about the Amazon being difficult for one person. Wallace himself had said as much. He had thrown in with the botanist Richard Spruce and the discoverer of animal mimicry, Walter Henry Bates, in order to do his Amazon exploring. But I was not whom I must seem to Heintz. I was no academic. I was an international fugitive with a price on my head. And also, I thought, what about my hippie girlfriend studying dance back on Bali, who was assuming we would travel on to Japan together? To mention any obligation to another person seemed almost ungrateful in the circumstance. And what about the Nazi connection? Did I really want to go off with a bunch of ex-SS types to the Amazonian rain forest? On the other hand I was running out of money. And my lady friend had a penchant for torrid affairs carried on in my absence. As for the Nazi matter, I was confused. I knew that Max Planck was supposedly the only person ever to stand up to Hitler, telling him to keep his hands off the pure science of the Institute. Heintz had also gone far out of his way to let me know that his brother, also part of FEMMI, was married to what he described as "a Nigerian lady so black she is almost blue," and his own choice of women was definitely non-Nordic.

I thought to myself. "Here is the knock of fate and opportunity. What now, McKenna?" I looked from his face to hers. They both seemed truly expectant. "This is a generous offer, extraordinary really."

"Then you accept?"

"Yes."

"Excellent. You have chosen well. You are no shoemaker. This I like."

"Yes. Thank you. As you know, I am returning to Bali this afternoon. I have collections and obligations there that I must attend to. Also I confess that I am without much money."

"This is no problem. Set your affairs in order in Bali. I will cable Singapore to arrange money for your air passage from Bali to the home office. There is only one thing." At this his steely gaze became even harder and he fixed me in a glacial stare. "You must be interviewed by Bockermann himself. He can see into the soul of a human being. If there is one iota of falsity in your character or your story he will detect it. Then there is no deal. This is terribly important, we must have no shoemakers!" The schmiss had become an angry line once more.

This last speech was heart sinking. "No deal. I understand." But I was thinking, "Oh shit, what have I gotten myself into." We shook hands on it, and I left to pack my things at the hotel and hurry to the airport.

My mind was in turmoil on the flight back to Bali. One by one the Lesser Sunda Islands slid past beneath me, and as they did, so did my doubts and my objections to Heintz's offer. "This has the feeling of fate," I thought to myself. "Play it out, give it a chance, and see what happens."

Over the next week I made my arrangements. I told the story to the freaks of Kuta Beach and most people encouraged me. My lady friend even supported me. We had agreed months before that Bali might be the parting of the ways for us. Each day I walked to Poste Restante in Denpasar expecting to find my tickets and the five hundred dollars in travel money that Heintz had promised. Three days went by, then five, and then seven.

On the morning of the seventh day, I awoke with the conviction that I had been had. It had all been some kind of weird mind game. I decided that Heintz must be nuts, a weirdo whose idea of fun was to get American freaks to buy into his secret Nazi mega-corporation fantasy and then drop them into reality just to see how far they would fall. Of course there was another possibility; that somehow they had been able to check up on me and had discovered my false history. That I was sure would put me in the shoemaker class and effectively cook my goose. Anyway, I had certainly made an ass of myself by telling everyone in Bali that I was about to board the *Rotterdam* for a corporate-sponsored trip to the Amazon.

I had to endure lots of good-natured kidding for the next couple of weeks as I returned to my original plan, outfitting myself for a final Indonesian collecting expedition out to Ambon and Seram in the Moluccas.

And there the matter rested. I buried the whole episode in a tomb in the back of my mind marked "Weird People You Meet on the Road." But it was an unquiet grave. A year later, in the aftermath of La Chorrera, I decided that it had been a precursive reflection of the true craziness that did finally find me in the Amazon. It had been an anticipation, a wavering in the time field, a kind of living prophetic dream, an instance of the cosmic giggle. But it wasn't the last I would see of Herr Heintz either.

A year after the events at La Chorrera and two years after my visit to Timor, in the spring of 1972, I was in Boulder, Colorado. I had returned from South America to settle my legal status and try to put life on the road behind me. Dennis and I were working together on the manuscript of *The Invisible Landscape* and spending a lot of time at the university library, studying the various disciplines that had to be mastered if our ideas were to stand a chance of being taken seriously.

One day I was scanning the student newspaper when I came upon a startling announcement. A full page had been reserved to announce that the University of Colorado, in association with the Max Planck Institute for Neurophysiology, would co-sponsor the next meeting of the World Congress of the Neurosciences. At the words "Max Planck Institute" my attention sharpened and I read on. Seven hundred scientists from around the world would be converging in Boulder for ten days of meetings and seminars. All the greats would be in attendance: Sir John Eccles, John Smythies, Solomon Snyder, and all the rest, the gods of the very Valhalla that we dreamed of conquering. The catch was that all the meetings would be closed to the general public with the single exception of the opening address, which would be titled "Autocatalytic Hypercycles" and would be delivered by the then-reigning star in the world of neuroscience, Manfred Eigen of the Max Planck Institute.

I was familiar with the outlines of Eigen's ideas. Autocatalytic hypercycles seemed to me an obvious necessary correlative to the ideas that I was working out concerning the timewave and the way in which it was expressed and reflected in living organisms. This was something that Ev, Dennis, and I simply had to attend. However, I did not give the Planck Institute much thought, as it is the major, pure science research outfit in Germany with hundreds of researchers on its payroll.

The lecture was to be held on campus in the Physical Science Lecture Hall, a barrel-shaped enclosure that placed the lecturer at the bottom of a deep well surrounded on three sides by tiers of seats, somewhat in the manner of an old style operating theater. There had apparently been a black tie dinner for the invited speakers before the lecture, and as we filed in to take our places I was impressed that the usually dowdy science crowd had dressed to the nines for the event. There was a babble of languages. From where I sat I could hear German, Italian, Japanese, Russian, a smattering of Hindi, Spanish, and Chinese.

As my eyes roved over the crowd, I suddenly experienced something very close to a physical jolt. There, less than fifty feet away from me and nearly directly across the intervening open space, sat Dr. Karl Heintz! I felt absolute amazement. Heintz! Here! Could it be? Somehow I must have betrayed my agitation to him, for as I watched in near disbelief I saw him move his hand to the pocket of his jacket and with a faultlessly smooth motion remove his name tag and drop it into his pocket. He did not even interrupt the animated German conversation he was carrying on with the person sitting to his right. I looked away, trying to pretend that I was unaware of him, had noticed nothing. The house lights dimmed and Manfred Eigen, magnificent with his swept back shock of white hair, began his lecture.

My mind raced. Was it all true then? Here he was! This was a Planck Institute event. It must all be true. He recognized me! And he was intent on concealing his identity! I felt completely weird as I scribbled a note outlining the situation and handed it to Dennis and to Ev. They both responded with looks that said plainly "Are you losing it, or is this a joke?" I sat there in the dark pondering the situation. Whatever Eigen was saying I would have to get it off Dennis's hand-held tape recorder later. I finally figured, nothing ventured, nothing gained. I knew there would be an opportunity to approach him immediately following the lecture. That was when I would make my move.

While Eigen brought his talk to a brilliant conclusion, I fidgeted. As the applause died down and the lights went up, people began to move toward the exits. Heintz was about fifty feet away talking animatedly to a couple of rather toad-like colleagues. But I could see that he was watching me, and as I began to approach he excused himself and began to move toward me. It was transparently clear to me that this maneuver was executed to make certain that we would be alone and our conversation unheard when we met. I moved directly into his oncoming path.

"Dr. Heintz. I believe that we met on Timor." I extended my hand.

Ignoring my outstretched hand, he smiled broadly, but the schmiss perceptibly reddened. "Heintz? Heintz? My name is not Heintz. And I have never been in Kupang."

Then he turned quickly and rejoined his departing colleagues, adding to their animated assessment of Eigen's performance. The word "Kupang" rang in my ears. The bastard was rubbing my nose in it!

As the king said to Mozart, "So there you have it." Madman, a creature of my fevered imagination, a charlatan, or the tip of a Nazi iceberg of scheming dreamers? To this I have no answer. That's how it is with the cosmic giggle.

CHAPTER EIGHTEEN

SAY WHAT DOES
IT MEAN?

*In which I attempt to link our experiences to a
science that is anything but normal.*

THOUGH HAVING LEFT the Amazon, this wild and
woolly tale continues on a little further. It is time to try to distill
some conclusions out of the ideas that were generated in La Chorrera. A model of the world is a way of seeing, and to assimilate the
timewave theory that was forced upon us there is to see the world
differently. My approach has been to grant the possibility that the
theory is true. It may someday be disproved, but until then, I shall
believe it, albeit with tongue in cheek. Perhaps, if it is given a hearing, others will strengthen and contextualize the idea. Many good
ideas simply perish for lack of a context. But this idea proposes a
fundamental reconstruction of the way in which we see reality. And
it can be taught. It fulfills my spiritual aspirations because it is understanding, simply and purely understanding.

The theory elaborated in the wake of the experiment at La
Chorrera doesn't deny any body of knowledge; it augments. There
is an argument for it on the physical level, though the idea is very
complicated, touching as it does on areas involving quantum physics,
submolecular biology, and the DNA structure. These notions are

laid out with what is hoped is care and attention in *The Invisible Landscape*.

While what Dennis did in the Amazon may not have caused the idea that I developed, I have the strong intuition that it did. In the wake of the experiment, my ordinary private concerns were replaced with such utterly strange musings that I could not recognize them as products of my own personality. He performed his experiment and it seemed as though I got a kind of informational feedback off my DNA, or some other molecular storage site of information. This happened precisely because the psychedelic molecules bound themselves to the DNA and then behaved in the way that we had expected; they did broadcast a totality symbol whose deep structure reflects the organizational principles of the molecules of life itself. This totality entered linear time disguised, in the presence of ordinary consciousness, as a dialogue with the Logos. The Logos provided a narrative voice able to frame and give coherency to the flood of new insights that otherwise would have overwhelmed me. My task became to unearth and replicate the symbolic structure behind the voice and to discover if it had any significance beyond myself and my own small circle of acquaintances. I felt as if I was creating a file system for a newly revealed world of infinite variety. The timewave is a kind of mathematical mandala describing the organization of time and space. It is a picture of the patterns of energy and intent within DNA. The DNA unfolds those mysteries over time like a record or a song. This song is one's life, and it is all life. But without a conceptual overview one cannot understand the melody as it plays. The timewave theory is like the score of the biocosmic symphony.

I am interested in disproving this theory. A good idea is not fragile and can withstand a lot of pressure. What happened at La Chorrera cannot be explained away; rather it asks simply to be explained. If it is not what I say it is, then what *is* the concrescence, the scintilla, the encounter with the wholly Other? What does it really represent?

Is it, as it appears to be, an ingression of a higher-dimensional epoch that reverberates through history? Is it a shock wave being generated by an eschatological event at the end of time? Natural laws are easier to understand if we assume that they are not universal constants, but rather slowly evolving flux phenomena. After all, the speed of light, which is taken as a universal constant, has only been measured in the last hundred years. It is pure inductive thinking to extrapolate the principle of the invariance of the speed of light to all times and places. Any good scientist knows that induction is a leap of faith. Nevertheless, science is founded on the principle of induction. That principle is what the timewave theory challenges. Induction assumes that the fact that one did A, and B resulted, means that whenever one does A, B will always result. The fact is that in the real world no A or B occurs in a vacuum. Other factors can intrude into any real situation sending it toward a different or unusual conclusion.

Before Einstein, space was thought to be a dimension where one put things; it was analogous to emptiness. Einstein pointed out that space is a thing that has a torque and is affected by matter and by gravitational fields. Light passing through a gravitational field in space will be bent because the space through which it travels is bent. In other words, space is a thing, not a place where you put things.

What I propose, in a nutshell, is that time, which was also previously considered a necessary abstraction, is also a thing. Time not only changes, there are different kinds of time. And these kinds of time come and go in cyclical progression on many levels; situations evolve as matter responds to the conditioning of time and space. These two *patterns* condition matter. Science has long been aware of the patterns of space—we call these "natural laws"—but the patterns of time? That is another consideration entirely.

Matter has always been assumed to epitomize reality, but it actually has some qualities more nearly like thought. Changes in matter are defined by two dynamic patterning agencies that are in a co-relationship: space and time. This idea has certain axioms, one of which is taken from the philosopher-lensmaker Gottfried Wilhelm von Leibnitz. Leibnitz described monads, which he envisioned as tiny particles that are infinitely reduplicated everywhere in the universe and contain all places within themselves. Monads are not merely here and now; they are everywhere all the time, or they have all space and time within them, depending on your point of view. All monads are identical, but they interconnect to build up a larger continuum while at the same time maintaining their individual, unique perspectives. These Leibnitzian ideas anticipated the new field of fractal mathematics, an exotic example of which is my idea of a temporal pattern.

Ideas such as this offer a possible explanation for the otherwise mysterious mechanisms of memory and recall. Destruction of up to 95 percent of the brain does not impair memory function. It appears that memory isn't stored anywhere; memory seems to permeate the brain. Like a hologram, all of the memory seems to be in each part. Similarly, one can take a holographic plate of Mount Fuji and cut it in half; when a half is illuminated, the entire image is present. One can do this again and again: the holograph is made up of a nearly infinite number of tiny images, each of which in combination with its fellows presents one image.

This "holographic" aspect of memory has been assumed to be of central importance by such thinkers as David Bohm and Karl Pribram. But it was Dennis and I who went so far as to suggest that this form of organization could be extended beyond the brain to include the cosmos at large.

Quantum physics makes similar pronouncements when it states that the electron is not somewhere or sometime; it is a cloud of probabilities and that is all one can say about it. A similar quality adheres to my idea of time and the comparison of time to an object. If time is an object, then the obvious question to be asked is what is the smallest duration relevant to physical processes? The scientific approach would be to keep dividing time into still smaller increments in order to find out if a discrete unit exists. What one is looking for by doing this is a *chronon*, or a particle of time. I believe the chronon exists, but it is not distinct from the atom. Atomic systems *are* chronons; atoms are simply far more complicated than had been suspected. I believe that atoms have undescribed properties that can account not only for the properties of matter, but for the behavior of space/time as well.

Chronons may *not* be reducible to atoms, but I suspect that what we will find is a wave/particle that composes matter, space/time, and energy. The chronon is more complicated than the classical Heisenberg/Bohr description of atomic systems. The chronon has properties that make it uniquely capable of functioning as a fundamental constituent of a universe within which minds and organisms arise. So far we have been unable to define the dynamic properties that would allow a particle to participate as a necessary part of a living or thinking organism. Even a bacterium like *E. coli* is a staggering accomplishment for the atom of Heisenberg and Bohr.

The Heisenberg/Bohr model allows us to simulate the physical universe of stars, galaxies, and quasars; but it doesn't explain organisms or mind. We have to overlay that atomic model with different qualities in order to represent more complex phenomena. We must imagine an atom with new parameters if we wish to understand how we could exist, how thinking, tool-using, human beings could arise out of the universal substratum.

I don't claim to have done this yet. But I do believe that I have stumbled upon an intellectual avenue that could be followed to achieve this understanding. The key lies in cycles of temporal variables nested in hierarchical structures, which generate various kinds of fractal relationships unfolding toward often surprising kinds of closure.

The person who has laid the most firm foundation for understanding this sort of notion philosophically is Alfred North Whitehead. Nothing we have suggested is beyond the power of his method to anticipate. Whitehead's formalism accounts for minds and organisms and a number of phenomena poorly resolved by the Cartesian approach.

Other visionary thinkers are probing these areas. Chaotic attractor dynamics is the idea that any process can be related through a mathematical equation to any other process simply by virtue of all processes being part of a common class. The overthrow of a dictator, the explosion of a star, the fertilization of an egg—all should be describable through one set of terms.

The most promising development in this area has been the emergence of the new evolutionary paradigm of Ilya Prigogine and Erich Jantsch. Their work has achieved nothing less than a new ordering principle in nature—the discovery and mathematical description of dissipative self-organization as a creative principle underlying the dynamics of an open and multi-leveled reality. Dissipative structures work their miracle of generating and preserving order through fluctuations—fluctuations whose ultimate ground is in quantum mechanical indeterminacy.

If you had a perfect understanding of the universe, you would be able, by applying this insight, to tell a man how much change was in his pocket. Since this amount is an accomplished fact, it would be, at least in principle, possible to calculate. What is important is to understand the true boundaries of reality, not the probable boundaries of possible future events. Although boundary conditions operate on the future, they are probabilistic constraints, not absolutely determined fact. We assume that ten minutes hence, the room we are in will still exist. It is a boundary condition that will define the next ten minutes in our space/time coordinate. But we cannot know who will be in the room ten minutes hence; that is free to be determined.

One may ask if we can really know that the room will exist at any future moment. This is where induction enters the picture, since in truth we cannot know with certainty. There is no absolutely rigorous way of establishing that. But we can make the inductive leap of faith that has to do with accumulated experience. We project that the existence of the room will remain a boundary condition, but in principle in the next ten minutes there could be an earthquake and this building might not be left standing. However, for that to happen, the boundary condition will have to be radically disrupted in some unexpected and improbable manner.

What is so curious is that such a thing *could* occur. That is what the timewave allows one to predict, that there are conditions under which events of great novelty may occur. There is, however, a problem with it. Because we suggest a model of time whose mathematics dictate a built-in spiral structure, events keep gathering themselves into tighter and tighter spirals that lead inevitably to a final time. Like the center of a black hole, the final time is a necessary singularity, a domain or an event in which the ordinary laws of physics do not function. Imagining what happens in the presence of a singularity is, in principle, impossible and so naturally science has shied away from such an idea. The ultimate singularity is the Big Bang, which physicists believe was responsible for the birth of the universe. We are asked by science to believe that the entire universe sprang from nothingness, at a single point and for no discernible reason. This notion is the limit case for credulity. In other words, if you can believe this, you can believe anything. It is a notion that is, in fact, utterly absurd, yet terribly important to all the rational assumptions that science wishes to preserve. Those so-called rational assumptions flow from this initial impossible situation.

Western religion has its own singularity in the form of the apocalypse, an event placed not at the beginning of the universe but at its end. This seems a more logical position than that of science. If singularities exist at all it seems easier to suppose that they might arise out of an ancient and highly complexified cosmos, such as our own, than out of a featureless and dimensionless mega-void.

Science looks down its nose at the apocalyptic fantasies of religion, thinking that the final time can only mean an entropic time of no change. The view of science is that all processes ultimately run down, but entropy is maximized only in some far, far away future. The idea of entropy makes an assumption that the laws of the space-time continuum are infinitely and linearly extendable into the future. In the spiral time scheme of the timewave this assumption is not made. Rather, final time means passing out of one set of laws that are conditioning existence and into another radically different set of laws. The universe is seen as a series of compartmentalized eras or epochs whose laws are quite different from one another, with transitions from one epoch to another occurring with unexpected suddenness.

To see through the eyes of this theory is to see one's place in the spiral scheme and to know and anticipate when the transition to new epochs will occur. One sees this in the physical world. The planet is five or six billion years old. The formation of the inorganic universe occupies the first turn of the spiral wave. Then life appears. If one examines this planet, which is the only planet we *can* examine in depth, one finds that processes are steadily accelerating in both speed and complexity.

A planet swings through space two billion years before life appears. Life represents a new emergent quality. The instant life gets started, a mad scramble is on. Species appear and disappear. This goes on for a billion and a half years and then suddenly a new emergent property takes the stage: thinking species. This new epoch of mind is brief in comparison to what preceded it; from the dumb confrontation with chipped flint to the starship is one hundred thousand years. What could that era be but the ingression of a new set of laws? An emergent new psychophysics is allowing our species to manifest very peculiar properties: language, writing, dreaming, and the spinning of philosophy.

Like rattlesnakes and poplar trees, human beings are made by DNA. Yet we trigger the same energies that light the stars. We do this on the surface of our planet. Or we can create a temperature of absolute zero. We do these things because, though we are made of mush and mud, our minds have taught us how to extend our reach through tools. With tools we can unleash energies that normally only occur under very different conditions. The center of stars is the usual site of fusion processes.

We do such things using mind. And what is mind? We haven't a clue. Twenty-thousand years from nomadic hunting and gathering to cybernetics and spaceflight. And we are still accelerating. There are yet more waves to come. From the Model-T Ford to the starship: one hundred years. From the fastest man on earth being able to move thirty miles per hour to nine miles per second: sixty years.

Most puzzling are the predictions the timewave theory makes of near term shifts of epochs made necessary by the congruence of the timewave and the historical record. The timewave seems to give a best fit configuration with the historical data when the assumption is made that the maximum ingression of novelty, or the end of the wave, will occur on December 22, 2012. Strangely enough this is the end date that the Mayans assigned to their calendar system as well. What is it that gives both a twentieth-century individual and an ancient Meso-American civilization the same date upon which to peg the transformation of the world? Is it that both used psychedelic mushrooms? Could the answer be so simple? I don't think so. Rather, I suspect that when we inspect the structure of our own deep unconscious we will make the unexpected discovery that we are ordered on the same principle as the larger universe in which we arose. This notion, surprising at first, quickly comes to be seen as obvious, natural, and inevitable.

The analogy that explains how this might be so is provided by looking at sand dunes. The interesting thing about such dunes is that they bear a resemblance to the force that created them, wind. It is as if each grain of sand were a bit inside the memory of a natural computer. The wind is the input that arranges the grains of sand so that they become a lower-dimensional template of a higher-dimensional phenomenon, in this case the wind. There is nothing magical about this, and it does not seem mysterious to us: wind, a pressure that is variable over time, creates a rippled dune, which is a structure regularly variable in space. In my thinking, the genes of organisms are grains of sand arranged by the ebb and flow of the winds of time. Naturally, then, organisms bear the imprint of the inherent variables in the temporal medium in which they arose. DNA is the blank slate upon which the changing temporal variables have had their sequence and relative differences recorded. Any technique that saw into the energetic relationships within a living organism, such as yoga or the use of psychedelic plants, would also give a deep insight concerning the variable nature of time. The King Wen sequence of the *I Ching* is the product of this kind of insight.

Human culture is a curve of expanding potentiality. In our own tormented century it has reached vertical gain. Human beings threaten every species on the planet. We have stockpiled radioactive materials everywhere, and every species on earth can feel this. The planet when viewed as a sentient entity can react to this kind of pressure. It is three billion years old, and it has many options.

Dualistic talk about humanity not being part of the natural order is foolish. We could not have arisen unless we served a purpose that fit into the planetary ecology. It is not clear what our purpose is, but it seems to have to do with our enormous research instruments. And crises! By stockpiling atomic weapons, we have claimed the capacity to destroy the earth like a stick of dynamite in a rotten apple. Why? We do not know why. Surely not for the political and social reasons that are given. We are simply a tool-building species that is itself the tool of a planetary ecology that is a higher intelligence. It knows what the dangers and limits on the cosmic scale are and it is furiously organizing life to both preserve and transform itself.

My story is a peculiar one. It is hard to know what to make of it. The notion of some kind of fantastically complicated visionary revelation that happens to put one at the very center of the action is a symptom of mental illness. This theory does that, and yet so does immediate experience, and so do the ontologies of Judaism, Islam, and Christianity. My theory may be clinically pathological, but unlike these religious systems, I have enough humor to realize this. It is important to appreciate the intrinsic comedy of privileged knowledge. It is also important to have recourse to the scientific method whenever appropriate. Most scientific theories can be disproven in the calm confines of the laboratory, evolution to the contrary.

To empathize with the visions at La Chorrera one must imagine what one *can* imagine. Imagine if wishes were horses, *how* beggars would ride. The ideas developed at La Chorrera were so compelling because they promised new dimensions of human freedom. The Amazonian rumors of time-binding magical fluids self-generated out of the bodies of master shamans are nothing less than intimations of the metamorphosis of the human body/mind into a higher-dimensional state. Were such a transformation of matter possible, one could do anything with it. One might spread it out and climb on it and take it up to any altitude, adding oxygen at will. It's the haunting image of the flying saucer yet again. One can climb inside it: putting on your mind like a mental wet suit. The flying saucer is an image of the perfected human mind: waiting, warmly humming, at the end of human history on this planet. When it is perfect, there will be an ontological mutation of the human form, nothing less than the resurrection-body that Christianity anticipates.

It is the genius of human technology to master and to serve the energies of life and death and time and space. The UFO holds out the possibility of mind become object, a ship that can cross the universe in the time it takes to think about it. Because that is what the universe is—a thought. And when thought becomes mobile and objectified, then humanity—novices in the mastery of thought—will begin to set out.

Of course we may discover that we are not to set out; the future may reveal instead that there is something out there calling us home. Then it will be our technology and the call of the Other that will move toward meeting. The saucer is an excellent metaphor for this. When Jung suggested that the saucer was the human soul, he was more correct than he may have supposed. It is not so far away. That is the other thing. The last shift of epochs gave us relativity theory and quantum mechanics. Another epochal shift looms, but whether or not it is the final epoch is hard to say. Our roles as parts of the process introduces an uncertainty in our observations that bedevils prediction.

All these themes are woven around DMT, possibly because DMT creates a microcosm of this very shift of epochs in the experience of a single individual. It seems to lift the perceiving mind out of the confines of ordinary space and time and give a glimpse of the largest frame of being possible. When Plato remarked that "Time is the moving image of Eternity," he made a statement every voyage into the DMT space reinforces. Like the shift of epoch called the apocalypse and anticipated by religious hysterics, DMT seems to illuminate the regions beyond death. And what is the dimension beyond life as illuminated by DMT? If we can trust our own perceptions, then it is a place in which thrives an ecology of souls whose stuff of being is more syntactical than material. It seems to be a nearby realm inhabited by eternal elfin entelechies made entirely of information and joyous self-expression. The afterlife is more Celtic fairyland than existential nonentity; at least that is the evidence of the DMT experience.

We human beings must admit that ours is a peculiar situation: having been born, we are autonomous, open chemical systems that maintain themselves through metabolism at a point far from equilibrium. And we are creatures of thought. What is that? What are the three dimensions? What is energy? We find ourselves in the strange position of being alive. Having been born, we know we are going to die. A lot of thinking says that this is not so strange, that this happens in the universe—living things appear. And yet our physics, which can light the fires of the stars in our deserts, cannot explain the strangeness of the phenomenon of our being alive.

Organisms are completely outside the realm of physical explanation at this point for science. So what is it for? Spenser and Shakespeare, quantum theory and the cave paintings at Altamira. Who are we? What is history? And what does it push toward? Now we have unleashed processes potentially fatal to the planet. We have triggered the final crises for all life. We have done this, but we do not control it. No single one of us. No leader or state can call a halt to the fact of our being trapped in history. We are moving toward the unimaginable as information piles up about the real nature of the situation we confront. To paraphrase J. B. S. Haldane: Our situation may not only be stranger than we suppose; it may be stranger that we *can* suppose.

CHAPTER NINETEEN

THE COMING OF
THE STROPHARIAD

*In which Ev and I part company and the mush-
room delivers an oration while turning into an
underground growth industry.*

SUCH ARE THE CONCERNS with which I navigated
the intervening years to the present. But during the two year period
after my second return from La Chorrera, before the publication of
The Invisible Landscape in 1975, I was not idle.

My brother and I concluded that the truly novel element, the
candidate for being the causal agent at La Chorrera, was the mushrooms. It was *Stropharia cubensis* that stood behind all of the effects
we had experienced. As this realization grew, so did the understanding that new expeditions into the unimaginable could be
launched only if a supply of mushrooms could be secured. It happened that on the second trip to La Chorrera the mushroom had
been much less abundant than before. This scarcity had impelled
me to take a number of spore prints from the few specimens that
we did run across. Those spore prints had been kept refrigerated
over the years while my brother and I pursued academic careers
and wrote our book.

During those years we dabbled with the thought of cultivating *Stropharia cubensis*, but the only work on the subject was Wasson and Heim's work in French, and it somehow seemed a remote and technically difficult thing to attempt. In the spring of 1972, we had already isolated the mycelium of the mushroom and had it growing on agar in petri dishes. But we could get nothing to happen. Then in the early spring of 1975 we encountered an article detailing a method for growing commercial mushrooms on rye in canning jars under very carefully controlled conditions. We wondered if perhaps this method would also work for *Stropharia cubensis* and get our stalled exploration of the invisible world moving again.

Ev and I had parted earlier in 1975. Our relationship of convenience formed on the road had not flowered after we returned to careers and school stateside. Ev quickly found work and I did not. Later she enrolled in secretarial school and I went back to Cal to finish my degree in Conservation of Natural Resources. How far we seemed to have fallen from the exaulted vistas revealed at La Chorrera. Our lives were financially marginal, intellectually constrained, and eventually our attachments and interests went elsewhere. When the breakup finally came it was ugly and heart-rending. We may have seen into the heart of the mysteries, but that did not mean that we were any wiser than ordinary people when it came to the affairs of our own hearts. Ev departed from my life in the company of an old friend of mine from my days at the Experimental College, and I was left confused and defensive by what felt like a double betrayal.

The awful conclusion of our long affair left me tormented with migraines and living alone. I was finishing up schooling that had lasted far too long, what with seven years of wandering around the world scheduled in. It was a time of loneliness, self-examination, and the pressure of pressure. During the weeks in which Ev and I were continuously fighting and struggling to find some sort of inner equilibrium, I had thrown myself into a state of hypermanic activity centered around the effort to grow the mushrooms. And then, when we finally parted, I dropped it completely and seemed to spend weeks either sitting staring at the walls or walking for hours in the Berkeley hills and Strawberry Canyon.

One day, returning from one of my long, introspective rambles, I thought of my abandoned experiments with a new method of growing mushrooms using beds of sterilized rye. Now the beds were doubtlessly dried out or rotting in the small, unattended greenhouse in the backyard. "I should clean out the greenhouse and empty the experimental beds," I thought. If I did that perhaps it would be the beginning of cleaning up my now excessively messy and unhappy psychic life. I had not so much as looked in the greenhouse for over two weeks. The reluctant greenhouse door was nearly swollen shut and only opened with a rending screech.

And there they were! By the dozens, by the hundreds, huge picture perfect specimens of *Stropharia*. The dark night of the soul had turned my attention elsewhere, and in that moment they had perfected themselves. I was neck deep in alchemical gold! The elf legions of hyperspace had ridden to my rescue again. I was saved! As I knelt to examine specimen after perfect specimen, tears of joy streamed down my face. Then I knew that the compact was still unbroken, the greatest adventure still lay ahead.

Working in close consultation with Dennis, who was back in Boulder, we determined within a matter of weeks that the hardy *Stropharia* not only grew and fruited with the new method, but that they could be more easily grown than the *Agaricas* species sold in grocery stores as food. The implications of all this were a constant topic of our endless telephone consultations.

From the spring of 1975 onward I was not without a continual supply of *Stropharia*. Into my world of humdrum grief suddenly appeared the perfected method for growing the same organism that had opened up the dimension of contact four years before. The very spores gathered at La Chorrera were now furiously producing mushroom psilocybin in my home. During the spring, I experimented with low dosages several times. The sense of peace and lightness that I associated with the halcyon days at La Chorrera was definitely there; so too was the presence of a teaching voice and a return to close consultation with a cosmic agency of complex intent.

Throughout the spring and summer of 1975, I took the mushroom at doses of five grams dried, or fifty grams fresh, as often as I felt was prudent, which worked out to about once every two weeks.

Each of these experiences was a lesson—a chilling, exhilarating plunge into an ocean of noetic images. I discovered my own mind like a topological manifold, lying before me, inviting me to rove and scan the reflective knot of past and future time that is each of us. Alien presences and translinguistic elves bent near to me in those trances. The mushroom stressed its age, its vast knowledge of the ebb and flow of historical forces in many civilizations through the millennia. Images of the past and future abounded.

Once I found myself on a hill with a crowd of people. The view looked out over a curved plain. It was the interior of a cylindrical space colony miles wide with vast sweeps of windows alternating with farmlands and towns scattered along the floors of the valleys. I knew somehow that in the particular future I was seeing, hundreds of millions of people lived in such cylindrical worlds. The teeming worlds that populate the galaxy in the minds of our science fiction writers had been recreated inside a sphere only twelve light-hours in diameter with the sun at its center. Within that sphere thousands of independent societies pursued their destinies and their evolution; thousands of independent cylinder worlds swarmed around the vast energy furnace of the sun. What a rich and endlessly creative force humanity had become in escaping the confines of the planet! Through the vast windows I could see more advanced machinery being made ready, glittering, obsidian machinery built to challenge the mind-numbing distances that lie between us and the suns of Centaurus. Before me was the spectacle of the departure preparations of a starship. In my mind Copeland's *Fanfare for the Common Man* was being played.

On other occasions I saw alternative futures where the knowledge of the mushroom was not fused with humanity's restless expansionism. I saw a planet covered with a society of slave-worker machine symbiots. I saw the life of North American society running through several hundred years of upheaval and political change, an image like a great animated, war-planning map. The dualism of fascism and democracy hung around North America's neck like an albatross. Again and again, nightmare police-state fascism would sweep like a fouled tide over the aspirations of the people, and again and again, the subtlety of the people would organize against the stupidity of the oppressor. They would rise in wild and bloody revolt to secure the space of a few generations in which to inaugurate attempts at democratic social reform.

The mushroom always returned to the theme that it was wise in the ways of evolution and sympathetic therefore to a symbiotic union with what it referred to as "the human beings." It was eager to share its own sense of the howness of things, a sense that had been developed over millions of years of conscious experience as an intelligent organism radiating through the galaxy. From its point of view, the mushroom is an elder life form, and as such it offers its tempering experience to a vibrant but naive child-race standing for the first time on the brink of flight to the stars. As our imagination has striven outward to attempt to encompass the possibility of the intelligent Other somewhere in the starry galaxy, so has the Other, observing this, revealed itself to be among us, when we are in the psilocybin trance, as an aspect of ourselves. In the phenomenon of *Stropharia cubensis*, we are confronted with an intelligent and seemingly alien life-form, not as we commonly imagine it, but an intelligent alien life nevertheless. In the often zany way that it does, popular culture has anticipated even this odd turn of events. *Invasion of the Mushroom People*, a schlocko-socko B science fiction film from those same good folks who brought us *Godzilla*, contains a final scene in which a team of Japanese explorers are transformed beyond the reach of audience identification into a group of mushrooms singing together in an islanded Asian rain forest.

Only an anachronistic lack of informed self-reflection would lead one to suppose that an intelligent, alien life-form would be even remotely like ourselves. Evolution is an unceasing river of forms and adaptive solutions to special conditions, and culture is even more so. It is far more likely that an alien intelligence would be barely recognizable to us than that it should overwhelm us with such similarities as humanoid form and an intimate knowledge of our gross industrial capacity. Star-traveling species could be presumed to have a sophisticated knowledge of genetics and DNA function and therefore would not necessarily bear the form that evolution on a native planet had given them. They might well look as they *wished* to look. The mushroom, with its habit of living off nonliving organic matter and its cobweb-fragile underground network of ephemeral mycelium, seems an organism designed with

Buddhist values of noninterference and low environmental impact in mind.

In the late summer of 1975, Dennis and I decided that the world we were exploring required a wider audience. We hoped to establish a community of consensus about what was going on. To that end we wrote and published a guide to the method we had developed cultivating the *Stropharia*. At the beginning of that little book, I introduced what we had personally learned about the world of the mushroom:

The mushroom speaks, and our opinions rest upon what it tells eloquently of itself in the cool night of the mind:

"I am old, older than thought in your species, which is itself fifty times older than your history. Though I have been on earth for ages, I am from the stars. My home is no one planet, for many worlds scattered through the shining disk of the galaxy have conditions which allow my spores an opportunity for life. The mushroom which you see is the part of my body given to sex thrills and sun bathing. My true body is a fine network of fibers growing through the soil. These networks may cover acres and may have far more connections than the number in a human brain. My mycelial network is nearly immortal—only the sudden toxification of a planet or the explosion of its parent star can wipe me out. By means impossible to explain because of certain misconceptions in your model of reality, all my mycelial networks in the galaxy are in hyperlight communication across space and time. The mycelial body is as fragile as a spider's web, but the collective hypermind and memory is a huge historical archive of the career of evolving intelligence on many worlds in our spiral star swarm. Space, you see, is a vast ocean to those hardy life forms that have the ability to reproduce from spores, for spores are covered with the hardest organic substance known. Across the aeons of time and space drift many spore-forming life-forms in suspended animation for millions of years until contact is made with a suitable environment. Few such species are minded, only myself and my recently

evolved near relatives have achieved the hypercommunication mode and memory capacity that makes us leading
members in the community of galactic intelligence. How
the hypercommunication mode operates is a secret which
will not be lightly given to man. But the means should be
obvious: It is the occurrence of psilocybin and psilocin in
the biosynthetic pathways of my living body that opens for
me and my symbiots the vision screens to many worlds.
You as an individual and humanity as a species are on the
brink of the formation of a symbiotic relationship with my
genetic material that will eventually carry humanity and
earth into the galactic mainstream of the higher civilizations.

"Since it is not easy for you to recognize other vari-
eties of intelligence around you, your most advanced theories of politics and society have advanced only as far as
the notion of collectivism. But beyond the cohesion of the
members of a species into a single social organism there lie
richer and even more baroque evolutionary possibilities.
Symbiosis is one of these. Symbiosis is a relation of mutual
dependence and positive benefits for both the species involved. Symbiotic relationships between myself and civi-
lized forms of higher animals have been established many
times and in many places throughout the long ages of my
development. These relationships have been mutually useful; within my memory is the knowledge of hyperlight-
drive ships and how to build them. I will trade this knowledge
for a free ticket to new worlds around suns less forsaken
and nearer galaxy center. To secure an eternal existence
down the long river of cosmic time, I again and again offer
this agreement to higher beings and thereby have spread
throughout the galaxy over the long millennia. A mycelial
network has no organs to move the world, no hands; but
higher animals with manipulative abilities can become
partners with the star knowledge within me and if they act
in good faith can return both themselves and their humble
mushroom teacher to the million worlds all citizens of our
star swarm are heir to."

Something that refers to itself as being as fragile and diaphanous as a spider's web—for such is the mycelial network of the mushroom—was not only able to communicate with me but was able to convey a vision of greater grandure and more transcendent hope than I had ever dared to dream possible. It was moving and breathtaking, but was it true?

My own reaction to the mushroom's claims concerning the extraterrestrial origin of tryptamine hallucinogens and the visions that they bear has taken many forms. I think that it is possible that certain of these compounds could be "seeded genes" injected into the planetary ecology eons ago by an automated space-probe arriving here from a civilization somewhere else in the galaxy. Such genes could have been carried along in the genome of a mushroom or some other plant, awaiting only the advent of another intelligence and its discovery of them to begin reading out a message that opens with the bizarre dimension familiar to shamans everywhere. The point of such a message could only be made clear when those for whom the message was intended had advanced to a sufficient level of technical achievement to appreciate it. The exponential growth of analytical tools and methods over the past century may indicate that we are now approaching such a level. I speculate that the final content of the message will be instructions—it will be called a "discovery"—of how to build a matter-transmitter or some other device that will allow us direct contact with the civilization that sent the message-bearing hallucinogen genes to earth so many aeons ago. The trances imply that such a civilization has a faster-than-light technology for information, if not for matter itself, but a receiver is required at the arrival point, otherwise the alien presence within the mushroom is as bound by the constraints of general relativity, as are we.

Something, someone, has seeded intragalactic space with automatic biomechanical probes. These probes are immensely sophisticated by our standards, able to tailor-make message-bearing hallucinogens for the special ecological conditions that the probe may encounter and to release virus-like pseudo-organisms able to carry the artificial genes into the nucleoplasm of the target species and to implant them there. This is a far more enduring form of message than a solid-state monolith on the moon or an orbiting monitor. The artificial genes may be carried along in the stream of evolution for literally hundreds of millions of years without substantial degradation of their message. The information carried by the probe and broadcast by the hallucinogens is modulated by the needs of evolving intelligent life on whatever planet is contacted. Gradually the emphasis of the information available from the probe shifts. Predictions of good hunting, simple divinatory results like the finding of lost objects, and the provision of medical advice are slowly superseded by the revelation of the extraterrestrial source of this information and the purpose behind it: construction of the star antenna and the entry into the Logos of galactic civilization that it will bring.

Speculative ideas indeed! But strangely enough many of the most current calculations and ideas about the density of life and intelligence in the galaxy confront exobiologists with the dilemma of why we have *not yet* been contacted. Cyril Ponnamperuma and A. G. W. Cameron's *Scientific Perspectives on Extraterrestrial Communication* gives an excellent overview of current thinking on the subject. R. N. Bracewell's contribution printed in the same work was the basis of my own ideas about interstellar probes.

I will summarize the state of the art thus: current thinking concludes that the peak of the emergence of intelligence in the galaxy was achieved ten to one hundred million years ago, that most races in the galaxy are very old and sophisticated. We cannot expect such races to appear with a trumpet-blast over every city on earth. Such an entry into history is tantamount to crashing into someone's house completely unannounced—hardly the sort of thing that one would expect from a subtle and ancient galactic civilization. Perhaps they have always been here, or rather their presence has always been here in the hallucinogens—when we understand this on our own, we will be signaling to them that we are now ready for the contact.

We can send that signal only by following the instructions contained in the seeded genes and building the necessary apparatus, social system, or vehicle. When that is done, somewhere in the galaxy lights will flash the message that yet another of the millions upon millions of seeded planets in the galaxy has achieved the threshold of galactic citizenship. Current estimates are that even in a galaxy teeming with intelligence, such a threshold is passed by an intelligent species only once every hundred or thousand years. It is a joyous moment, even for galactarians. If such a speculation has any validity at all, then its very articulation signifies the final moment of the pre-contact phase—and signifies also the pressing need to explore the psilocybin trance and to understand the role that it is playing in the psychology of the human species.*

* New light has been thrown on the phenomenon of voices heard in the head and the role that they may play in the evolution of consciousness. In 1977, Julian Jaynes of Princeton University published a most provocative book, *The Origin of Consciousness in the Breakdown of the Bicameral Mind.* Jaynes uses four hundred and forty-five pages to lay out his ideas concerning the role that hallucinations, especially audio hallucinations, have played in the structuring of mind. Jaynes believes that until the time of roughly the Iliad, around 1400 B.C., nothing at all like modern ego-centered and individuated consciousness existed. Instead he argues that people behaved like automata or social insects, unconsciously going about the tasks of the hive. Only in moments of great stress and personal danger was this regimen broken. In such moments an impersonal mind, outside the usual experience of the world, became manifest as a voice. According to Jaynes's theory, such voices were the guiding lights of human society, perhaps for millennia, whether they were understood to be the voice of an absent but living king, a dead king, an omnipresent god, or a personal deity. Migrations and the breakdown of the cultural insularity of the early human civilizations brought an end to man's relations to the bicameral mind, which is Jaynes's term for the cybernetic, god-like presence felt behind the hallucinated voices. Social prejudices against having a relationship with the bicameral mind in modern times has made "hearing voices" into a mystical phenomenon or a serious mental aberration—in any case something very rare.

The interested reader should study Jaynes's case carefully, although his book is exasperating, since in a treatise on the role of hallucinations in human history, he fails to offer any serious discussion of hallucinogenic plant use at all. This is a serious failing, especially if the effect triggered by psilocybin is not, as I have suggested, a contact with an intelligence entirely distinct from ourselves. Jaynes's theory opens up the possibility that psilocybin returns one to rapport with the transpersonal Other in a way that duplicates on some level the state of mind that was characteristic of early human populations. It is reasonable to suggest that a voice in the head, interpreted by ancient man as a god, might be interpreted by a naive, modern person as a telepathic contact with extraterrestrials. Whatever "facts" may eventually be known, psilocybin offers a tool that allows direct experience of this voice that explains all things, this Logos of the Other.

CHAPTER TWENTY

THE HAWAIIAN CONNECTION

*In which pirate Mantids from hyperspace attack
me and my new lover in the volcanic wastes of
Kau, Hawaii, and I deliver my last words on
the Unspeakable.*

THE FALL OF 1975 WAS a time of personal change
and consolidation. Kat, an old friend met years before in Jerusalem
during my opium and kabbala phase, became at last my lover. Eight
years had passed since we had circumambulated the Mosque of
Omar. She was a tide pool gazer and a solitary traveler. The mushroom had made good its promise to send another partner to share
the ongoing journey through the interior world. In October, we
went to Hawaii to write and to plan a trip to the Peruvian Amazon
in early 1976. And to languish in love.

We rented a house in the remote and desolate Kau district of the
big island of Hawaii. It was an area of twisted lava flows of all ages.
Kapukas were the only vegetation, islanded areas of ancient forest
surrounded by frothy seas of hardened rock, which had killed all low-
lying and less fortunate life. Slowly, nearly imperceptibly, Mauna
Loa's gentle bulk rose up to fourteen thousand feet in the distance
behind us. We were at approximately the twenty-five hundred foot

level. Our small house fronted the vast and forbidding cinder fields, but the lot ran back into a *kapuka* whose enclosing shade and many birds and insects provided welcome contrast to the primal devastation that stretched in all directions for miles. Our life was leisurely. I wrote and did some experiments with more arcane aspects of mushroom cultivation. Kat was immersed in doing line drawings for the book Dennis and I had written on *Stropharia cubensis* cultivation. A sun-filled erotic dream unfolded itself around us.

We were isolated, as we both love to be, and we took mushrooms together often. It was during that Hawaiian idyll that I determined to return again to the Amazon Basin to track down the *Banisteriopsis caapi* in its native setting, in order to satisfy myself as to the role that it and the beta-carboline hallucinogens that it contains played in the experience at La Chorrera. I was especially interested to know if other chemically different aboriginal hallucinogens provoked the same experiences as did the mushroom psilocybin. I wanted to determine if our experiences were part of the general phenomenology of hallucinogens or were unique to psilocybin.

At weekly or ten-day intervals throughout that October and November in Hawaii, we took the *Stropharia* that we had grown. We had an amazing series of experiences. The psilocybin definitely conveys the impression that sometimes other people can see with equal clarity the hallucinations that one is experiencing. Kat and I satisfied ourselves that this was true by taking turns describing the images in which we were immersed. During those times when the flow of images had a certain electric intensity, there was no doubt that we were seeing the same things. The relationship of the psyche to the surface of the body, the skin, is synesthetic and emotionally complex under the influence of psilocybin. Colors and feelings have a tactile quality that ordinary experience never hints of. By having large areas of skin in contact we seemed to somehow obviate the usual psychic individuality and integrity of the body; we would melt into each other's minds in a Tantric climax that was immensely pleasant and full of preposterous and hysterical potential for human growth and parapsychological studies.

Ev and I had had no mushrooms since returning to the States. It was wonderful to have someone to again share the mushrooms with, for until Kat joined me, most of my mushroom trips had been entirely alone, one soul adrift in the cosmic ocean. Happily, there were now two of us navigating together through the billows of jeweled and demonically scintillating geometries.

Two of those mushroom occasions stand out as especially memorable. The first occurred one evening late in November. We each ate five dried grams of *Stropharia* and sat inside by the fire watching the slow upwelling of hallucinations from behind closed eyelids. I seemed to see fleeting but prophetic images of the trip that we were planning into the Amazon. Camp fires and trails filled my head. The sound of nearby crickets seemed transformed into the roar of night jungle sounds that awaited us in Peru. We talked together of our plans and our future. The future seemed enormous and open before us. It was that evening that we both became committed to a family and a life together. It was a major turning point for me, I have no doubt. We walked together outside and stood beneath the stars near the sheds and gardens where we daily pursued the yet more perfect cultivation of *Stropharia*. The night was uncannily still and the sky blazing with stars.

Looking into the southern sky, I thought, "If you are out there; if you approve the course we have set our lives on, if the mystery is real, then give us a sign." I stepped toward Kat, who was walking in front of me, to say, "I asked them for a sign." But before I could speak, the sky was rent from mid-heaven to horizon with a crimson streak of meteoric fire. The depth of atunement of psyche and world must be very great for such synchronisms to occur.

"Such meteor-burns occur but once in all time," came the mushroom's comment, clear and unbidden into my mind.

We sat down then on the warm, receptive earth and abandoned ourselves to the waves of visions and vistas. At one point a revolving night wind whipped the leaves on the otherwise perfectly still trees. The district was a remote one, but borne on the still air over miles and miles, from neighbors and ranches scattered far, we could hear the mournful howl of every dog in that whole part of the island. For hours they moaned and howled in eerie, wavering ululation. We could not imagine what it meant, but we took it as a coincidence as inexplicable as the sky sign on our future.

Hours later, in the time of the false dawn, and at 4:49 local time according to seismic instruments scattered around the planet, an earthquake struck. A low, grinding roar moved through the lava fields stretching for miles all around and beneath us. Tidal waves and volcanic activity at Kilauea Caldera, near the epicenter and thirty miles away from us, followed fast on the first shock. An hour later another smaller shock wave occurred. Now the reason for the hours of howling was starkly explained. Thus it was that meteoric signs and a great earthquake—the most intense in Hawaii in a hundred years—attended our mushroom trip and our intensified exploration of the psilocybin deeps, just as we attended them.

The second, and in many ways more puzzling, major mushroom experience that we shared in Hawaii brought to an end any further exploration of psilocybin until after our return from the Peruvian Amazon. It was the twenty-third of December, the day before Dennis would arrive to spend the Christmas holidays with us. Kat and I each took five dried grams and settled down before the fireplace to await the first wave of images. Soon we were deep into it. The mushroom was showing me a watery, blue-green planet with no land except a globe-girdling archipelago at the equator—a kind of super-Indonesia. Accompanying the views of the planet was a narration explaining that this oxygen-rich world was within one hundred light years of earth and was totally uninhabited by higher animals. As the implications of this last bit of data came home, I felt a wave of acquisitiveness that seemed to come right out of my primate gonads, a reaction to a million years of nomadism and the restless swelling of human populations. The narration was explaining that when the symbiotic fusion of humanity and the *Stropharia* was completed, "the human beings" would be free to claim such planets for the Strophariad.

The narration had become personified into the inner voice that attends the mushroom trance. With it I began a discussion of the view of the watery planet and the technology such views implied. I wondered about the technology of star-travel and remote imaging. I asked the mushroom whether, for all the extravagant images it is able to bestow, could it produce any effect in the normal continuum?

I had the idea that if we should go outside, as we usually did at some point in our journeys, we might see some continuation of the cloud-related phenomenon that had been a part of the experience at La Chorrera. Kat complained of being very hot and agreed that we should go outdoors. We were very unsteady on our feet, and though Kat said very little, I felt considerable alarm for her. However I assumed that going outdoors would be sufficient to cool her off.

Outside, we stood unsteadily in the front yard. The night was overcast. Kat seemed to be lapsing in and out of consciousness. It was becoming harder and harder to rouse her. She kept saying that they were burning her, but that she thought she could hold them back. Finally, she collapsed altogether and I could not get any response. We were so isolated that it was impossible to get any sort of outside help. It would have taken hours to get anyone there, and doubtless no one on the entire island knew more than we did about psilocybin. The overwhelming *gestalt* of the situation was that somehow we had been placed in the scales of life and death, and that whatever was to be done was to be done by us alone and within the next very few minutes.

I remembered that at the back of the house, near where we were accustomed to sunbathing, there was a large tub of water, which held the overflow from our rainwater collecting system. Even though I knew that we were in the face of a mortal threat, it required a complete organization of my consciousness to think of emptying that water over Kat. But as soon as I thought of it, it seemed to give the swirling world a direction. I picked her up in a single, sweeping motion and carried her, lurching through the dark, past the spiky palms now fantastic in the darkness. The moment was excruciatingly grotesque: my drawstring pants had fallen about my ankles so that I walked bare-assed and stiff-legged like Frankenstein's monster, carrying unconscious Kat.

I laid her on the ground and began to empty can after can of clear, black and silver silken water over every inch of her. It was immediately apparent that we had found the antidote to whatever was making her feel a burning sensation and dragging her into unconsciousness. We tearfully and joyously embraced there in the water and mud, both sensing that this very uncharacteristic effect of the mushroom had been a close call. As we knelt together, realizing that we had surmounted the difficulty that had confronted us, a wild peal of unearthly sound—a howling laughter—split the air from the direction of the ancient woods behind the house. This laughter was like the scream of a panic-inducing god. Eldrich, amoral, mad—the throaty battle cackle of the unleashed fiend. We fled.

We stumbled back into the house, and I made us tea while Kat talked to me and candidly confided that what she was experiencing "must be what it is like to be insane." She described having very frank hallucinations with her eyes open, strange "tangible" fern and orchid-like forms were growing and twisting out of every available surface. The previous sensation of heat continued, but it had changed into a field of white-hot potential energy that could be held away from burning contact with her body only by allowing the hallucinogenic energy to spend itself in a chaos of weird and explicit images. Only by applied concentration could she hold the burning plasma at bay a few feet away from her, where it became a skin of vision that encompassed everything else. After a few minutes of this Kat again seemed to be fading, and so we drew a cold bath and she lay in that for awhile until the symptoms again abated.

When later we talked it became apparent that her experience had dimensions for her that had not been apparent to me. From the moment we had first stepped out of the house, she discovered that the sensation of heat had not diminished but grown stronger. She noticed that directly above her was a disk of light and color—a giant tinker-toy assemblage of softly glowing rods of light, with jewel-like connectors emanating every color.

"I understood," she told me, "that the relationships of the places—their lengths, their angles to each other—was infinitely complex and also the embodiment of perfect truth. By seeing it, I was understanding everything . . . but there were creatures inside the vehicle, mantis-like and made of light, that didn't want me to know. Bending over their instrument panels, the more I understood, the more they burned me with their ray. I couldn't stop looking, but I was being vaporized. I felt you pick me up and, as you carried me, I thought, 'I hope he hurries. I'm becoming a cloud. . . .' For a moment I was floating above and looking down at us—people bigger than life, out of time. Then I felt the water on my skin redefining the limits of my body and condensing me again."

Kat's impression of the situation was that this was not a threat conveyed by the mushroom, but a force inside the continuum that the mushroom makes available—a force that is seemingly morally ambiguous: pirates in hyperspace? Kat was having a UFO close-contact experience while I was seeing nothing. It was a contact fraught with danger and the threat of extinction. It had abruptly terminated when I had doused her with water.

We sat up all night discussing what had happened. It served to accentuate other odd things that we had noticed when taking psilocybin in that remote environment. We had particularly noticed small scratching and rustling noises at the periphery of sense and vision during the trips, not unlike the activation of a classic poltergeist phenomenon. These small movements and noises were so regular a feature of these experiences that I came simply to accept them. We also noticed waves of activity that seemed to sweep through animate and inanimate matter alike during the mushroom voyages. For instance, after a prolonged period of near-trance in contemplation of the visions, if we were to draw away from it in a collective motion to stretch or talk, the fire would suddenly flare and burn brighter and the rustling at the periphery would increase.

We were definitely at the brink of the same dimension that I had been plunged into at La Chorrera, again brought there by the agency of the mushroom. This time, however, we took our threat-laden brush with the thing as an admonition for us to ease up for a time. It was after this that we determined to go to Peru, to take *ayahuasca* and get some perspective on the nature of psilocybin relative to other visionary plant hallucinogens.

Our walks in the rain forests of Hawaii were a pale but real echo of Amazon trails once followed in the past and in a few months to be traveled again. It was during one of those walks, reflecting on her encounter with the mantis-beings and their machines of light, that Kat pointed out that a lens is the natural result of the overlapping of two spheres. Is there something to be learned by applying this idea to the lens-shaped UFO? Perhaps some topological truth is implied in the thought that the lens is caused by the over-lapping of one continuum with another. Lenticular clouds were a part of the UFO contact that occurred at La Chorrera in 1971. This theme reemerged during those psilocybin experiences in the desolate landscapes of rural Hawaii.

On yet another mushroom trip, when Kat and I stepped outside late at night, we beheld the stars through the moving interstices of a high lacework of thin clouds. Yet, hovering only a few hundred feet above and slightly in front of us, was a very dark, dense lenticular cloud. It grew more solid appearing as we watched; suddenly this tendency was reversed and it began to thin and fade very quickly. Then it was gone.

Years go by and there is little intrusion of the peculiar into daily life. Then suddenly it is with us again, effecting coincidence and appearing to channel the flow of events toward some end which is sensed but not possible to anticipate. The paranoiac patina that has formed over modern society makes feedback from the culture difficult to evaluate. From a certain perspective, humanity is always a creature in transformation, imparting to every moment the deeply felt mystery of the unrealized future. Is the present situation really any different from many others in the past?

Novelty is always in the process of emergence, but does it ever emerge explicitly, suddenly, from the events in which it is embedded? And what are we to make of it when it does emerge suddenly enough for us to recognize it as a true flux of the temporal continuum? I believe in miracles and ecstasy and in situations where "forces" are seen to be at work that are undescribed by today's physics. I felt it was necessary to retrace these familiar threads of my own life and thought. If I had not done this then no record would exist of the halting steps we took at La Chorrera, steps that lead us toward understanding psilocybin and its relation to the human soul—that knot of precious anomaly and fragile feeling that haunts our planet like a ghost.

EPILOGUE

*In which I return to the present, introduce my
fellow explorers as they are today, and genuflect
before the weirdness of it all.*

So WHERE DOES THIS all leave us today? Did the
cosmic giggle move on? Am I like an archaeologist, condemned
now to work diligently with toothbrush and nut-pick, attempting to
exhume and reassemble the broken shards of dreams and visions
obtained in long forgotten times and places? It was easy to look
back and to tell this story as if it were a completed cycle, something
finished and resplendent in its completion. The problem with that
approach is that this story is true, its actors real people, their lives
ongoing. The major mysteries of the experiment at La Chorrera remain just that, mysteries even to this date.

My colleagues, my friends and lovers, have changed and
moved on. Different fates have claimed each of us. Dave remained
in South America, having returned to the United States only once
in the last twenty years, for the briefest of visits. I have not seen
him since 1971. I know that he has lived in most of the countries of
Andean South America. For years he remained true to his itinerant
hippie roots, traveling from one high altitude village to the next
teaching the local women to crochet. By now I should imagine that
this minor art form is well established in places where before his

visits it must have been utterly unknown. He didn't make it to the West Coast during his short visit to the States, but he called me and we talked at length. Same old Dave as far as I could tell.

Ev married the friend for whom she left me in 1975, and they are still married, with a son soon old enough to be sent off to college. I have not seen Ev or her husband since her departure in 1975. We talked once on the phone years ago. I muttered something about how it might be nice to have dinner sometime, but it was up to me to follow through, and I never did. This avoidance has not been casual or unconsidered. There is still a reluctance on my part and a lingering pain that goes deep and puzzles me—but it is not to be lightly gone against.

Vanessa returned to the States from the Amazon and followed in the tradition of her father and sister by obtaining a medical degree. Today she lives in Berkeley, as does Ev, and is a psychiatrist with a thriving practice. We see each other too rarely, and when we do get together I am reluctant to raise the issue of La Chorrera for two reasons. The first is that we were at opposite ends of the spectrum in our judgments concerning those events. And the second is that I don't wish to have our friendship turn, as it easily could, into a review of what might be thought of as my "case." Vanessa is smart and fair and has no motivation to judge me harshly. Our original differences arose out of her belief that, at the time, my unwillingness to treat Dennis's condition at La Chorrera as a medical crisis was the result of my own callousness, selfishness, lack of character, or just plain nuttiness.

The only person who was part of the original team to whom I feel I can still rave at full bore with concerning the experiment at La Chorrera is Dennis. He obtained his degrees in botany, molecular biology, and neurochemistry years ago. He is now the scientist that at La Chorrera he could only aspire to be. He is married, has a precocious child, and works as a research pharmacologist for a Silicon Valley outfit called Shaman Pharmaceuticals. He tolerates my raving but is careful never to encourage me. I think that his attitude is still much as it was only a few months after the experiment, that whatever happened the toll on him was too great. He likes to rest with the facile argument that what happened was only a *folie a deux*, a delusion of two brothers grieving for their recently deceased mother and obsessed with conquering hyperspace. When I marshal my case against this and argue the evidence that something much more was going on, he reluctantly agrees, then shakes his head and turns away. To this day he remembers very little of what actually went on between the fourth and the twentieth of March 1971, and he prefers to keep it that way.

So without rancor or surprise I can say that the matter is pretty much in my keeping. The morning that we all flew out of La Chorrera in Tsalikas's small plane, I was twenty-four years old, penniless, without plans, considered mad by my closest friends, and with a price on my head. In the intervening years, I have done what I could to keep the issues surrounding the experiment at La Chorrera from being forgotten.

Together, during the mid-seventies, Dennis and I developed and promulgated the techniques for growing the mushrooms. Though others followed us into the field, we were the first and loudest to preach the home cultivation of psychedelic mushrooms. This technology brought to tens of thousands of dedicated and curious seekers the option of exploring what would otherwise have been an obscure and unobtainable tryptamine hallucinogen. Psilocybin-taking in the seventies was the major factor creating and sustaining a small but dedicated public following for ideas such as those developed at La Chorrera. Over the years, the story of La Chorrera and the ideas spawned there have slowly made their way into public awareness via my books, and a film soon to be planned around them.

My position is interesting but not enviable. Because the major idea to emerge out of this experience is the timewave and the computer software that supports it, I am in the absurd position of being either an unsung Newton or completely nuts. There is very little room to maneuver between those two positions. The timewave paints a radical picture of how time works and what history is. It provides a map of the global ebb and flow of novelty over the next twenty years and it also makes a prediction of a major transformational event in 2012. This is only as far in the future as La Chorrera lies in the past. It is soon.

These personal developments have taken place against a background of deepening problems in the real world and a rising interest in the psychedelic experience by young people. I am, I am told, a minor icon in the culture of the underground. Is this all simply due to my schizophrenic tenaciousness in promulgating what are ultimately really only my ideas? Or do I have the winds of history blowing at my back and really did befriend the Logos and learn the secret of the universe, or at least one of many secrets, in the chaos at La Chorrera?

I honestly confess that I do not know. As I write these words my marriage to Kat of nearly sixteen years seems caught up in a process of dissolution painful to both of us. This despite our two children, the house we built together, and both our efforts to be decent people. Apparently the presence of the Logos has done nothing to mitigate or ward off the ordinary vicissitudes of life. Like the Soul in Yeats's poem I am still an eternal thing fastened to the body of a dying animal.

Yet if my sense of a special destiny and a way to save the world from the more dangerous and vulgar parts of itself is a delusion, then it is a grand delusion and one that is dying in me only slowly and by inches. I am assured by the people around me—publishers, editors, agents, marketing experts—people who are obviously uninformed as to the whispered promise of a special destiny made to me by the elves of hyperspace, that I am going to be big, have influence, and change the way people think.

Perhaps this will be true. I hope so. *Something* happened at La Chorrera, something extraordinary. I was extremely fortunate to have briefly glimpsed a strange, beautiful, and better sort of world and to have made a marvelous pact with the alien gods who dwell there. The timewave, created over years of work, is both a prophecy concerning, and a map to, that better world. That I am an unworthy vessel for such high-minded work, I am sure. I have tried to make these transcendent fantasies return to normal and take their place in the mundane and dying worldview in which we all are imprisoned by late twentieth-century culture. But the job has been more than I could do.

My fear is that if these ideas are less than true then our world is destined for a very final and ordinary death, for reason has grown too feeble to save us from the demons we have set loose. My hope is that I may bear witness to the fact that there is a great mystery calling to us all, beckoning across the landscape of our history, promising to realize itself and to give real meaning to what is otherwise only the confusion of our lives and our collective past. Twenty years after the experiment at La Chorrera, I still cannot say that it shall not be.

ACKNOWLEDGMENTS

THE AUTHOR WISHES to express appreciation to
the many friends who encouraged the writing of this book. Twenty
years in the writing means their names are legion, but especially
important are Ernest Waugh and Kat Harrison McKenna, both of
whom read and criticized the manuscript at various stages. Thanks
also to Dennis McKenna, who encouraged the telling of our adventures, and to the other members of our expedition, who offered no
objections to a public revealing of our story. Special and very deep
thanks is due to Dan Levy, who believed in this project from the
first moment that he encountered my work and who did a superb
job in editing and criticizing these pages. Without his support this
tale would still be an embryonic manuscript. Special thanks also to
Tom Grady, my in-house editor at Harper San Francisco, to Jeff
Campbell, who did the copyediting, to Leslie Rossman, my inde-
fatigable publicist, and to Jaime Robles, who oversaw the design of
the book. Also grateful thanks to my agent, John Brockman, and
his assistant, Katinka Matson. Sincere thanks also to Sara Hartley,
who allowed her photograph to be used as the frontispiece. And
finally thanks to all the fans, friends, and colleagues who over the
years have insisted that the story of La Chorrera reach all those
who sense the importance of the psychedelic experience and the
strange dimensions that is makes accessible.

FURTHER READING

Abraham, Ralph, Terence McKenna, and Rupert Sheldrake. *Trialogues at the Edge of the West.* Albuquerque: Bear & Co., 1992.

Burroughs, William, and Allen Ginsberg. *The Yagé Letters.* San Francisco: City Lights, 1963.

Dee, John. *The Hieroglyphic Monad.* Translated by J. W. Hamilton-Jones. London: Stuart & Watkins, 1947.

Dick, Phillip K. *The Three Stigmata of Palmer Eldritch.* London: Triad Panther, 1964.

———. *Valis.* New York: Bantam Books, 1979.

———. *The Transmigration of Timothy Archer.* New York: Simon & Schuster, 1982.

Eliade, Mircea. *Shamanism: Archaic Techniques of Ecstasy.* New York: Pantheon Books, 1964.

Evans-Wentz, W. E. *The Fairy Faith in Celtic Countries.* New York: University Books, 1966.

Ghosal, S., Dutta, S. K., Sanyal, A. K., and Bhattacharya. "Arundo Donex L. (Graminae), Phytochemical and Pharmacological Evaluation." In the *Journal of Medical Chemistry*, vol. 12 (1969), p. 480.

Gibson, William. *Burning Chrome*. New York: Arbor House, 1986.

———. *Count Zero*. New York: Arbor House, 1986.

———. *Neuromancer*. New York: Ave Books, 1985.

Graves, Robert. *Difficult Questions, Easy Answers*. New York: Doubleday, 1964.

———. *Food for Centaurs*. New York: Doubleday, 1960.

Graves, Robert. *The White Goddess*. New York: Creative Age, 1948.

Guenther, Herbert V. *Tibetan Buddhism Without Mystification*. Leiden: E. J. Brill, 1966.

Hardenburg, W. E. *The Putumayo: The Devil's Paradise*. London: T. Fisher Unwin, 1912.

Harner, Michael. "The Sound of Rushing Water." In *Natural History*, July, 1968.

Huxley, Aldous. *The Doors of Perception*. New York: Harper & Brothers, 1954.

Jaynes, Julian. *The Origin of Consciousness in the Breakdown of the Bicameral Mind*. Boston: Houghton Mifflin, 1977.

Joyce, James. *Finnegans Wake*. London: Faber & Faber, 1939.

———. *Ulysses*. New York: Random House, 1922.

Jantsch, Eric. *The Self-Organizing Universe*. New York: Pergamon Press, 1980.

Jung, C. G. *Flying Saucers: A Modern Myth of Things Seen in The Sky*. New York: Pantheon, 1954.

———. *Mysterium Coniunctionis*. New York: Pantheon, 1963.

Leibnitz, Gottfried Wilhelm von. "Monadology." In the *Philosophical Works of Leibnitz*. Translated by G. Martin Duncan. New Haven, CT: Tuttle, Morehouse & Taylor, 1890.

Lewis, Wyndham. *The Human Age*. London: Methuen, 1928.

Ludlow, Fitz Hugh. *The Hashish Eater*. New York: Harper & Brothers, 1857.

Maier, Michael. *Atlanta fugiens. hoc est. emblemata nova de secretis naturae chymica.* Oppenheim, 1618.

McKenna, Dennis, and Terence McKenna. *The Invisible Landscape.* New York: Seabury Press, 1975.

McKenna, Terence. *The Archaic Revival.* San Francisco: Harper SanFrancisco, 1992.

———. *Food of The Gods.* New York: Bantam Books, 1992.

———. *Synesthesia.* New York: Granary Books, 1992.

Munn, Henry. "The Mushrooms of Language." In *Shamanism and Hallucinogens.* Edited by Michael Harner. London: Oxford Univ. Press, 1973.

Nabokov, Vladimir. *Ada.* New York: McGraw-Hill, 1969.

———. *Pale Fire.* New York: Lancer, 1963.

Oss, O. T., and O. N. Oeric. *Psilocybin: Magic Mushroom Grower's Guide.* Berkeley, CA: And/Or Press, 1975, rev. 1985.

Ponnamperuma, Cyril, and A. G. W. Cameron. *Scientific Perspectives on Extraterrestrial Communication.* Boston: MIT Press, 1974.

Prigogine, Ilya. *From Being to Becoming.* San Francisco: Freeman, 1980.

———. *Self-Organization in Nonequilibrium Systems.* New York: Wiley Interscience, 1977.

Pynchon, Thomas. *Gravity's Rainbow.* New York: Viking, 1974.

———. *V.,* New York: Bantam Books, 1963.

Rilke, Ranier Maria. *The Duino Elegies.* New York: Norton, 1939.

Schultes, R. E. "Virola as an Orally Administered Hallucinogen." In the *Botanical Museum Leaflets of Harvard University.* vol. 22, no. 6, pp. 229–40.

Sheldrake, Rupert. *A New Science of Life.* Los Angeles: Tarcher, 1981.

———. *The Presence of the Past.* New York: Times Books, 1988.

Stapleton, Olaf. *The Starmaker*. London, 1937.

Taussig, Michael. *Shamanism Colonialism and the Wildman*. Chicago: Univ. of Chicago Press, 1987.

Templeton, Alex. *The Sirius Mystery*. New York: St. Martin's Press, 1976.

Valentine, Basil. *The Triumphal Chariot of Antimony*. London, 1685.

Vallee, Jacques. *The Invisible College*. New York: Dutton, 1975.

Wasson, R. Gordon. *Soma: Divine Mushroom of Immortality*. New York: Harcourt Brace Jovanovich, 1971.

Wasson, R. G., Albert Hoffman, and Carl Ruck. *The Road to Eleusis*. New York: Harcourt Brace Jovanovich, 1978.

Wells, H. G. *The Time Machine*. London, 1895.

Whiffen, Col. *Explorations of the Upper Amazon*. London: Constable, 1915.

Whitehead, A. N. *Process and Reality*. New York: Macmillan, 1929.

Wilson, Robert Anton. *Cosmic Trigger*. Berkeley, CA: And/Or Press, 1977.

BY DENNIS MCKENNA

Dennis J. McKenna. "DMT: Nature's Ubiquitous Hallucinogen." *Interdependences*, in press.

———. "Tryptamine Hallucinogens of the New World: An Ethnopharmacological Survey." *Interdependences*, in press.

Constantino M. Torres, David B. Repke, Kelvin Chan, Dennis McKenna, Augustin Llagostera, and Richard E. Schultes. "Botanical, chemical, and contextual analysis of archaeological snuff powders from San Pedro de Atacama, Northern Chile." *Current Anthropology* 32 (1992): 640–49.

Dennis J. McKenna, X.-M. Guan, and A. T. Shulgin. "3,4-methylenedioxyamphetamine (MDA) analogues exhibit differential effects on synaptosomal release of ^{3}H-dopamine and ^{3}H-5-

hydroxytryptamine." *Pharmacology, Biochemistry, and Behavior* 38 (1991): 505–12.

Chester A. Mathis, John M. Gerdes, Joel D. Enas, John M. Whitney, Yi Zhang, Scott E. Taylor, Dennis J. McKenna, Sona Havlick, and Stephen J. Peroutka. "Binding potency of paroxetine anaolgues for the serotonin uptake complex." *Journal of Pharmacy and Pharmacology*. Submitted.

David E. Nichols, Robert Oberlender, and Dennis J. McKenna. "Stereochemical Aspects of Hallucinogenesis." In *Biochemistry and Physiology of Substance Abuse*, vol. III, edited by R. R. Watson, pp. 1–39. Boca Raton, FL: CRC Press, 1991.

Dennis J. McKenna and Stephen J. Peroutka. "Serotonin neurotoxins: Focus on MDMA (3,4-methylenedioxymethamphetamine, 'Ecstasy')." In *Serotonin Receptor Subtypes: Basic and Clinical Aspects*, edited by S. J. Peroutka, pp. 127–48. New York: Alan R. Liss Publishers, 1990.

———. "The neurochemistry and neurotoxicity of 3,4-methylenedioxymethamphetamine (MDMA, 'Ecstasy')." *Journal of Neurochemistry* 54 (1990): 14–22.

———. "Differentiation of 5-hydroxytryptamine$_2$ receptor subtypes using ^{125}I-R-(-)2,5,-dimethoxyphenylisopropylamine (^{125}I-R-(-)DOI) and ^{3}H-ketanserin." *Journal of Neuroscience* 9 (1989): 3482–90.

Dennis J. McKenna, David B. Repke, Leland Lo, and Stephen J. Peroutka. "Differential interactions of indolealkylamines with 5-hydroxytryptamine receptor subtypes." *Neuropharmacology* 29 (1990): 193–98.

Dennis J. McKenna. "It's a Jungle Out There: Biochemical Conflict and Co-operation in the Ecosphere." *Whole Earth Review* 64 (1989): 40–47.

———. "Plant Wisdom Resources." *Whole Earth Review* 64 (1989): 48–49.

Cameron R. Hekmatpanath, Dennis J. McKenna, and Stephen J. Peroutka. "Reserpine does not prevent 3,4-methylenedioxymethamphetamine-induced neurotoxicity." *Neuroscience Letters* 104 (1989): 178–82.

Dennis J. McKenna, David B. Repke, and Stephen J. Peroutka. "Hallucinogenic indolealkylamines are selective for $5HT_{2A}$ binding sites." *Neuroscience Abstract* 15 (1989): 485.

Dennis J. McKenna, Adil J. Nazarali, Andrew J. Hoffman, David E. Nichols, C. A. Mathis, and Juan M. Saavedra. "Common receptors for hallucinogens in rat brain: a comparative autoradiographic study using [^{125}I]LSD and [^{125}I]-DOI, a new psychotomimetic radioligand." *Brain Research* 476 (1989): 45–56.

Dennis J. McKenna, Adil J. Nazarali, Akihiko Himeno, and Juan M. Saavedra. "Chronic treatment with (+_)DOI, a psychotomimetic $5HT_2$ agonist, downregulates $5HT_2$ receptors in rat brain." *Neuropsychopharmacology* 2 (1989): 81–87.

Adil J. Nazarali, Dennis J. McKenna, and Juan M. Saavedra. "Autoradiographic localization of $5HT_2$ receptors in rat brain using [^{125}I]-DOI, a selective psychotomimetic radioligand." *Progressive Neuropsychopharmacology and Biological Psychiatry* 13 (1989): 573–81.

Dennis J. McKenna, C. A. Mathis, and Stephen J. Peroutka. "Characterization of ^{125}I-DOI binding sites in rat brain." *Neuroscience Abstracts* 14 (1988), no. 247.12.

Akihiko Himeno, Dennis J. McKenna, Adil J. Nazarali, and Juan M. Saavedra. "(+_)DOI, a hallucinogenic phenylalkylamine, downregulates $5HT_2$ receptors in rat brain." *Neuroscience Abstracts* 14 (1988), no. 229.2.

Dennis J. McKenna and Juan M. Saavedra. "Autoradiography of LSD and 2,5-dimethoxyphenylisopropylamine psychotomimetics demonstrates regional, specific cross-displacement in the rat brain." *European Journal of Pharmacology* 142 (1987): 313–15.

Dennis J. McKenna, C. A. Mathis, A. T. Shulgin, and J. M. Saavedra. "Hallucinogens bind to common receptors in the rat forebrain: a comparative study using ^{125}I-LSD and ^{125}I-DOI, a new psychotomimetic radioligand." *Neuroscience Abstracts* 13 (1987), no. 311.14.

Dennis J. McKenna, C. A. Mathis, A. T. Shulgin, Thornton Sargent III, and J. M. Saavedra. "Autoradiographic localization of binding sites for ^{125}I-(-)DOI, a new psychotomimetic radioligand, in the rat brain." *European Journal of Pharmacology* 137 (1987): 289–90.

Dennis J. McKenna, L. E. Luna, and G. H. N. Towers. "Biodynamic constituents in Ayahuasca admixture plants: an uninvestigated folk pharmacopoeia." *America Indigena* 46 (1986): 73–101.

Dennis J. McKenna and G. H. N. Towers. "On the comparative ethnopharmacology of the Malpighiaceous and Myristicaceous hallucinogens." *Journal of Psychoactive Drugs* 17 (1985): 35–39.

———. "Biochemistry and pharmacology of tryptamine and B-carboline derivatives: A minireview." *Journal of Psychoactive Drugs* 16 (1984): 347–58.

Dennis J. McKenna, G. H. N. Towers, and F. S. Abbott. "Monoamine oxidase inhibitors in South American hallucinogenic plants: Tryptamine and B-carboline constituents of Ayahuasca." *Journal of Ethnopharmacology* 10 (1984): 195–223.

———. "Monoamine oxidase inhibitors in South American hallucinogenic plants, Part II: Constituents of orally active Myristicaceous hallucinogens." *Journal of Ethnopharmacology* 12 (1984): 179–211.

Dennis J. McKenna and G. H. N. Towers. "Ultra-violet mediated cytotoxic activity of B-carboline alkaloids." *Phytochemistry* 20 (1981): 1001–1004.

Dennis J. McKenna and T. K. McKenna. *The Invisible Landscape.* New York: Seabury Press, 1975.